CRIMINAL RIVER

By the same author

Tyranny and the Lash

CRIMINAL RIVER

THE HISTORY OF THE THAMES RIVER POLICE

STEPHEN WADE

ROBERT HALE · LONDON

© Stephen Wade 2012
First published in Great Britain 2012

ISBN 978-0-7090-9327-5

Robert Hale Limited
Clerkenwell House
Clerkenwell Green
London EC1R 0HT

www.halebooks.com

The right of Stephen Wade to be identified as
author of this work has been asserted by him
in accordance with the Copyright, Designs and
Patents Act 1988

A catalogue record for this book is available from the British Library

2 4 6 8 10 9 7 5 3 1

All images of Wapping station, police craft and working scenes are
courtesy of the Thames Police Association. Other illustrations are from
the author's own collection, or from contemporary literature, as credited.

Typeset by e-type, Liverpool
Printed in Great Britain by the MPG Books Group,
Bodmin and King's Lynn

Contents

Acknowledgements

THANKS ARE DUE to a number of people who have helped with the research for this book. At the Wapping office, special thanks are due to John 'Joz' Joslin who is joint honorary curator of everything that remains of the Thames Police from the early days, with Robert Jeffries, the other honorary curator, who is also involved with the care and preservation of the artefacts and records of the force. Jean Fullerton, the East London novelist, inspired me to make imaginative engagement with the location and the people from the Victorian era, with a walk around Wapping and to the Ratcliffe Highway.

My first foray into London police history, on the City of London Police, has also been useful here, so I must again thank Roger Appleby, who formerly kept the museum for the City officers at Wood Street. I have to add that his display – which included the gun used in an attempt to murder Leo Rothschild – has given me a formative experience in exploring this area of social history, on a par with my visit to Wapping and the amazing sight of the resuscitation equipment from Victorian times. Police work, in spite of all the accounts of the bigger picture and national events, comes to life through artefacts – the objects, possessions and equipment used by men and women on the beat.

Other historians and writers have offered ideas and suggestions in conversation and correspondence, and these include Stewart Evans, Richard Whittington-Egan, Brian Longbone and Richard Jones. As for writers who have been on this journey through the river law history before, I have to acknowledge Geoffrey Budworth and Tom Fallon, and also Martin Stallion and David Wall for their indispensable reference work on the British police forces, spanning the years 1829–2000. Without Geoffrey Budworth's book, *River Beat,* it would have been an enormous task to understand the more technical side of the development of the boats used by the Thames Division and its earlier identities. Staff at the London Metropolitan Archives were very helpful, as were other crime history enthusiasts who expressed interest in the project from the beginning. Also, thanks to Rob Jerrard, whose work on the City of London Police first kindled my interest in this area of research.

I am grateful to the Thames Police Association for permission to use the images of Wapping station, police craft and working scenes that appear within these pages.

Thanks are also due to Nikki Edwards at Robert Hale, for her help with the editing and final stages of work with the text.

Introduction

A WALK FROM the Tower of London to Wapping today along the new waterfront means that the visitor sees smart restaurants, new riverside flats, expensive craft at anchor, attractive designs of avant-garde retail and business edifices; but just a little way beyond, to turn off the waterfront to head for the old tobacco dock is to step into the vestiges of Georgian London. Greyish-yellow stock bricks abound, with ground-level buildings sometimes faced with stucco; there are rubbed brick arches on windows. Another few minutes walk takes one to the Town of Ramsgate pub, on Wapping Stairs, a place where the past lies heavy and exciting, the Thames lapping its edge at the rear.

Then, in a few minutes, turning left gradually, the dock-lands of the past come into view, and beyond them the road that was, in 1800 when the first River Police walked around here looking for known 'faces', the Ratcliffe Highway, scene of the horrendous mass-murder of 1811 in which two households were slaughtered. Today, the Highway at this point, near the tobacco dock, is dominated by the church of St George in the East, and there are a few small remains of the past centuries of London life. But if we dig deeper and look into the glowering shadows of the Thames and its past, there are tales of sensation, drama and fear waiting for us.

Inextricably mixed into that past are the officers of the Thames River Police, a constabulary pre-dating Sir Robert Peel's first Metropolitan force by thirty-one years. These new men were to take on the smugglers and the pirates, the gangs dealing in contraband and the hard cases who wanted to rule their 'patch'. These police would also face disasters: fires,

© THAMES POLICE ASSOCIATION

The headquarters at Wapping c.1900. To one visitor at that time, the blue lamp outside was a welcome reminder of law and order because men were 'standing at the top of some neighbouring steps, wearing slouched hats and with anything but a comforting expression on their faces.'

explosions and terrible nautical accidents. They learned to cope, and their professionalism was steadily honed and refined until they became one of the most impressive and capable forces for law and order in the land.

In August 1823, John Jennings stretched to cut some rushes by the Thames shore; he fell into the water, and every attempt was made to restore him to life, but he died, and this young man, who could have been a celebrity of his age, was just one more brief report in the press under the listings of coroners' inquests. His parents had been offered a large sum of money to exhibit him as 'a prodigy of nature' on account of his huge frame.

A much more mundane death in the great river of London was that of John Abbot, who, a month later, jumped off

Waterloo Bridge. He was a compositor, the son of the Mayor of Athlone. A workmate testified that, on the day of his death, John had been 'irritated in his mind'. He had asked the witness if anyone there had any reason to find fault with him and was told that no, his employers were happy with his work. But the same witness saw him later, in a public house, and saw that John was 'bad in his mind'.

In both cases, the verdict was 'found drowned' and that kind of event was to be a weekly job for the Thames River Police, formed in 1798 in the midst of the Georgian crisis of crime, dissent, public unrest and social anarchy. The force had been created as demand had increased from the river merchants and the massive East India Company for protection and crime prevention at a time in which petty theft, smuggling and assault on the river were everyday affairs.

Although dealing with suicides was routine – what was more of a challenge, and often packed with high drama, was policing the gangs, fights and disorder along the embankment and in the docks. In 1797 half a million men were employed along the wharves in the dockland, stretching from the Pool of London to Gravesend. Estimates of the river traffic at the turn of the eighteenth century suggest that there were over 22,000 craft working on the docks. Theft from boats was common and easy to achieve. A man aged eighty, called Goss, stole a mainsail from a vessel owned by William Broughton in 1817, and the old man was then tried on another indictment of stealing a tarpaulin, two sculls, a seat-board and other goods from a Mr Harbottle. He had stolen the mainsail while Mr Broughton had left his boat for a short time; Broughton had then found out where the thief had stored the goods and informed the Thames Police. The old thief was sent to Newgate.

That kind of easy crime had reached massive proportions before the River Police arrived; the officers of Customs and Excise had done their best, but something radical was needed. Trade was suffering extreme losses. Patrick Colquhoun, the mastermind behind the new police, wrote an account of the 'depredations' in the Port of London in a tract of 1799, in which he identified and described the main categories of criminal along the Thames. He started with river pirates, the 'most desperate and depraved characters', who were not usually restrained 'by any sense of turpitude of their actions'; then he referred to 'night plunderers' who assailed any victim in their way and who stole anything of any size or value that they could snatch and carry away.

Colquhoun's great work, *Treatise on the Police of the Metropolis* (1797) further elaborated on the crisis of crime in London, and he included: 'River pilferers, fraudulent lumpers, scuffle-hunters, mudlarks, lightermen, riggers, artificers and labourers in the docks and arsenals.' In other words, all workers were subject to criminality. It was a world of bribes, receiving, gangland allegiances, corrupt officials, nepotism and sinecures; people would fall into crime for gin, gaming, small profits and preferment.

In Regency London there were several reasons why breaking the law was so common and so frequent. There were vast areas

Patrick Colquhoun: joint first magistrate and theorist of river policing. Colquhoun realized that avoiding increases in police costs was crucial to change, and in 1798 his proposals were recommended to Parliament.

of the city into which thieves could run and hide in the dark; the forces of law were few and inefficient and, most of all, the criminals were organized in varieties of self-help groups and support networks. In the century before the establishment of the River Police, there had been only a few limited attempts to combat the crime wave. The Fielding brothers, Henry and John, had made Bow Street a magistrates' court of some power and achievement; they had created a publication which was the forerunner of the *Police Gazette*, recording crimes and giving descriptions of suspects but, when John died in 1780, their good work declined.

By the last decade of the eighteenth century, the British criminal justice system was in chaos. In the 1790s, fear and horror at the events of the recent French Revolution led the government to pass a series of repressive Acts to limit gatherings in the streets. In 1780 the Gordon Riots had shown that a London mob could do terrible damage and almost create a revolution; the anarchy then had destroyed buildings (including the King's Bench prison) and terrified the populace. The intellectual left were writing seditious publications and talking of political reform; the working classes, their numbers swelled in the towns and cities after the acceleration of enclosure in the shires and the growth of mechanized production, presented the authorities with all kinds of problems in housing and employment, in addition to a rise in violent crime.

A glance at the newspapers of the Regency period soon gives the reader an impression of the range and diversity of violent crime at this time. A typical crime report from London would include attacks by highwaymen, thefts from shops, murder, violent robbery, forgery, riots, duels, piracy, smuggling and, on a higher scale, treason and sedition. Following anti-militia riots in 1796, in 1797 there were mutinies in the dockyards at Spithead and the Nore, and in 1801 there were widespread food riots. In 1798, the year in which the River Police were formed, the United Englishmen and the committee of the London Corresponding Society were seized and arrested, and James O'Coiley was executed for high treason. There were over two hundred capital offences on the statutes. The mass of criminals before the justices at the Old Bailey led the government to seek alternatives to hanging and life imprisonment as the prisons were filling up rapidly, and most death sentences were commuted. From 1787 transportation to Australia began and on the Thames the prison hulk ships were soon crammed with villains.

The Thames was at the very heart of this seething, restless, greedy mass of citizens at odds with the law. The worst, most disturbing element of all this for those who obeyed and respected the law was that there was no policing in place in a regular, organized form. The Bow Street Runners, limited in number, did a reasonable job in tackling some of the more serious crime, but the 'watch'– known as 'Charlies' – who were supposed to patrol streets by day and night were ineffectual and outnumbered by the criminal fraternity. The river ran through the centre of the warrens, cellars and rookeries where rogues and footpads hid from the law. The professionals who knew the river were to be the backbone of the new police. Within the ranks of the first corps of men, there were watermen, who rowed the boats, surveyors, who acted as inspectors, and lumpers, who were to supervise the actions of the loaders and unloaders from the craft.

The river and the vessels bobbing on the water in many ways defined London. Lord Byron's lines from *Don Juan* give a vivid account of this thriving port:

> *A mighty mass of brick and smoke and shipping,*
> *Dirty and dusky, but as wide as eye*
> *Could reach, with here and there a sail just skipping*
> *In sight, then lost amid the forestry*
> *Of masts, a wilderness of steeples peeping*
> *On tiptoe through their sea coal canopy.*

The Thames in the early nineteenth century was beginning to show the ill-effects of the rapid growth of London and the accompanying pollution of the water. Salmon, once thriving in the Thames, were no longer in the river by the end of the Regency; the last salmon caught there (until one was caught in 1974 near Thurrock power station) was recorded in 1833. In

1807 the poet Robert Southey wrote *Letters from England*, in which he fabricated an outsider's view of his native land, and there he describes the pollution of the river: 'A fine sweep of steps ascends from the river to Blackfriars – the second of three bridges, close by which the common sewers discharge themselves, and blacken the water round about.' Others have written about the greenish coffee-colour of the water at this time, and noted that the river water was covered by a foul scum which was exposed at full tide.

Most people in the city needed the river for their living; all kinds of secondary companies grew up, linked to the maritime trades and the massive scale of exports which kept on growing as the Empire expanded. Close up, it may have been an unhealthy and foul waterway, but in 1800 the Thames was still essential for pleasure trips as well as for functional journeys. For the artist, Thomas Rowlandson, for instance, one of his greatest delights was to take a boat from near his home in the Strand out to Greenwich to spend the day in a pleasant place, along the waterfront.

The city along the stretch from the Strand to all the new docks of the Regency was a mix of terrible but sometimes glorious extremes: artists and writers languished in debtors' prisons along with the underclass; the gaming tables were packed, exclusive clubs thrived, in which young aristocrats lost fortunes, and, outside, the working girls plied their trade. One of the sharpest examples of these contrasts is the new Regent Street designed by John Nash, from which the Haymarket runs: the former a wonderful, stylish artistic achievement for the 'new London' and the latter a haunt of prostitutes and pimps. The city had room for every type of vice, intrigue and exploitation.

There were even categories of thieves who worked as receivers of stolen goods ('fences') and Colquhoun identified twelve of these ranging from 'Opulent receivers' to 'Receivers who travel with carts'. These were the managers of crime, the leaders and masterminds, with another portion of their lives given over to 'respectable' cover for their nefarious trade.

Two men are credited with the establishment and success of the Thames River Police: Patrick Colquhoun and John Harriott.

Colquhoun was a Scot who had been Lord Provost of Glasgow; he was born in 1745, the son of a judge. After his father's death he left to seek his fortune in America and there he succeeded in business, returned to Glasgow and founded the Glasgow Chamber of Commerce. He must have been a natural and tireless campaigner for social improvement, because he took on the challenge of establishing soup kitchens for the poor in London after coming south and taking up the office of magistrate at Worship Street.

His flair for documentation and planning combined in his writing of the *Treatise*; he was as meticulous and thorough as the later Victorian social investigators such as Mayhew and Binny were to be. The more he studied London, the more he began to see how crime and poverty were related, and he described and explained the functions of criminal networks. His powerful and well-expressed conclusions and recommendations regarding professional police were largely ignored and he was certainly ahead of his time. But then along came the powerbase representatives of the riverside companies, and his river police theory was to become a reality.

John Harriott was born in the same year as Colquhoun, and he too had devised a plan for a new river police force. Earlier he had been a farmer in Essex, where he had also served as a magistrate. He had served in both the army and the navy, being a soldier in the army of the East India Company and seeing active service in a sepoy battalion, during which he was shot and severely wounded. His army service certainly prepared him for future work within the operation of criminal law, but he also acted as a judge advocate, despite the fact that he was not qualified in law.

Colquhoun and Harriott met and shared ideas and opinions, and when the dock companies realized that their own method of trying to combat crime – a reward scheme – had failed, they approached Colquhoun and Harriott. The government agreed to a trial period, with the two creators of the new force as magistrates. Parliament itself had not been involved, but the first steps were taken: initially the force would comprise a group of civilians who had powers of arrest.

© WAPPING MUSEUM, THAMES POLICE ASSOCIATION

John Harriott, entrepreneur and adventurer, who was a founding magistrate, along with Patrick Colquhoun.

This happened at the time when the 'wet docks' system started to be devised and developed. The old system had been for vessels to dock side by side, and then small craft would work with them, taking goods to quays and docks. This practice was, of course, open to theft, as it was difficult to control and supervise. More efficient and usable docks were planned and the West India Dock Company Act of 1799 was passed; after that, other new docks were built at Wapping (the London Dock) and at Blackwall (the East India Dock). Later came the Regent's Canal, which linked these docks to commerce further across the land, joining the Grand Union Canal. The docks were to be some of the most magnificent sights in the country, the subject of artists and writers of the new age to come.

The old street keepers and private constables employed in years past to try to stop petty theft on the docks had failed. The professionals had now arrived. Their creation was slow, however; both Colquhoun and Harriott had developed their plans independently, and Colquhoun had sent his plans to the Secretary of

State, but for months no reply came. Finally, a letter was sent to Lord Dundas at the Naval Board of Control and events began to unfold, leading to an agreement by the Chancellor of the Exchequer that the government would part-fund the new force, if the merchants of the West India Dock would pay their share. John Harriott was made magistrate on 15 June 1798 and the police office for the Thames was founded. The 'River Police' were to open their doors for business.

The criminal community did not exactly quake in their boots. But, generally, the country overall had a hatred and suspicion of any police force. Taking a wider picture, this was a bad time for England: the country was almost certainly about to go to war with France; there were frequent troubles in the north and various dignitaries were causing a stir about the inhumane criminal justice system and the disgusting state of the prisons and local gaols. With hindsight, it is a simple matter to see that another reason for a police force, particularly during that period, was to take up some of the strain on men and resources otherwise put on the armed forces. There had been a standing army in the north and the midlands for many decades, ready to deal with radicals and riots. Soldiers were based in most main Yorkshire towns, for instance, ready to assemble in trouble 'hotspots' at any time. As late as the mid-1830s, the 'Physical Force' Chartists under Feargus O'Connor were drilling with weapons on Woodhouse Moor, in Leeds.

Nothing provides a sharper contrast between the French and British ideologies of criminal law and the morality of policing than the French concept of detectives 'in the system'. In France, there had always been the 'King's Police' and these had contained *agents provocateurs*. The *Ancien Régime* in France had established the idea of the police as an integral part of an espionage network, used to spy on the radical elements of society. When Joseph Fouche took over the French Ministry of Police in 1799 the old tradition of detective work being essentially espionage was carried on. Fouche recruited 300 officers to use as spies; when Vidocq took over the *Brigade de Sûreté* he was a part of Fouche's organization, something that worked organically, with excellent communications between different *arondissements* in

Paris. In England, the problem with the notion of police was that the word suggested a repressive state and a system of spies among the ordinary people. The hatred and resentment of police officers by the people in the streets was one of the main obstacles to success, and the new magistrates and constables knew this.

Nevertheless, measures were taken to support the process of detection, arrest and trial. Shortly after the new force began their work, in 1798, an Act was passed to create magistrates in Middlesex and Surrey near the city: seven offices were established, with paid justices. These included offices at Shadwell and Whitechapel, and they could handle affairs on the Thames as well as on land.

Officially, what was born in the midst of all this was the Marine Police Institution. In the first instance, the role of the West India Merchants and Planters Marine Police Institute – to use the full title – was to protect the shipping of the West India Company, but it was clear that the duties would soon multiply.

1 Crime and the Thames in the Eighteenth Century

WHAT KIND OF society existed before Britain had a regular police force and before the Thames had its own dedicated professional law enforcers? It would be wrong to say that people lived in a fearful state of anarchy, but plenty of records and autobiographies testify to a state of fear, especially at night, when families had to secure their homes and hope that the night watch would not fall asleep or drink too much beer. On the surface, it appears that law was preserved more by ties of kinship and allegiances than by civic order, and there is an element of truth in that. In most parts of Britain, the investigation of crime and legal redress were actions taken by the victims and their friends and family. Community transgressions were often dealt with by the community itself, particularly if there was a moral offence which might not go before the courts, but needed to be punished. The church courts also attended to many of these types of offence.

As far as the rivers and the coastline were concerned, legal jurisdiction and efficiency were patchy at best; the basic problem was a lack of finance and a longstanding reliance on calling out the militia for any serious crime such as public disorder. Smuggling was rife and contraband activities were big business. On the Thames, local constables tried their best to deal with petty crime, but were always outnumbered and isolated.

When we think of the popular images of crime in the 'long' eighteenth century (c.1700–1837), the aspects of the period that come to mind are probably Dick Turpin the highwayman, smugglers and horrible hangings at Tyburn. These kinds of images stem partly from more recent popular culture – mainly film and novels – but also from countless illustrations in books, magazines and documentaries depicting the sheer vicious lawlessness of that period.

But, in fact, the most dominant criminal events of the years were arguably the Jacobite insurrections of 1715 and 1745; the riots and disorder which occurred for all kinds of reasons; sedition; and offences against the Game Laws, and the most significant new remedies were the introduction of transportation and the birth of professional police forces. Although there was a high level of homicide, and many crimes against the person in that period, and also a series of repressive Murder Acts, what captures the limelight in terms of the history of crime is the political narrative.

If we look at some of the major legislation of the time, we find a hugely influential statute in 1715, The Riot Act; then the 1718 Transportation Act, which gave courts the power to transport some felons to the American colonies; the Black Act of 1723 which added a large number of offences to the established 'Bloody Code' of repressive capital offence statutes discussed in the last chapter; and finally the various Acts against sedition and radicalism in the Regency years, all aimed at preventing the open or secret dissemination of radical political ideas during and after the French Revolution of 1789.

The period is marked at every level of crime as one of horrendous repression and punishment. Nevertheless, the British citizen was under threat from robbers and muggers at all times in the towns and, of course, in London, with nocturnal fears being particularly severe – after all, a man and his household were only protected by the 'watch and ward' officers, who were generally ineffective. Although the Bow Street magistrates and 'Runners' were operating in London, and at the end of the period there was Sir Robert Peel's Police Act of 1829, for Britain in general, there were perils everywhere.

In 1728, for instance, John Byrom had a meeting with a highwayman. He wrote a letter to his wife describing this: 'About half a mile or less of Epping, a highwayman in a red rug upon a black horse came out of the bushes up to the coach, and presenting pistol, first at the coachman and then at the corporation within, with a volley of oaths demanded our money.' Shots were fired and the passengers parted with cash and silver. But the robberies went on daily: copies of *The Gentleman's Magazine* and *The Annual Register* are peppered with reports of nasty and brutal attacks, dreadful murders and brutal hangings.

The number of capital crimes gradually increased throughout this period, until the offences included many varieties of theft, including from rivers. Judges on the assize circuits found a procession of culprits standing before them – often very young – who could technically be hanged for what we would think of as small thefts. For a 'grand larceny' the sentence was death, so courts and judges often humanely changed the value of stolen goods so that they would be related to simple larceny. (Until 1827 grand larceny referred to stealing goods valued at over twelve pence).

Despite the many offences on the statute book, for which penalties were severe, it was a time when there was much trouble in the streets, in the country, and in the new mills. In 1769 attacks on mills were included in the offences subject to the Riot Act, and later in this period, political radicalism triggered further extreme measures. In 1799 and 1800 the Combination Act outlawed meetings in streets of more than six people; after the Luddite troubles of 1812, when machine-wreckers (named after a fabled figure called Ned Ludd) set about destroying mills in Yorkshire, a new offence of administering an illegal oath was created, so that more felons could be hanged or sent to Van Diemen's Land (Tasmania).

Some riots were not merely responses to the price of corn; the 1780 Gordon Riots in London, triggered when Lord George Gordon presented a petition to Parliament against Catholic rights, lasted for six days. Deaths occurred and in the end 135 people stood trial. Riots were also linked to sedition, and in 1792 there was a proclamation against seditious publications, and even the great statesman Thomas Paine was tried (*in absentia*) and convicted of sedition.

Another aspect of this unrest was mutiny. The Napoleonic Wars had numerous side-effects, of which mutiny was one: in 1797, after a dangerous mutiny at the Nore, men were tried and hanged. In the area of political protest, assembly for political reasons received its most brutal response from the authorities when the Peterloo Massacre occurred in 1819 in Manchester: here, the famous speaker Henry 'Orator' Hunt addressed an immense crowd, gathered peaceably, but the yeomanry intervened and, in that bloody encounter, eleven people were killed and many more wounded.

But riots could break out for all kinds of reasons: there were food riots in Cornwall in 1727; anti-enclosure riots in the Forest of Dean in 1735, and election riots in several places in 1734. Crowds gathered to destroy turnpikes in Bristol in 1749 and, in 1751, two women suspected of being witches were murdered by a crowd in Tring.

One report in the press from 1755 gives some idea of the trouble that was often experienced: 'May, Selby, Yorks. The bellman made proclamation for the inhabitants to bring their hatchets and axes at 12 o'clock that night to cut down the turnpike erected by Act of Parliament. Accordingly, the great gate with five rails was totally destroyed by some riotous persons.'

The abiding image of the criminal justice system in the Georgian years is one of trials at the Old Bailey and hangings at Newgate or Tyburn, accompanied by huge crowds. Of course, there is some truth in this, but we have to recall that although many were sentenced to die (and did), many were also reprieved. Between 1814 and 1834, for instance, almost 5,000 people were sentenced to hang for burglary, but only 233 did so. Nevertheless, the hangman was busy. Following the Murder Act of 1752, a felon was to be hanged within just forty-eight hours of sentencing. Until 1760, a 'triple tree', a wooden frame with three sides, was used at Tyburn, so that several people could be hanged at once; this was replaced by a portable gallows in that year. Hangings at Tyburn (now Marble Arch) ended in 1783, and from December of that year executions took place at Newgate. The so-called 'new drop' there was the scene of a multiple hanging in 1783, when nine men and a woman were on the scaffold.

Until 1784, a wife murdering a husband would be burned at the stake rather than hanged, as her crime was petty treason, not murder. In that year Mary Bailey was the last to suffer that horrible fate – although it was common practice for the hangman, for a small bribe, to strangle the women before she was tied to the stake. For treason, a person could be hanged, drawn and quartered until 1820, when the famous Cato Street conspirators suffered that fate.

After the loss of the American colonies, transportation was to Australia, beginning in 1787. Between 1815 and 1829, around 12,000 convicts were transported to Australia. The process involved a period in a specific colony, and then work on probation teams, so that, for instance, convicts in Tasmania would at times be allocated to gaols in Richmond and be engaged in public works, such as bridge-building.

Prisons in this period were seriously dangerous places to be. The assize system meant that prisoners on remand awaiting trial had to languish in disease-ridden cells until the judges arrived on the circuit to clear the gaols. Local gaols and houses of correction were, however, the subject of a study and survey by the great prison reformer John Howard. His book, *The State of the Prisons* (1777) was the first step in the movement towards making prisons more humane and open to some notions of rehabilitation and reform rather than mere punishment and hard work in a 'silent system'.

Much work relating to public safety was done by the Vestry Committees, who employed constables for 'watch and ward': running a day watch and a night watch in the community. As with the quarter sessions, at which magistrates presided, their business included everything from dealing with robberies to heaps of dung deposited on the highway.

A useful way to gain an insight into the workings of the Vestry Committees is to take a case study. In Richmond, the Teddington Association for Proper Persons met in the Vestry Room in 1822 to organize its police patrols. Two patrols (a 'watch and ward' beat system) followed the precedent of the London night patrols, which had emerged from the work of John Coloquhoun before Peel's Act. It cost Richmond around

£50 to maintain that vigilant group in their night streets. Twickenham Reference Library has detailed material on this Vestry work and on the constables, and their minutes open up their work for the modern historian:

> Richard William Cook and John Harris having been proposed as proper persons to act as patrols –
>
> Resolved – That they be appointed accordingly, and paid at the rate of one guinea per week each, and that they be provided with proper arms at the expense of this Association.... It is extremely desirable that the said persons should be appointed constables.
>
> Resolved – That an application be made to Mr Sergeant Marshall, requesting that he will swear them in accordingly.

The Watch in Richmond was superseded by the new V Division of the Metropolitan Police in January 1840 and its watch-houses were taken over as police stations. For the family historian, the accounts and minutes of the Vestry subscription fund provide names, even in small detail such as: 'Nov. to the parish constable and his assistants of Kingston who apprehended Brown ... £3.3. 0.'

However, the watch was not exactly effective. The reign of the Hanoverians was riddled with crime. Statistics are not always reliable, but we have glimpses of the scale of this. In 1788, for instance, the *Morning Herald* published a list of the offences committed by the prisoners in Newgate covering the two years ending in September 1787. The list includes 13 murders, 114 cases of housebreaking, 109 of shoplifting, 132 of privately stealing from persons and just 15 for robbery on the Thames. The reason for this small number of offences committed on the river is that robberies were happening all the time, and very few persons were ever caught and arrested. The newspapers for the eighteenth century are peppered with short reports of robberies on boats on the Thames, often very simple matters of men with guns or knives entering a boat and robbing the occupants on pain of death, usually stealing money, jewels, clothes and especially buckles.

The most fruitful strategy for the victims was to offer a reward and publish an advert describing the crime and the stolen goods, such as this piece from *The World* in 1782:

> Two hundred pounds reward: Whereas in September a most daring robbery was committed on the Thames a little below Gravesend by four men in an open boat, armed with pistols and cutlasses. The above villains, between five and six in the evening, boarded an American brig laden with stores for Virginia, and after confining the crew, stole goods to the value of 30 shillings....Whoever can give information ... to Mr Silvester at 3 Pump Court in the Temple ... shall receive upon conviction of the villains, two hundred pounds.

Any and every kind of item was stolen from boats, even ropes and sails. Sometimes men would board a ship, set her afloat and then cut the sails. Bow Street and its patrols did their best in such cases; sometimes constables from that base would stop suspects and question them, as happened on Tower Hill in 1792 when Constable Shallard stopped a man in connection with a murder committed on the Thames the week before. But there were several impediments to success: before the Middlesex Justices Act, there were difficulties of prosecution, such as occurred in 1751 when two men were indicted for stealing 50 lb of hemp from a ship commanded by a Captain Peter. Late one night the two men had approached in their bumboat (a small, wide boat to carry provisions to vessels from the shore), shouting that they had drink for sale. When there was no response from the ship, one of them boarded and started to steal the hemp. The crew were alerted and chased the two men, one sailor diving into the water in pursuit. This all happened near the Tower, and the judge at the Old Bailey asked, 'Was it above the Tower or below it?' When the reply came that it was below the Tower, the judge acquitted the men because the robbery had happened in Middlesex, and so in London there was no authority to try the case.

There were many cases that involved arbitration, common sense and an understanding of the rules and culture pertaining specifically to the Thames: the kind of rules the Thames office magistrates in the next century were to understand and apply in their judgments. But in the years before the Marine Police, matters were clear-cut because that gave little complication for the bench. So punishment was severe in most cases; for instance, in 1748 Richard Ford and Connell Neal were convicted of respectively stealing (amounting to grand larceny) and receiving bags of sugar. They claimed at their trial that custom allowed that they could keep 'sweepings up' but the Master of the ship from which the sugar was taken said at the trial that this was not so. 'Sweepings' had to be defined and the Master obliged: 'After the cargo is delivered, [it is] that which is left, trod under foot.' But the accused had filled bags and put log-wood shavings at the top, above the sugar (which was very valuable). They clearly knew that they were not allowed the sugar. Ford was fined thirty-nine shillings and Neal was transported for seven years.

The most straightforward, everyday offence on the river was theft from lighters. Entirely typical is the case of three men of Wapping who, in 1748, stole twenty-four bushels of beans at a value of forty-eight shillings and four sacks valued at ten shillings. It was most often the case at this time that pursuit and arrest were by the victim, perhaps aided by friends; in this instance, the lighterman heard where his stolen goods were and obtained a search warrant from a justice. At the trial, a watchman at Execution Dock, where the accused's cart with the stolen goods in it had been reported, said that he had seen the goods and had been asked to lock them up until the law was brought. Both men in the dock were transported.

Of course, robbery and theft on the Thames were just one part of the crime wave of these years. Smuggling was also rife, and river piracy, together with the petty offences Patrick Colquhoun describes in great detail in his *Treatise on the Police of the Metropolis* of 1796. There had been attempts to combat this crime wave by legislation, as in 1784 when a statute was passed ruling that no six-oared boat would be allowed on the Thames, on forfeiture of the boat and what was in it. In early February the next year, more than twenty boats of that type were seized, and so zealous were the constables that one of the craft taken belonged to the water bailiff. This office had a long history and was one of the key positions in the maintenance of law on the Thames before the Marine Police. It was a dangerous occupation: in 1755 the water bailiff at Richmond cut some nets which had been left by fishermen to catch salmon, and he was caught, his boat was destroyed, and he was then beaten to death.

The Court of Conservancy, which had the water bailiff working with it, had the remit of dealing with regulations governing wharves, fishing and offences of fouling the river; juries presented cases to the water bailiff. Traditionally, water bailiffs were appointed in seaport towns to search vessels; in London the bailiff mainly supervised fishing, gathered taxes, and could also arrest for debt. After the Thames Conservation Board was established in 1857, a number of retired police officers took up the role of water bailiff.

There had been earlier legislation too: under the Hovering Act of 1718, vessels of less than 50 tons could not drop anchor within 6 miles of the shore; then in 1736 attacks on preventive officers – the excise men – was made a capital offence. This was the Act of Indemnity and it included a number of extreme punishments for any involvement in smuggling, even the act of resisting arrest (which could be punishable by transportation). As is so often the case with repressive legislation, there was also the notion of a free pardon for a smuggler who gave names of other accomplices.

It is possible to trace the beginnings of the customs system to the Winchester Assize of 1203, and as early as 1298 there were officers appointed to work in the role we now think of as that of a customs officer; the actual Board of Customs was established in 1643. After that, revenue cutters worked the coasts and estuaries, being merged with the Board of Taxes in 1849. On the Thames, revenue officers were always working alongside the River Police, and in that same year, for instance, the revenue cutter *Vigilant* took hold of a barge with a crew of five, for having a contraband cargo: It was a seizure of a very large amount of tobacco: *The Times* reported that the tobacco taken amounted to 14,402 lb. The court convicted the five men, with a penalty of £100 each, which was not paid, and they were sent to Maidstone gaol.

Yet small-time robbery from river craft was constantly in progress, and a menace. There was a black market for luxury goods, any type of valuable possessions, and even for a variety of equipment and tools. The situation before the police were established was basically one of the use of informers (nick-named 'stags'), and that successful way of working continued. Colquhoun had an informer called John Branham, a waterman, paid not only by Colquhoun but also by the West India Company merchants. He was a local character of some influence, being part of a group called the Wapping Boat Society. He was ideally placed to know and report on the movements of goods in bumboats, barges and other small craft. He had also served in the navy and for Customs and Excise. Reading between the lines in the story of this man, it seems clear that he knew the seamier side of life, could move freely across different communities on the river and communicate well. In an age when the government employed spies in contexts of industrial and political unrest, he would do well for himself.

Most of the river depredations were small-scale; Peter Linebaugh, in his book *The London Hanged*, notes that in the Old Bailey sessions papers from the 1790s, at least eighteen men were reported as being tried, as in the 'sweepings' case mentioned earlier, for the theft of sugar. Other goods taken in small amounts were all varieties of clothing. As to punishments, at the less severe end of the spectrum, there were whippings; then there were custodial sentences at a house of correction, and the most draconian measures were mainly transportation.

Stealing from river craft involved a range of tricks and ruses, depending on different ways of hiding goods on the person. Even by 1890, as a feature in the *Strand Magazine* makes clear, crime had barely changed, as in this account of an imagined thief:

The ingenious docker is responsible for more than one quaint artifice; and as the secretion of tobacco or spirit on his part may at times involve an accusation of theft as well as smuggling, a sharp look-out is kept for him. Let us imagine ourselves at the dock gates ... To ordinary observation he is a plain and innocent docker, with the customary amount of hard wear in his clothes... Now we should never notice, unless our attention were directed to it, that he wears very large boots. The constable has observed it however, and makes a pointed allusion to the fact... The fact is, he has been making anti-damp socks, like cork soles, for himself, but they are made of tobacco-cake.

The article goes on to describe 'a pigeon box' in which a secret compartment hides stolen goods; an 'accordion' (a case with stolen goods inside) and oil tins used to smuggle in brandy.

When the new wet docks were built, they were designed to be fortresses in terms of their security, mainly because they had high walls around them. Also, as work in the new docks was more streamlined, loading and unloading times were reduced, and supervision was made easier. The West India Merchants Committee was well aware of what measures needed to be taken to further reduce crime, such as stopping men working on vessels from going ashore in daytime and making sure that lumpers (labourers loading and unloading cargo),were searched in transit from river craft. Colquhoun worked for and with the Committee and knew their mindset; he had long been aware of the methods of work used by the criminal underclass in cities, and was full of new ideas. After all, Henry and John Fielding, magistrates at Bow Street, had shown how to use communication channels and information to do police work. Colquhoun saw that, despite the good work done in the new docks in terms of protection, there was still a gap – men qualified and skilled enough to apply vigilance on the wharves and on the water were needed.

When the Fielding brothers started their innovative investigative methods, they had established the first kind of police intelligence that actually gave insights into the offences in their area. They printed handbills giving details of wanted men and these were sent to all postmasters in the land; this was followed by a quarterly list of London criminals and a weekly bulletin.

Henry Fielding's publications, the *Quarterly Pursuit* and the *Weekly Pursuit*, were followed by *Public Hue and Cry* in 1786, issued by Sir Sampson Wright, who followed the Fielding brothers at Bow Street. What was happening – and Colquhoun would have seen this – was that middle-class, educated men were faced with writing, describing and distributing information mostly on members of the labouring population and the criminal underclass. For Colquhoun, as he prepared to write his *Treatise*, one of the most important elements in his task was to be sure who the criminals of London were. Were they in organized gangs? Were they often wealthier men out for an adventure? In fact, as Professor Clive Emsley has concluded, that was not the case. He summarizes the topic by saying that most of the criminals in the trial reports were 'runaway apprentices, small-time whores, pilferers and sneak-thieves, drunkards and cheats' and that 'any simplistic idea of London as a crucible of advanced professional, organized criminality [is] not easy to maintain'.

Patrick Colquhoun knew this, also. He gained an accurate insight into the fact that the bulk of crime on and by the river was opportunist, desperate and small-scale: facts which made it highly likely that the small crimes would be repeated endlessly. What we see in the 1790s is something like the later situation when there was an actual detective force (although the Bow Street Runners had worked largely as detectives, albeit on a small scale). Colquhoun and everyone else who planned regular and organized police forces knew very well what common attitudes to such things were. After the Ratcliffe Highway murders of 1811, the Earl of Dudley wrote: 'They have an admirable police at Paris but they pay for it dear enough. I had rather have half a dozen people's throats be cut in Ratcliffe Highway every three or four years than be subject to domiciliary visits, spies and all the rest.' The fact was that crime could not be addressed and prevented without 'knowledge of the enemy' and it took a very long time for people to understand that.

Arguably, more so than with any other variety of local crime prevention in the land, the various officials who desperately tried to thwart the activities of the Thames criminals and then punish them, represented the wrong-headed thinking of the time – the notion that a succession of repressive statutes would instil fear and all would be well. Throughout the eighteenth century, law after law was passed, pinpointing specific offences in all regions and areas of criminal activity, as well as regulating trade and industry. As these were enacted, so the number of capital offences increased dramatically. When the law reformers of the 1790–1830 period, such as Samuel Romilly and Robert Peel, began to address this problem, they saw a system in operation in which death or transportation for life awaited offenders guilty of numerous offences.

With this background in mind, the achievements of Patrick Colquhoun (and before him, Henry and John Fielding), are all the more impressive and significant. The criminal justice system in London had worked by the use of informers, watchmen and a variety of men in other trades who welcomed additional income in part-time work with the magistrate and the customs men; but the British Empire was expanding in leaps and bounds, and the docks and wharves of London were the very life-blood of that cosmopolitan enterprise. Colquhoun knew, as a businessman and as a criminologist, that matters could only degenerate as the new century arrived and the population expanded; his remedy was for the city, and historians have to speculate what would have been the results if the authorities of London had listened to him and acted before the Marine Police initiative. At least, by the Regency period, London had the Bow Street Magistrates and Runners, a horse patrol, and the Marine Police in their probation period. Alongside this there were still local constables, trying to cope with myriad small offences and nuisances in their parish.

The dock merchants and the men of business around the river may have had no idea just what kind of quiet revolution in law enforcement was taking place around them. A little later, Peel was to meet the same resistance as Colquhoun. In 1822 a Select Committee sat to consider a police force for London. Called to meet by Peel when he became Home Secretary, its report argued that it was hard to reconcile an effective system of police 'as was consistent with the character of a free country'. The Committee members had not looked to the river and the docks to see what was slowly starting to happen. It was by no means an instant success, and the new constables were reviled, outnumbered and resisted, but they were working as Bow Street had worked: a police office and magistrates in conjunction with men who knew their clients, their local geography and the nature of the crimes on their beat.

It would take several decades from the beginning of the new century for the word 'police' to become an acceptable part of the world of crime, law and order. With hindsight, it may be seen that the Marine Police at Wapping were an experiment – one hardly noticed at all, but doing invaluable work, not only on the river but in neighbouring parishes, backing up the watch and the constables when needed, going beyond their necessary and essential duties on the wharves and on the water.

2 Early Days

The new force had been established for only a few months when one of its first major challenges occurred: a murder case involving a violent mob and Patrick Colquhoun reading the Riot Act. It all began when the two magistrates were questioning some coalheavers charged with the unlawful possession of coal. They were doing this under the Bumboat Act of 1761, which made it easier for magistrates to stop and question persons suspected of taking goods from vessels. A bumboat was a scavenger's craft, used for carrying filth from vessels lying in the river, and was also a term used for boats that carried provisions out to ships, so it is plain to see why the Act was so called: these craft were clearly suitable for small-time theft. The coalheavers of the area, numbering around 1,400 at the time, were in the habit of taking several bushels of coal every time they unloaded a collier ship.

With their power to stop and question, with a summary offence as a possible outcome, Colquhoun and Harriott were busy trying to get the truth out of the coalheavers, when a mob gathered outside and started shouting for their blood. Soon, they were throwing paving stones. One of the men detained was named Charles Eyres, and his brother James was one of the leaders of the mob outside. But the magistrates would not be intimidated and imposed a fine on the men detained. That enraged the mob still further and matters escalated to such an extent that later, when more suspects were being interrogated for theft from a ship, the mob came closer and threw huge stones at the police office windows.

Despite the fury outside, Colquhoun went out to face them

and he read the Riot Act. The police also fired pistol shots out, and that frightened the mob for a while, but they returned and threatened murder. James Eyres was in one group as the mob were separated into two areas – the Ding Wharf and the Cooperage – and there, matters got totally out of hand, as the lawyer at the Old Bailey later described:

> I understand that the mob which retreated to the Cooperage never returned, but those who retreated to the Dung Wharf were rallied again and in consequence this unfortunate man, Gabriel Franks, and also one of the rioters, were killed....It will be found that Franks going towards the Dung Wharf, for the purpose of making observations on the rioters was shot by some person.

At the new police office that day there were various members of staff besides the two magistrates: Henry Lang was a clerk, Franks, although he worked as a lumper, was a part-time official but not a sworn-in constable, Richard Perry and Thomas Mitchell were constables, and Bartholomew Peacock appears to have been a part-time assistant, as this was the first phase of the force, when citizens were part of the team.

Lang, the clerk, saw and heard virtually everything, and his testimony in court gives us a clear picture of events. After Charles Eyres and his friend were fined, the cash was given to Lang, and he recalled a row about that and then a noise outside. He told the court that the mob started to batter the office windows and then they destroyed the shutters outside. He saw Constable Mitchell run to the office, wounded in his hand. Lang noted that Colquhoun had sent someone to call out the volunteer force of London militia.

Lang heard the noise increase, and he said that Franks asked for a cutlass but was refused, then he and Franks went outside to front the mob and back up Colquhoun. Franks turned around to tell Perry to take care, and at that moment he was shot and he fell. Before he fell he had picked out Eyres and said that they should take note of him. Lang was sure that the pistol could not have been fired from the police office. Franks was carried to the Rose and Crown and there, after some time, a surgeon called William Blizard from the London Hospital attended but knew that nothing could be done to save Franks' life. He testified that the victim was bleeding internally, having been struck by a bullet on the right side of his breast. Blizard took the man's dying declaration, and then, amazingly, Franks did not die until two days later.

In the early confrontation with the new force, Colquhoun and Harriott had come through with flying colours: not only had they preserved the office against massive odds, but they had caught the perpetrator of a wilful murder. Colquhoun had bravely read the Riot Act, and his constables and other staff had stood their ground. It is clear from the trial that the people in the local mob hated the police; they had shouted murderous threats to them, and words were recorded and noted in court, such as: 'Bring the arms and let us shoot all the buggers!' A man called Webb who had property dealings with the police was advised to go home because, as the witness said, 'it was ten to one they [the angry mob] would pick him out'.

It had been a serious riot: one civilian had died, with one officer killed and another injured. Yet one thing was now sure in the minds of the locals: the new River Police were not a pushover, and their commanders were tough and resolute.

The power and importance of the magistrates in and around London definitely increased at this time; in fact the magistrates appointed, without knowledge of the law, were well catered for in terms of education and publications available. Dr John Burns' book, *The Justice of the Peace and Parish Officer* had reached its sixth edition by 1801. It was produced in four volumes, octavo, and was widely known and used. Shortly after this, the standard work for coroners, by Jervis, was to appear, and *Jervis on Coroners* was to be the *vade mecum* for that profession. In a climate of escalation of crime in London, it was very important that the magistrates, police constables and coroners worked together. In the riot involving Eyres, the bodies of both men who had mortal wounds were taken to the nearest public house, as was the custom for most coroners' inquiries. The police and the coroners would be together, with witnesses, for future reference, particularly when the case was destined to be heard at the Old Bailey, which is what happened with the Eyres murder.

In the first years of the police force, there was such a plethora of petty crime, both on the river and amongst the neighbourhoods along the wharves, that at times the new River Police had to turn people away. This happened in the case of William Inglis in 1801. He was a black sailor, found by a labourer called Hughes, in the New Cut, weeping and desperate for a home and food. He said he did not know London and needed help. Hughes was kind and took him home, then gave him food and a bed for the night. But early the next morning, as he told the judge at trial, 'I looked about my room and found my box broke open.'

He went to look for Inglis and found him in Church Lane; Inglis tried to run but was caught, and then taken to the Thames Police office, but was turned away. Hughes had to find a constable at Whitechapel who would arrest him and lock him up. It was a serious offence, and Inglis was transported for seven years. Clearly the River Police were too overworked to cope. One reason for this was the sheer volume of crime; offences actually committed on the river were a special challenge. In June 1801 at 4 a.m., the *Themis* was lying in Bell Wharfways when a gang of pirates boarded her while the captain and mates were asleep, and made off with £10 in bank notes (a large sum then). They were unseen by anyone and were never traced. The new police were never involved.

In fact, on several occasions at this early stage in the history of the force, serious offences were dealt with by the sailors involved: the trials would take place in an Admiralty Court, with death sentences carried out on Execution Dock – the destination for pirates and others who committed serious felonies.

In the first few decades of the new River Police, much of the crime dealt with was, of course, theft from vessels and wharves or warehouses. Typical of this was the case of John Weight, who stole two hempen sacks, two bushels of split peas and half a bushel of oats from a warehouse at Bow. He was seen rowing a boat to the shore, by a watchman who followed him, with an assistant, and took him into custody. He was sent to Van Diemen's Land for seven years.

But there were plenty of serious and violent encounters, and sometimes these involved the navy. In 1803, the navy needed to keep their press gangs active and maintain recruitment for the war against France. A press gang of three men set out in June that year to look for potential recruits around the taverns. They went to Wapping and saw two mariners going into a public house kept by a man called Quin, and they followed them. The gang immediately took hold of one of the men, but Quin began to fight with them, saying that 'No rascally crew would his friend have pressed' and a brawl ensued. Quin, and his friends Bell and Noel, were arrested by officers and taken to the Thames Police office. The press gang had a warrant, so they had infringed no law and the men resisting the pressing were in the wrong. A press gang man called Trevallion had been badly beaten. At the trial at Hicks Hall, an account of the fight was given:

> Trevallion pointed out a man of the name of McCarty as the person who had knocked him down and beat him. Morse, another officer assaulted, said that that was not the man, but Noel was. The former also said that the moon had not gone down and that there was a lamp near and that he had light enough to distinguish the countenances of those who were beating him.

Trevallion was a man with a violent past and had, in fact, been a constable with the River Police but had been sacked. He then worked for the Admiralty and in the pressing work he had fired a pistol at a man being taken for the navy.

This gives a glimpse of the sheer overload of duties and responsibilities of the new force. Not only did Harriott and Colquhoun have to constantly question arrested suspects and deal with the huge amount of larceny taking place, but they also had to handle events such as riots and fights – some, as in this case, involving friction caused by the Admiralty and their staff.

Yet the work went on, and the Old Bailey was supplied with a regular flow of culprits standing in the dock for offences committed on or beside the river. The prosecutions were not always successful, of course, and sometimes the crime was on a vast scale. In 1815 there was a massive theft of material from a ship on the Thames owned by a man called Oliver Wilcock. The thieves stole 267 shawls, 22 dozen handkerchiefs and 6 cotton cambrics. Three men were caught and charged with receiving the goods, and the value was given as £100 – in today's values, around £20,000. Wilcock had transported all his goods onto a ship, ready for export to Surinam, but the next day a check revealed that two-thirds of the whole consignment had been stolen.

What happened shows just how difficult it was for the police to convict the 'fences' in the network of thievery that went on. The lawyers argued that there was no solid evidence and witnesses called by the defence provided alibis, in spite of other witnesses stating that they had bought goods later shown to have been stolen. In the end, the legal issue was whether there had been one or two felonies, and whether or not all the men indicted were proved to have been there at the time of the theft. The jury acquitted without even retiring from the box to consider the case.

It is not difficult to imagine the frustration of the magistrates back at Wapping. What became evident in the first twenty years of the force was that the only way to succeed in future would be to have investigations involving informers, detective work and the use of established networks of lookouts and customs officers all working together. But this was something that did not start to happen until the middle of the Victorian era. In 1815, the only detectives at work were the Bow Street Runners, and they were a small number, often recruited to work on special cases and to operate as protection and security for the wealthy.

The river was now firmly in the hands of the new magistrates and their men, but the learning process was going to be very long, and fraught with troubles and problems. One of the most common and recurrent hurdles in the way of success was, as the Metropolitan Police were later to learn, the drop-out rate among new constables. In the case just mentioned, Trevallion had been sacked from the force and had still been employed by the Admiralty. It was a time when a man useful with his fists and a pistol or a cutlass was employable despite his tendency to go beyond legal and acceptable behaviour.

Later, when police constabularies set up across the land, recruitment was more streamlined and qualifications were applied. But in 1800, there was more of an element of desperation and urgency. For some years, the force was still dependent on part-timers, volunteers and private citizens. Of the four sections of the new River Police, the 'Marine' was to be the strike force (initially a force of sixty-two men), but there was support from the other departments: the Judicial, the General and the Discharge groups.

The new force existed as a strange mixture of various agencies of the law for its first thirty years until it amalgamated with the Peelers in 1839: in the first years of the new century this small group of magistrates and constables, with supporting watermen, operated alongside the watchmen, the beadles and the constables, who were ineffective amateurs and part-timers, and the prestigious Bow Street Runners, who really were an efficient and widely respected body of men, working across the land on special assignments in addition to their work in London.

Nevertheless, the new Marine Police had their foothold in the brave and frightening new world of policing the long, tortuous and stinking river, rife with crime: it must have been with a feeling of excitement and anticipation that the new men set up for police business at 259 Wapping New Stairs on 2 July 1798. Having arrived along with the new docks, part of their brief was to attend to that area as well as to the river commerce. The new officers had to be all things to all men: the instructions issued by statute specified the various elements in their role, stressing the necessary vigilance: 'You shall well and truly serve our Sovereign Lord King ... for the special and express purpose, and no other, of detecting felonies, larcenies and misdemeanours in ships, vessels and lighters in and upon the River Thames.'

At amalgamation the Marine men, as they became part of the Thames Division, were differentiated from other Metropolitan men by their uniform. They wanted to appear 'marine' insofar as their dress should suggest something nautical rather than municipal; hence the hierarchy had their respective attire. The structure was that of inspector, superintendent, surveyors, sergeants (also called second and third class inspectors) and constables. Dress was a straw hat for the constabulary and silver crowns on hats and coat collars for sergeants, while senior inspectors were in a black, peaked cap and a braided jacket (the latter similar to that of warders in some prisons and asylums later). Superintendents and surveyors wore three-quarter length coats, with peaked caps or boaters, all in black.

The sergeants who worked as inspectors second and third class were paid less than the inspectors *per se*. Geoffrey Budworth explained this in his book, *River Beat*, in 1997: 'This was deliberate contrivance. Since 1833 Surveyors had carried Customs warrants with formidable extra powers of search and seizure to combat smuggling and Sergeants were designated Inspectors so that they too could be issued with Customs warrants.'

The new century was only just beginning when it became clear that the new men would have to be involved in any number of cases in a range of localities bordering the river. They were, in fact, in the very heart of a tough, lawless society, as Boyd Hilton explains in his survey of the Regency situation in this context:

> The concept of lawlessness was elusive. About 5,000 people were committed for trial in England and Wales in 1810, and more than 18,000 in 1830. Yet policemen were virtually non-existent ... Soldiers stood by in urban barracks to curb radical discontent, but played no part in law enforcement. Affluent people who walked the streets were at perpetual risk from pickpockets or worse.

Early success and cohesion of the Marine Police was going to depend on the magistrates, men who had a solid and respectable precedent in the achievements of the Fielding brothers, Henry and John, who had made Bow Street a model of the road to success in prosecution and administration, but these men were to be overstretched and always in demand as the nineteenth century began.

3 Magistrates, Murder and Mayhem

IF WE TAKE a closer look at the state of the crime committed on the Thames at the turn of the eighteenth century, it becomes clear that theft and depredation were rife, and that the sheer scale of estuary and river trade left everyone on the water and on the riverside vulnerable to any number of nefarious activities, from bribery and concealed items taken off vessels to outright attack and daytime robbery. When Colquhoun itemized the scale of the situation in 1800 he wrote that there was 75 million pounds worth of property on the water and that all of this was subject to one of a number of crimes, mainly acts of 'peculation, fraud and pillage'. He also provided statistics on the nature and number of vessels coming and going: for the year ending 5 January 1798 he noted that 346 vessels made repeated voyages to the West Indies, 608 travelled to and from Prussia, and in the coastal trade of coal transport there were 3,676 ships involved. The total value of goods from imports and exports in the coastal work alone came to around eleven million pounds. Today that would be a figure in the billions.

Colquhoun certainly knew how to tender for a job: his words, read by the merchants of the great trading companies, told of 'millions of packages, many of which contain very valuable articles of merchandise, greatly exposed to depredations, not only from the criminal habits of many of the aquatic labourers … but from the temptations to plunder arising from the confusion unavoidable in a crowded port'. The companies using the docks had previously known some limited kind of policing – the Customs and Excise already existed – but their officers had little success against a crime wave. Also, as far back as 1711, there had been constables in place along the quays to try to stop theft, but despite the existence of a five-shilling reward for capture of thieves, they had little impact. The basic fact, pertinent to all principal avenues of criminal activity there, was that the Pool of London, designed to take just over five hundred ships in the Tudor years, by 1800 had almost eight hundred crammed into the available space. By Regency times, the ships' tonnage had increased considerably.

On the streets of London, although crime was just as frequent and varied as on the river, at least there was a topography which played a part in basic security at times, but on water, with vessels so open to assault and theft, policing was a major logistical challenge. Colquhoun, when he finally persuaded the merchants to acquire a police force, concentrated on having officers who could supervise the loading and unloading of cargo, particularly of sugar and rum, the staple products of the West India businessmen; the new officers were paid by the merchants, and the results were impressive.

After the initial period, the force became official, slightly more numerous and also a little better-known. The most important element in advancing further was to have the right kind of magistrates. The Fieldings had achieved great things in the previous generation, making Bow Street a respected focus for properly regulated judicial administration. John Fielding knew the importance of efficient co-operation and intelligence on criminal activity. In *The Public Advertiser* for August 1767, he described for the public (and for villains) how his publications worked: 'The collecting into one point of all information of fraud and felony committed in or near this metropolis by constant advertisements and the correspondence carried on at this office ... with the acting magistrates in the county ... had ever been deemed a valuable acquisition to this country.' He made a special point about the magistrates, men hard pressed and overworked. There had been statutes issued to attempt to give the magistrates and constables, the very heart of the justice system, more protection, notably an Act of 1751 which explained their major problems.

Magistrates were always open to litigation and complaint, to say nothing of actual physical assault and the 1751 Act noted that: 'No writ shall be sued out against, nor any copy of any process, at the suit of a subject, shall be served on any justice of the peace for any thing done by him in the execution of his office ... at least one calendar month before the suing of the same.' What was happening was that justices were 'discouraged in the execution of their office by vexatious actions brought against them for small and involuntary errors in their proceedings.' When they were not overworked and making errors, they were still objects of hatred and murderous intent. A particular example of this was in the horrendous years of 1811–1812 when the Luddites were in action, but they were vulnerable at all times. In 1791, for instance, there was a horrible attack in Yorkshire as a result of a move to enclose the common land of Crookes Moor, where working men could spend their small leisure time profitably and freely. The area of land in question was vast – 6,000 acres. An Act of Parliament had been gained by some powerful landowners who had land in the Moor, men such as the Duke of Norfolk and the clergyman Wilkinson. The workers were furious. On 13 July 1791, when the commissioners arrived to enclose the land, they were confronted by some local die-hard workers who terrified them with threats. As usual in those affairs of public disorder, men in the wealthier classes asked for help from London, some writing to the newly established Home Office, demanding militia. (Not long prior to this, major riots in Birmingham had been quelled by militia.) The request was acceded to, and some dragoons arrived from Nottingham.

There was a massive crowd in the streets when the dragoons arrived; riots were commonplace for all kinds of reasons. In this instance, the occasion was used to free a man who had been arrested for debt, and that boosted the crowd's morale. But the powder-keg was lit when the officer who had arrested the debtor insisted on getting his man. When the man was retaken, the officer, one Schofield, was effectively under siege from the crowd. The riot spread to other centres of resentment, such as Broom Hall, the home of Wilkinson, who was a magistrate as well as a member of the clergy. The mob descended, intending to burn the place down. As some men were inside, others went out into the enclosed garth to burn four haystacks, and a servant there saw what happened.

People arrived to help put out the fires, and the mob moved on to attack other property, including that of Eyre, the constable. By morning, more soldiers arrived, and the land and property involved was retaken, and of course arrests were made. Among the arrested men was John Bennet, who was only eighteen, and there were three or four others, some of whom had merely been in the wrong place at the wrong time. Bennet and a man called Ellis were charged with riot and arson and committed to York for trial.

Crimes of this sort were, in that period, the easiest methods by which the poor or those with grievances could wreak havoc and fear in the ranks of the wealthy, landed classes, and were thus taken very seriously. Four men were in the dock, Bennet among them, as the trials began. Something familiar happened: someone (Ellis) turned King's evidence and testified that Bennet had been the main offender when the stacks were set alight. Other witnesses were called, and we have to suspect that these were paid 'yes men', all a part of the process to ensure that someone would swing for such a terrifying offence.

Bennet was young, and he was also an apprentice with some years still to serve under his master. But supportive statements mattered not one jot: he would have to be seen to be punished severely for such an offence and he received the sentence of death from Baron Thompson. Bennet was hanged, along with another arsonist and a forger, on 6 September. Another man, Johnson, was luckier, being acquitted as he was, as one witness said, 'ever considered weak in the head and easily persuaded'.

The local men of power who had been hated and had been the targets of the crowd's anger appear to have deserved much of the poor opinion. The clergyman Wilkinson, for instance, was recorded as having put a little girl in the stocks for repeating some scurrilous verse about him: 'They burnt his books/and scared his rooks/ and set his stacks on fire.'

This episode shows that the regional power base of the criminal justice system depended on the magistrates, but the county sheriff and the Lord Lieutenant, who supervised the army resources in local barracks in case of large-scale trouble also played their part, providing back-up.

In London the force most prominent in the days before the police was the Volunteers, a body often ridiculed, as for instance in a caricature by the Strand-based artist Thomas Rowlandson. Magistrates were at the very centre of confronting all criminal activity and, at least in London, forces for the suppression of riot and disorder were near at hand, but the terrifying Gordon Riots of 1780 had shown how fragile the King's peace was.

For these reasons, Colquhoun and Harriott needed good, reliable men as magistrates for their part of Middlesex and the City. In the first thirty years of the force, there was a succession of busy, solid, dependable men as magistrates: their names are now forgotten except in the footnotes of police history, but Richbell, Clarkson, Coombs, Broderip and Ballantine, who succeeded the first and famous founders of the force, were involved in a dizzyingly large number of cases, from minor thefts to mutiny and murder. The son of John Ballantine, writing as Mr Serjeant Ballantine in 1883, recalled these men and his father:

> At the time I was called to the bar my father was a magistrate and was residing at the official residence of the Thames Police ... opposite to what was called Execution Dock, where it was customary to hang pirates in chains. He had for a colleague an old sea captain of the name of Richbell. It was thought in those days that the experiences of navigating a ship on the sea would be a good preparation for administering the law in connection with the river.

Young Ballantine often visited the Thames Police office, and the magistrate Broderip was to provide the young lawyer with a reference later on. Ballantine commented that the magistrates were 'an admirable body of men, joining discipline with much of the knowledge possessed by the old Bow Street Runners.'

Ballantine Snr worked with Richbell until the latter died on 24 April 1833. But before we trace the cases and activities of these men, a closer look at John Harriott in the first decade or so of the century will throw light on the position of these magistrates, caught between the everyday duties when cases before them were clearly river business, and the other world of often terrible crimes inland from Wapping. In fact, the clearest way to show this is to look at what Harriott did when he played his part in one of the most notorious mass murders in British history; the Ratcliffe Highway murders. This slaughter of two families just before Christmas 1811 was discussed in one of the nineteenth century's most innovative essays, the classic true crime piece written by Thomas de Quincey, 'Murder Considered as one of the Fine Arts' (1827) in which he wrote, attaching blame to the magistrates involved:

> You all remember that the instruments with which he executed his first great work [the murder of the Marrs] were a ship-carpenter's mallet and a knife. Now the mallet belonged to an old Swede, one John Petersen and it bore his initials. This instrument Williams left behind him, and it fell into the hands of the magistrates. Now, gentlemen, it is a fact that the publication of this circumstance of the initials led immediately to the apprehension of Williams and if made earlier, would have prevented his second great work [the murder of the Williamsons] which took place twelve days after.

The first murder, of the Marr family, was very close to the Wapping Thames Police office, being just beyond the tobacco docks and close to St George in the East church. There was a dangerous byway called Old Gravel Lane close by and, of course, the night of the murder was very dark, with only the night watchman around. Timothy Marr was a linen draper on the Ratcliffe Highway, and on the night when the killer murdered him and his family, he had been tidying up his shop after a long day. He was a retired seaman, working hard at his new trade, and his locality at the time, Wapping and neighbouring Shadwell, was an atmospheric place, close to Execution Dock where pirates' corpses, as Ballantine had noted, hung in chains on the marsh. But it was a slum area, too, and this bloody tale enlightens the status and responsibilities of Harriott and his colleagues.

A worker called Jewell had been sent out to buy food for the Marrs but found shops closed. When she came back to the door, she was seen by the watchman, George Olney. Inside, Marr, his apprentice boy, his wife and their baby lay dead, brutally killed by the intruders in the dark. Eventually, entry was made into the shop via a neighbour's property, and the bodies found. The question was: who could be consulted? Who was in authority and who could help? The Thames Police office was the nearest location where the forces of law could be found, so news reached the office, and Police Constable Charles Horton, who was on duty then, hastened to the scene of carnage. Horton, regardless of his duties and his 'patch' as an officer of the law, did what any true constable would do: he hurried to the Marrs' shop. He saw the bodies and found the iron mallet, and then assumed this was the work of a gang, though the motive was unclear. He reckoned that the killers had run off down Old Gravel Lane.

Harriott was at the centre of the matter, in spite of other magistrates being close by in Shadwell, and it was he who had some Greek sailors arrested and questioned, though they proved to have an alibi. This was eighteen years before the establishment of the Metropolitan Police, so, in such circumstances, it was the magistrates who represented authority and the law. Harriott and his officers were, in effect, the real professionals in the area: the old watchmen and their supervisory beadle had no experience of dealing with serious crime and, although the Shadwell magistrates were not far away, they had responsibility for a vast locality with a very large population – mainly Shadwell, Wapping and Poplar as well as the stretch of the Ratcliffe Highway.

Harriott also had relevant previous experience: in his military career out East he had been a deputy judge advocate. P.D. James has summed up the situation regarding the operation of the law at the time of the Ratcliffe Highway murders, and she places Harriott and Horton in context:

In 1811 the forces available in Ratcliffe Highway to detect and apprehend the murderers of the Marrs comprised: one night beadle, one High Constable, one constable, thirty-five old night watchmen and twenty-four night patrols employed by the vestry of St George's in the East; three magistrates at their public office in Shadwell … and an inquisitive old adventurer, Harriott, with a force of river police.

But Harriott was the most active, even writing to the Home Secretary and monitoring his actions, mainly playing at being a detective. Harriott offered a reward leading to the arrest of the killers, while the Shadwell magistrates did nothing, but, for his pains, Harriott was reprimanded by Ryder, the Home Secretary. He was censured for showing too much 'zeal'. It was a case of his being involved in something so large-scale that the higher authorities wanted to be seen to be doing more to track down the killers than rely on an old man whose real job was supervising theft from vessels – although, of course, people generally knew the amounts of cash and value of goods involved in that daily work, as in the 1815 case of Taylor and Hastings, who had stolen shawls and cambric worth a huge amount of money.

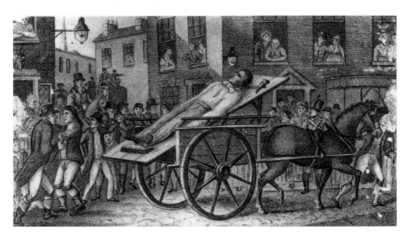

The burial procession of John Williams, the
Ratcliffe Highway murderer

The work as a Thames Police magistrate had certainly helped Harriott escape his financial worries. But through his life, trouble and controversy dogged him. He was in the habit of using the police boats for leisure trips and he also contracted maintenance work from a firm called Hurry & Co. When he sacked staff in 1809, they wanted revenge on him and they reported certain irregularities in accounts to the Home Secretary. Harriott appeared before the court of the King's Bench and, although he was acquitted of all but a minor charge, his health declined with the stress involved. One of the sacked men was a Mr Gullifer, a clerk. There was an inquiry into the administration of the office and, in the end, Harriott was strongly advised to appear in court, so that his name (and that of the force as a whole) could be cleared in public. He appeared in court on 15 June 1810, with fifty-three counts on the indictment. But in the end, the minor charge was simply that of having his name on a few billheads of the force. He was fined, but the affair was more significant in its effects than in the fact of a trial *per se*. Such a matter always leaves a dark shadow of suspicion over an individual, of course. Accounts had not been properly and meticulously kept, that seems sure. As the Thames Police Museum literature points out, 'The only hint of anything of the kind which has survived is a letter written by the magistrates in May, 1825, to an account which was "kept entirely by Mr Harriott and was not left in the office but continued in his possession until his death".'

After this, Harriott's life declined; he lost two of his children, and in 1816 he was found to have prostate cancer. Even in his death there was dissension and drama, because when found, his body had stab-wounds, clearly self-inflicted. He signed a will in a period of remission, and his suicide then took place in the Thames Police office. The jury was aware of the tragic personal situation and a verdict of death by natural causes, rather than suicide, was returned.

In the trial period of the Thames Police, in which the fledgling force had been tested by the West India Company, there had been a designation of the 'Judicial Department' consisting of a resident magistrate, two clerks, a chief constable and seven petty constables. The magistrates were to sit mornings and evenings and commit offenders to trial. An accounts department supported this administration, with a cashier, a collecting clerk, office- and house keepers and other supporting clerks. The office and judicial staff were linked to a residential solicitor for prosecutions.

In addition to these administrative elements, there was the business of direct action regarding the river craft and the attached occupations, with the daily supervision and protection of the trades by and on the river. This was the province of the Discharge Department, run by a superintendent and two clerks. Their main tactic was to operate a system of licensed workers – the lumpers. At the end of the eighteenth century, when this was being established, there were 820 licensed workers.

The magistrates who succeeded Harriott were to be involved in masses of petty crime but also in major, sometimes international, crime. In the ten years after Harriott's death, Richbell, for instance, found himself in every conceivable situation of judgment and arbitration that could be imagined, his work covering matters which, in other times and places, would be dealt with by other professionals. In 1819 he was faced with a brutal sea captain, one Charles MacGlashan, who was summoned to appear with regard to non-payment of wages to a seaman called Alex Campbell. The seaman had been beaten while their ship lay at Tobago, and then given strokes of the lash. As the court report states, Campbell was then in dire straits:

> He went on shore up the island, a distance of 25 miles, to make his complaint to a magistrate, from whom he could neither obtain a hearing or any redress; rather than starve on the island he tendered himself to the captain … who refused to receive him unless he signed a paper whereby he promised to pay all expenses the ship had been at on his account.

The issue at law was: had Campbell deserted, and so forfeited all wages? Richbell and his bench decided that it was not a desertion and ordered the captain to pay the balance of wages – the huge sum of almost £10 – and the costs of the application.

In contrast to this, Richbell had to handle numerous truly

ghastly cases, including the 'Hat-Box Mystery' of 1826. Generally, the magistrates were able to sort out any argument, dilemma, atrocity or accident that came before them, but this case illustrates the puzzling and random nature of their daily routine. Two bargemen, Jacam and Pearse, who worked for a firm in Brentford run by a Mr Townsend, came into the office and asked to see Captain Richbell. They wanted to show him a hat box and its gory contents, which they had brought out of the river as they were going up with the tide between Southwark Bridge and Blackfriars. They opened it and found two blood-stained shirts inside, so they went to a magistrate called Clark, who told them to take it to Bow Street, clearly assuming that this was a horrible London murder and therefore should be Bow Street business.

The bargemen decided to take the box to the Thames Police instead. The full contents proved to be a mysterious collection of items worthy of a murder from a thriller or a Ripper tale:

> It was found to contain two shirts marked all over with blood, one of them greatly torn, and the blood on them greatly coagulated; they were frilled and marked with the letters J.R. in blue silk thread ... an old towel, marked L.C., a pair of calico drawers, marked as the shirt, a coarse apron with no particular mark ... a collar stained with blood, besides several small bits of paper, some of which were found to be apothecary's directions to take medicine ... also a printed card on which there was H.B. Plowright, retail ironmonger, Lynn.

The box had been in the hands of a traveller at some point, because on the lid there were the words, 'Mr Robertson, Passenger'. There was also a note from a Mr Bell of Duke Street, London, and that seemed to be the first port of call, but it led nowhere.

Richbell directed his men to start some detective work; in an age well before computers or any kind of mass communication, unravelling identities and locations was a gargantuan task. However, two days later the street keeper of All Hallows Lane reported at the office and told a tale about finding a 'quantity of blood' on the All Hallows Lane Stairs ten days earlier. Basic forensics on the scene led to the belief that there had been a struggle there, and the conclusion was that the blood smears came from the right-hand side of the person who had apparently been attacked. The bloody shirt in the box was indeed torn on the right-hand side only.

This was, however, a case that petered out, with a final comment in the newspaper report on the matter that: 'It is rather singular how such a fragile article as a hat-box with such weight in it should float.' The story became one of the many potentially dramatic and sensational cases left frustratingly unclosed in the annals of the force.

Sometimes the magistrates and the new police were openly and viciously attacked in riots and disorder. In 1831, Ballantine and Broderip sat in judgement on a case involving a violent confrontation of police with some street roughs. It started when Sergeant Wheeler and Constables Lee and Higginbotham from K Division of the new Metropolitan Police, which covered West Ham, witnessed a mass brawl involving some five hundred people on the Ratcliffe Highway. Wheeler somehow managed to part the main combatants in the fray, a man called Sullivan, his brother and a boxer called Crawley. Then the press reported that a crowd of Irish set about attacking the police and, as this was happening, Crawley insisted that he and Sullivan move to Old Gravel Lane to finish their fight. Constable Lee followed them, having avoided being killed at the hands of the mob.

Sergeant Wheeler was brutally kicked and trampled on, and a man called Hicks led a particularly savage group of Irish to continue the assault on both the officers. But, impossible though it seems, the officers calmed people down, except for Crawley, who was heard to shout out, 'Murder the police! Down with the peelers!' One factor that had exacerbated the affair was that Hicks had been carrying the coffin of his son to burial when the fight started, and he, along with his friends, put down the coffin and joined in. The police were seen to have been interfering where they were not wanted.

Following up on the incident, Thames Police became involved; an officer called Boyd Sylvester led a search for the main culprits, going on board a ship, *The Magpie,* to look for Crawley and Hicks. Sullivan was found in the hold, and several constables of the River Police and of K Division gathered to arrest him, but then the lieutenant on board ship refused to give up Sullivan. There was a confrontation, and Officer Sylvester, told to go, ignored the naval officer and grabbed Sullivan. In the stand-off, sailors armed with cutlasses and knives stood threateningly before the police officers. The man who saved the day was Evans, the Principal Surveyor at the Thames Police office, who managed to calm things down.

Before magistrates Ballantine and Broderip, the naval officers were reprimanded and their conduct reported to the Admiralty. As for the rioters, Sullivan and Hicks were heavily fined, with a two-month prison sentence if they could not pay up.

The affair was not exactly a rare occurrence at the time. The new police attracted a number of attacks and assaults, as fear of a police state spread among the populace of London. But what this case does show is that the new Metropolitan Police were mixing with the River Police. The 1829 Police Act created the divisional structure and this added a new dimension to the Thames Police office work and the everyday tasks of the officers. Although the River Police were not to become the Thames Division of the Metropolitan Police until 1839, it is clear that the 1829 organization was helpful in many ways to the Thames office. For example, the Divisions from K to S covered West Ham, Lambeth, Southwark, Islington, Peckham and Greenwich. T Division covered Hammersmith and V Division dealt with Wandsworth. In addition, the new police were responsible for the Royal Dockyards and military installations, covering Woolwich and Chatham in terms of areas bordering the Thames locality. There was also the Bow Street Horse Patrol, which had to work in liaison with the River Police, and they were incorporated into the force in 1836.

All this meant that, in the first years of work by the magistrates Ballantine and Broderip, they were in action at a massive turning point in police history, and such confrontations as the one just mentioned were common; the 1830s was a time of general unrest across the land, and public disorder was on a large scale. By the middle years of that decade, the Chartists would also be active, and their activities were perceived by the establishment as being a daunting threat to law and order. The decade also included the escalating nefarious trade of body-snatching. London *c.*1830 was indeed a terribly threatening and formidable place for all the arms of the law: around that time there were the 'water rats' robbing the Thames' shipping of goods worth £300,000 a year, and besides them were the trades of counterfeiting and passing stolen goods. It was a time that desperately needed a detective force, to increase the success rate of preventing crime and discouraging criminals, but, aside from the Bow Street Runners, who had been working successfully (albeit on a small scale) for more than half a century, it was not until 1842 that the first detective force arrived in the city.

The new River Police also had to work in very unsavoury and depressing conditions. The old 'lost' rivers of London were, at that time, still there and in use. As is evident in Alexander Pope's poem *The Dunciad* (1728) the old river fleet was an example of the nasty environment:

> *Fleet Ditch, with disemboguing streams*
> *Rolls the large tribute of dead dogs to Thames,*
> *The King of dykes! Than whom no sluice of mud*
> *With deeper sable blots the silver flood.*

In their patch, at the very heart of their domain, the Thames officers also witnessed the expansion of the docks, and the first magistrates would have seen the construction of five major docks by 1828: the West India, the East India, London, Surrey Commercial and St Katharine Docks. In this context, it is no wonder that the new force, particularly prior to the Police Act of 1829, had to cope with any number of events and crises around its base: crime emanating from sources on water and on land, and comprising both white collar crime and crimes against the person and property. The magistrates and constables experienced a baptism of fire in those early years, and, in modern language, their teamwork and sense of satisfaction at taking on such a challenging task were most impressive.

In Georgian Britain, the various elements in the criminal justice system had taken a very long time to mature and form a viable and reasonably efficient mode of work and co-operation. In fact, nothing significant happened in this respect until outstanding individuals took prominent parts in the struggle against endemic and deeply-rooted criminal activities and attitudes. In the Regency years, Patrick Colquhoun and John Harriott's achievements stand alongside those of such luminaries as John Howard, who began a process of prison investigation and reform, Samuel Romilly, who fought to change the criminal law regarding execution, and Robert Peel, who led the way in respect of legislation to rationalize police, gaols and judicial administration.

Yet, in spite of all the hard work done by these individuals, in 1829 there were still posters and handbills around the city with opinions such as this:

The New Police

Parishioners — ask yourselves the following questions:

Why is an Englishman, if he complains of an outrage or an insult, referred for redress to a Commissioner of Police?

Why is a Commissioner of Police delegated to administer justice?

Why are the proceedings of this new Police Court unpublished and unknown? And by what law of the land is it recognized?

Why is the sword of justice placed in the hand of a military man?

Robert Peel, along with Colquhoun and Harriott, wanted 'a police force that shall act by night and day' and by 1830, as the new Metropolitan Police were on their beats in the rather frightening streets of the city, the Thames men were patrolling fifty-four miles up and down river, from Staines Bridge to Dartford Creek in Kent. Unless the good people of the metropolis read the police and law reports down to the small print, they would have no idea of just how varied and demanding the work of the magistrates and officers based at Wapping was: they were asked to be courageous, adaptable and resourceful in a thousand different ways in an average week, always expecting the unexpected.

4 Everyday Policing: Suicide, Pirates and Theft

A S MENTIONED IN the introduction, the unpleasant business of 'found drowned' – suicides and accidental deaths in the river – was as normal and familiar to the Thames officers as eating dinner. Clearly, the task of preventing suicide around the river was always going to be impossible. Suicide was a common remedy in the hard times of Regency and Victorian England, when problems included insuperable ones of debt, depression, dire medical conditions and the dilemma of pregnancy outside wedlock. Apart from the religious issues, involving the sin against God and Creation and the fact that one's life was not one's own to take, prior to the Forfeiture Act of 1870, suicide or *felo de se* as it was called (self-murder) was a felony, and felonies entailed the loss of property and inherited wealth. (Suicide actually remained a crime until 1961 and, even after that, a suicide pact was still illegal.)

The police officers and the coroner at the inquests following suicides had to deal with a succession of sad cases, such as that of Emily Nott, a servant girl of just twenty-one who, in 1850, plunged into the river off Blackfriars Bridge. There was a certain professional interest in this because, as *Household Narrative* journal reported: 'The girl had formed an attachment to a police constable who, being engaged to another woman, gave no encouragement to her passion.' Emily left a suicide note of direct simplicity: 'Dear madam, by the time you receive this I shall be no more.' What happened typifies the helplessness of the police: 'She enquired the way to Blackfriars Bridge and having reached it, mounted to the top, and plunged head foremost onto the causeway below. The policeman at the bridge saw her fall and on going to her, found her head battered in.' The coroner's verdict was sympathetic, returning 'Temporarily insane'.

Suicides and accidental drownings provided a challenge to all interested humanitarian and legal parties that might be involved. Since 1774 there had been the Royal Humane Society, established by two doctors, William Hawes and Thomas Cogan, who were worried about the high incidence of people being assumed to be drowned and dead when in fact they were still alive. The doctors and other interested parties met at the Chapter Coffee House and invited public support. The society was, initially, known as The Society for the Recovery of Persons Apparently Drowned and had five aims: to publish information about resuscitation; to make a payment of two guineas to anyone trying to save a life; to pay four guineas to those who succeeded in that task; to pay a guinea to anyone who allowed a body to be treated in their house, and to provide volunteers with medical equipment.

In London, in 1773, 123 people drowned and the society's simple rhetorical question with regard to the situation was: 'Suppose but one in ten restored, what man would think the designs of the Society unimportant, were himself, his relation, or his friend, that one?' Later, a succession of receiving houses was established, and these were a valuable support for the Thames officers. In 1816, the secretary of what was by then the Royal Humane Society, T.J. Pettigrew, wrote to *The Times* to list the receiving houses, after a coroner's inquest at Millbank had revealed a general ignorance of the places. He added a reference to an issue at Rochester: 'Where an unfortunate occurrence lately took place, there are no less than five medical assistants with whom the apparatus has been lodged for years, but which could not possibly be employed, life being extinct.' The list comprised taverns such as The Angel at Rotherhithe, The City of Quebec at Wapping Wall and The White Hart at Chelsea. The 'apparatus' Pettigrew referred to was a set of bellows with a brass box enclosed in wood, which contained heated tobacco, with a flexible pipe attached; this was used as early as 1771 for artificial respiration. Jennifer Breen has explained how this apparatus was used:

> This process of artificial respiration ... consisted of the infla-
> tion of the victim's lungs with a bellows, which was followed
> by pressure on the chest.... After some time, if the patient
> showed no sign of breathing, a further method was to blow a
> small amount of tobacco smoke into the rectum or lungs with
> a pipe or fumigator, because tobacco smoke had been found
> to stimulate respiration.

There is no doubt that the police officers learned from the Society. A kit of a similar kind was adopted by the Thames Police, and one of these is preserved in the museum at Wapping today.

Officers were certainly busy. Returns on suicides from coroners' courts in Middlesex and Southwark for 1859 show 204 deaths and, between 1859 and 1865, the average annual figure was 210. Statistics of deaths are not the whole story though, because the returns of the Metropolitan Police for 1859 show 49 attempted suicides within the City of London and 2 in the Thames Police district, but by 1865 the figures for both forces combined exceeded a hundred.

As mentioned earlier, suicide in the middle years of Victoria's reign was on an immense scale. Blackfriars Bridge was notorious as a haunt of would-be suicides; in 1841 *The Times* reported that at least one person, not a police officer, was something of a specialist in saving lives at that place:

> The mania for attempts at suicide at this bridge has unfortu-
> nately not ceased, and the motives which have actuated the
> greater number of the persons who have been taken out of the
> river, singularly to say, through the brave conduct of two or
> three of the watermen who ply there, have hardly in one
> instance been explained. Yesterday morning ... John Ware,
> who has been the means of saving the lives of upwards of 20
> individuals, was successful in rescuing another, after a most
> determined suicidal attempt.

Ware saved a young woman who was seen on the steps at the Surrey side; she had leapt into the water and he went after her in his boat, retrieving her swiftly. As the report continues, 'The exertions that had been made to save her life were so prompt and effectual that she was very speedily rescued.'

No sooner was this woman taken to a nearby workhouse than another woman attempted suicide on the south side. This time the police got to the spot and acted quickly; but the newspaper criticized the arm of the law: 'These repeated occurrences on the bridge have caused a great sensation in the neighbourhood and are likely to be of very serious consequence.... It will be necessary that the police do more than they have hitherto done.'

In 1852 the Royal Humane Society prepared a report and their court of governors heard that in the previous six months there had been sixty-three cases of apparent death treated and lives saved, and that twelve out of sixteen attempted suicides had been saved. Ten people were singled out for achieving heroic rescue, but none of these were police officers. The fact is that the police looking after the Thames were mostly concerned with crime on the vessels, and there was too much of that to cope with.

Henry Mayhew, the great documentary writer, produced his study of the London underworld in the 1850s in which he itemized and described the kinds of offences the Thames Police office staff had to deal with. Mayhew commented: 'When we look at the long lines of shipping along each side of the river, and the crowds of barges and steamers that daily pass along its bosom, and the dense shipping in its docks, laden with untold wealth, we are surprised at the comparatively small aggregate amount of these felonies.' Nevertheless, he listed criminals in the groups of mudlarks, sweeping boys, sellers of small wares, labourers on board ship, dredgermen, smugglers, and added felonies by lightermen and river pirates.

Mudlarks were mostly children and older people who worked between the barges and knocked coal down into the mud, to be collected later and sold at very cheap prices, to the poor. Mayhew commented: 'One of them [who] may be seen beside the Thames Police office, Wapping, picking up coals in the bed of the river, appears to be about sixty-five years of age.' These scavengers worked on all the coal wharves, and Mayhew adds: 'Their fathers are robust men. By going too often to the public house they keep their families in destitution, and the mothers of the poor children are glad to get a few pence in whatever way they can.'

The sweeping boys went on empty craft, supposedly to clean them, but of course they stole whatever they could. Some of them cut bags and took quantities of such items as sugar, rice or coffee, to sell to shopkeepers. These were mostly teenagers, and they dwelt in old barges, living life in the open and never going to any school. Mayhew noted that two such boys lived in an old barge at Bermondsey and sometimes in an old deserted house, and that: 'At night they covered themselves with old mats and sacks, their clothes being in a wretched state ... The magistrate sent them to the workhouse for shelter.'

The sellers of small wares were similarly scavengers, taking anything they could from the staff on ships and barges; their main trick was to board and rob ships about to sail, so that prosecutions rarely followed. Similarly, labourers on board ship pilfered regularly, and as noted earlier in the job descriptions of the marine officers, the most important part of the policing role was to supervise all workers on board ship in an effort to prevent such thefts.

Smuggling was ubiquitous, of course. Mayhew tells a story of an officer who was successful in uncovering a typical smuggling plan:

> Several years ago an officer of the Thames Police was on duty at five in the morning. While rowing by the Tower he saw in the dusk two chimney sweeps in a boat leaving a steam vessel, having with them two bags of soot. He boarded the boat along with two officers and asked them if they had anything in their possession liable to custom-house duty. They answered they had not. Upon searching the bags of soot he found several packages of foreign manufactured tobacco weighing 48 pounds. The parties were arrested and taken to the police

station, and were fined £100 each or six months' imprisonment. Not being able to pay, they were imprisoned.

Officers were always alert and vigilant, and one advantage of
smuggling being so common and so easy was that officers of the
law began to notice patterns of behaviour and scams. In 1858
an officer in Bermondsey saw a bag which had apparently been
left in the street, and as he looked more closely, he saw a man
carrying a bag from the river. With the help of some back-up
and a waterman, he followed the man and came across bags
containing 229 lb of tobacco. The men were later prosecuted by
the Board of Customs and sentenced to six months in prison.

One of the most successful cases leading to prosecution took
place in 1860, when details became known at the Wapping
office of smuggling going on in the Shadwell Basin in London
Docks, from an American vessel, the *Amazon*. It was noticed
that the steward of the ship was daily carrying a bag of tobacco
through a gate in the early hours; an inspector and a constable
followed another man who had received the goods and tracked
him to a shop in Shadwell. Prison sentences followed the arrest.
The same intrepid inspector of the Thames force, Henry Dyers,
also saw two people, Thomas Roskarts and Pauline Smastars,
crossing a road. Dyers told the court later that 'Immediately they
saw me, the female spoke to the male prisoner and dropped a
bag containing about 5 pounds of tobacco and cigars.' He
arrested them, and we learn from this how the officers sometimes worked: he called a cab and took them to Wapping. Dyers
also said that he had been looking out for them for eight months.

There was clearly an intelligence system in operation by this
time; from the very beginning, the new police had realized that
a network of informers was essential, and also rewards for vigilance on the part of various men in occupations that enabled
them to watch and note comings and goings along the river.
This was obviously useful in respect of many of the petty
crimes Mayhew mentions, such as thefts by lightermen, those
employed to navigate barges through the river and docks. These
men were trusted with cargoes, and so could exploit the situation. Mayhew noted that such thefts were not too difficult to

trace as the police became increasingly aware of 'fences' and communication channels among thieves:

> In one instance a barge was taken up at Bow Creek, with about twenty bundles of whalebone and twenty bags of salt-petre, which were conveyed away in a van to the city. The police traced the booty to a marine store-dealer. The value of the property was £4,000. Two well-known thieves were tried for the robbery, but were acquitted.

Sometimes the zeal and efficiency of the officers in search of contraband brought with it some humour in the courts, as was the case when a certain William Duncombe, a seaman, was charged with appropriating 9 oz of cigars before any customs duties had been paid. Duncombe had been stopped in London Docks and argued that he was not aware he was doing wrong. At the Mansion House he argued sheer ignorance of the law and this interchange followed:

> Yardley: (magistrate) I am bound by the law. If a person is brought up before me for smuggling a single cigar I must hear the case and if a conviction is pressed, fine the person charged. What is the value of the duty?
>
> (Officer Haynes hesitated)
>
> Yardley: Tell me directly, or I will dismiss the case.
>
> (Officer Haynes paused)
>
> Yardley: Now sir, shall I not ask you again?
>
> Haynes: Six shillings.
>
> Yardley: What would they sell for outside the gates after payment of duty?
>
> Haynes: Well I don't know.
>
> Yardley: Yes you do.
>
> Haynes: About four shillings.

Yardley: I fine the prisoner four shillings or two days imprisonment ... I say it publicly and I don't care how widely it is known, that a man should not be dragged through the streets in custody for smuggling half a pound of cigars. Tell your superiors what I say.

It must be asked: what about the work actually on the river, done by the Thames Police in the 1850s? We know a lot about that, partly thanks to the writers of the time. It is noteworthy that 'the detective' had arrived and the phenomenon drew the attention of the public and the media. One man who saw the allure of the detective's life and character was Charles Dickens. Not only did Dickens invent the first substantial characterization of a detective in English literature in the person of Inspector Bucket in *Bleak House*; he also wrote thousands of words in non-fictional genres to give his public a relish for this new breed of man. When writing his *Uncommercial Traveller* sketches he went out for a night with the Liverpool police, but in 'The Modern Science of Thief-Taking', written for the periodical *Household Words* in July 1850, he begins to use his knowledge of the new men in print. He met Jonathan Whicher and calls him 'Whichem' in various essays. Dickens understood the spirit of the human nexus in the nature of thief-taking. That is that relationships have to be forged across the line, into the no-man's-land between the established police practice and the risk-taking double-identity of this 'new science':

> In order to counteract the plans of the swell mob, two of the sergeants of the detective police make it their business to know every one of them personally. The consequence is, that the appearance of either of these officers upon any scene of operations is a bar to anything or anybody being 'done'. This is an excellent characteristic of the detective, for they thus become as well a Preventive Police.

There is more than this in what Dickens understood, however. As a man who knew the physical aspects of London from his interminable nocturnal rambles, he saw the new crimes and instinctively sensed their subtlety:

> But the tricks and contrivances of those who wheedle money out of your pocket rather than steal it; who cheat you with eyes open; who clear every vestige of plate out of your pantry while your servant is on the stairs ... for the detection and punishment of such impostors a superior order of police is requisite.

When Dickens actually met these intriguing gentlemen who had to provide this new policing, he celebrated it with a piece on 'The Detective Police Party' and here he used his novelist's acute sixth sense about people to give his public an insight, as when he described 'Stalker': 'Stalker is a shrewd, hard-headed Scotchman – in appearance not at all unlike an acute, thoroughly-trained schoolmaster from the Normal Establishment at Glasgow.'

After a few years of operational experience, patterns of detective duties were instituted, such as the measure of assigning two constables to keep watch on known offenders in pubs. Such men as Jonathan Whicher, a weathered and tough ex-labourer only just over the minimum height of 5 ft 7 in, worked hard to cultivate contacts and slipped easily between the police office and the sleazy world of urban crime. When it came to watching known offenders, men like him would gradually become the teachers and guides of the new men who came along. It was a school of the streets and only by walking the 'manor' and being a presence in it could a foothold be made.

Dickens had the same fascination for the police on the river, and in his piece 'Down with the Tide,' written in February 1853 for his *Household Words* magazine, he described a night-time trip on the river with a police patrol. He sets the scene neatly: 'We were in a four-oared police galley lying on our oars in the deep shadow of Southwark Bridge – under the corner arch on the Surrey side – having come down with the tide from Vauxhall.' In the boat with the officers, he soon learns how they work: they wait and observe: 'We had been lying here some half an hour. With our backs to the wind, it is true; but the wind being in a determined temper blew straight through us. I would have boarded a fire-ship to get into action, and mildly suggested as much to my friend Pea [the officer].'

The officer described to Dickens what their approach was: 'Shore-going tactics wouldn't do with us. River-thieves can always get rid of stolen property in a moment by dropping it overboard. We want to take them *with* the property, so we lurk about and come out upon 'em sharp. If they see us or hear us, over it goes.'

Dickens explained to his readers how the police worked the river; in the dark corners, watching and waiting, were the so-called 'duty boats', while the mobile 'supervision boats' patrolled, and then both sets of galleys signalled regularly by flashing lights. Dickens explained in more detail: 'These duty boats had one sitter in each: an inspector, and were rowed "ran-dan" which … may be explained as being rowed by three men, two pulling an oar each. And one a pair of sculls.'

We also have the basic manpower statistics as at 1850, given in Dickens' essay. He wrote that the figures were: 'Ninety-eight men, eight duty boats, two supervision boats.' Ten years later, a correspondent to *The Times* stated that the Thames Police force was woefully inadequate: 'It appears that the whole of the Thames police force includes only about 120 constables, of whom probably not more than 50 are on duty at any given time. It is believed that 1,000 are scarcely adequate to cope with the depredators who now infest the river.' But whatever the truth of that, the officers giving Dickens his nocturnal tour were certainly impressive, as they weaved around the moored boats in silence, noting every movement and sound.

We also have a picture of the Wapping office from the essay, as Dickens met the well-respected Superintendent Evans and inspected everything he could see:

We … went ashore at Wapping, where the old Thames Police office is now a station house, and where the old court with its cabin windows looking on the river, is a quaint charge-room: with nothing worse in it usually than a stuffed cat in a glass case, and a portrait of a rare old police officer, Mr. Superintendent Evans, now succeeded by his son. We looked over the charge-books, admirably kept, and found the prevention so good that there were not five hundred entries (including drunk and disorderly) in a whole year.

It would not be unreasonable to read between the lines of this passage and suspect that Dickens is really giving his readers a picture of an outdated, cosy and rather ineffective outfit. There is a certain ambiguity in the tone. But he adds a positive note too, after looking at the cell and seeing a drunk lying there: 'Then into a better sort of watch and ward room, where there was a squadron of stone bottles drawn up, ready to be filled with hot water and applied to any unfortunate creature who might be brought up apparently drowned.'

Certainly, the writer of 1860, complaining of the shortcomings of the Thames Police, nevertheless had very good things to say of Evans, and his remedy of the situation was, 'It is only requisite that the Hon. Board of Customs should confer that most able officer, Superintendent Evans, to add the whole staff of tidewaiters practically to the force of the Thames Police, without much addition to the cost of the constabulary, and with a great increase to the security of the revenue of the property of the public.' The 'tidewaiters' were the men employed at Gravesend to board every arriving ship. When one considers that in 1800 the force had consisted of just 8 professionals with 50 assistants from the body of watermen, lighters and lumpers, the advance in fifty years had been quite impressive. By 1829 there were almost 900 constables and 88 sergeants in the Metropolitan Police, so there was also a massive resource for the River Police to call on if needed.

As Dickens made clear, the main work of the force was either in patrolling in galleys to prevent crime, or dealing with suicides or accidents, of which there were plenty. The staff had the stone bottles Dickens described, and they had the Royal Humane Society, who were so proactive in their determination to save lives that they even reprimanded a landlord who, in 1821, had refused to let a dying man taken from the river be brought into his tavern by the Regent's Canal. The police also worked with bridge watchmen, and so at least that part of their role was working well in the mid-nineteenth century.

Between the establishment of the Metropolitan Police in 1829 and the important changes in policing generally with further legislation on borough forces in 1856, society had experienced accelerated change. The social and economic consequences of the Industrial Revolution presented the new police with the challenge of coping with social disorder on a large scale. From the beginning, for both the Thames and the Metropolitan Police, there had been danger, threats and violence. Within the first year of the 1829 Police Act, the first death of a police constable occurred when PC Joseph Grantham was killed in Somers Town, and in 1833, PC Robert Culley was killed in the midst of the riots at Coldbath Fields. We can gather some idea of the fears felt by ordinary householders in London from a pamphlet written in 1831 called *Householders in Danger from the Populace* by E. Wakefield. Mr Wakefield noted: 'The moment that the system of pillaging the people seemed to be drawing to a close, a new apprehension sprung up, that the rich were about to be pillaged by the poor.' He adds, 'Because law ceases to be an instrument of pillage, must anarchy, riot and general scramble ensue?' In other words, he was writing after the reforms of the 'bloody code' of the eighteenth century, which had placed well over two hundred capital crimes on the statute books. The wealthy naturally looked to the law to protect them and their property, but often saw the function of the officers of the law as being oppressive and brutal – meeting kind with kind.

The capital punishment and transportation meted out before Robert Peel's reduction of the number of capital crimes appeared to many to solve the problems of the mob and of gangs; this was largely because, for many of the underclass, prison was preferable to a life of mendicancy. The area between the Mansion House and Cheapside and Poultry was notorious at the time for disorder and threats of violence to persons. In his book, *I Spy Blue*, historian Donald Rumbelow makes it clear that, by 1848, the windows of the Mansion House had been smashed so many times that a special lookout had to be hired to watch for the beggar women who daily milled outside and who had baskets of paving stones to hurl through the Lord Mayor's windows.

But crimes of violence were not the only cause for concern. Forgery and the 'clipping' of coins were common; in 1833, for instance, a certain Robert Spencer appeared in the Mansion House charged with 'having forged the acceptance of T W Coke Esq. of Norfolk, for the sum of 405 pounds'. Notes with practised forged signatures were found on the prisoner, and he had also sent begging letters. The Lord Mayor commented that 'a great deal of ingenuity had been practised in this case', and as *The Times* reported, 'He believed a great deal of mischief was created by the facility of getting the handwriting of gentlemen of property.' Again, the Mayor noted that the abolition of capital punishment for forgery and uttering had encouraged crooks like Spencer to try their hand in the forgery business. But he did add that the government had resolved that 'forgers should undergo all the hardships of the convict's life'.

There had been many committees in the decade before the Police Act of 1829, all dedicated to forming some kind of police force. In the City, 1838 saw the arrival of a force of 500 men who formed the Day Police and Nightly Watch, with a superintendent in charge. But there was a clamour for greater numbers and more of a presence on the increasingly dangerous streets and in the alleys of the City wards, and in 1839 the City of London Police was created, with Daniel Whittle Harvey as the first Commissioner.

Therefore, after the introduction of the first magistrates and then the amalgamation of the Thames force into the Metropolitan force, there was the further addition of the City Police, to add to the chain of police forces. These were soon to be working together by sheer necessity, but that state of affairs would not materialize until the growth of larger-scale crime, such as the advent of anarchism and Fenian bombings, which made co-operation so urgent.

In the years from around 1840–1860, then, the Thames Police office and its force of officers and helpers was in the thick of the everyday crime generated constantly from all kinds of sources; much of the work was concerned with establishing intelligence networks, observation and public order; the new docks and the massive scale of river traffic certainly kept them busy and the occurrence books full.

But there were more dramatic moments, of course. Two of the major problems facing them were violence and robbery, from different sources, but often involving piracy, riots, mutinies and serious assaults. In 1844 there was a confrontation which highlighted the kind of violence was always close and imminent. In that year a floating pier was built at the bottom of Essex Street. The old pier was not sanctioned by the City authorities, nor by the Commission of Sewers and, as the new pier was in place, it was arranged that the old pier should be destroyed. The locals, however, wanted the old pier moved as quickly as possible before permission for demolition had been obtained and so a group of men determined to smash it up. A newspaper report describes what happened next: 'On Friday morning a gang of 50 ruffians from Execution Dock, Wapping, the stone pier at Greenwich and other places, began cutting away the supports of the old pier, and swore with dreadful imprecations that they would murder anyone who interrupted them.' Two of the owner's men were assaulted and knocked to the ground. It was then a job for the police. The first constables to arrive were from F Division (Kensington) but there were only eight of them and the rioters threatened to kill them, waving their crowbars, hammers and boat-hooks, as the fight went on with more of the pier owners' men.

It was a situation which called for co-operation between the police forces, and that is what happened. Warrants were issued for the arrest of individuals seen to be leading the trouble, and the forces of the Thames Police and other divisions assembled to face the riot again. Culprits were taken to Bow Street and, for some days after this, a strong police presence was maintained to allow the old pier to continue its work until legal demolition occurred.

There were also murders on the river, a typical instance being a case that came before Captain Richbell in July 1832 and eventually led to a trial at the Old Bailey. This occurred when Thomas Smales, a printer, and William Wilkinson, a clerk, both in their twenties, hired a boat by Blackfriars Bridge and set off to row against the tide, aiming to stop at the Spread Eagle for a drink. They had been having a quiet drink at another inn before setting off, but were not inebriated at all. As they were rowing, they noticed two boats coming after them, and as they came within thirty yards of the inn Smales noticed that one of the pursuing boats went rapidly past them. The boat then turned and came back at them, ramming into their side, and one of the two men in the craft skilfully reached across and stole their coats. Smales told the court what happened next:

> Mr Wilkinson jumped up in our boat, and endeavoured to jump into the strange boat – the two boats were at that time about six feet apart; I was looking at him when he made the jump, and he did not get close to their boat … he caught the gunnel [gunwhale] so as to keep his head above water … he did not strike any part of his person against the boat…. I saw both men in the boat strike him on the head. I cannot say how many blows they struck … they seemed to strike in turn.

Wilkinson fell back into the water and Smales put out a scull for him to hold, but he went under the water.

We learn a lot about how the Thames Police worked from this case, because at the Spread Eagle there was a police officer and soon galleys were in action, with drags, to try to find the body. There followed some detective work, led by Alexander Mitchell, a surveyor with the Thames force, who made inquiries and, having discovered that the boat in which the killers chased the young men was stolen from Moore's yard at Lambeth, later found that boat in Battersea. Constable Isbister then went to find the culprits and make an arrest; he found them in a Lambeth beer shop, and one of them, Kennedy, tried to escape, but Isbister collared him.

What had happened was essentially detective work, and from this case it is apparent that plenty of searching for evidence had been done. Officers Fogg and Evans had searched for and found the stolen coats at a barge's head in Talbot's Yard. Later, some papers were found, as one of the culprits was trying to burn them, and these were taken to Surveyor Mitchell. The court report ends with a sad footnote regarding these papers: 'One bit contained part of a line of poetry'. Mr Smales, his friend and another gentleman had been engaged in writing poetry earlier on the fateful day.

In due course, four men were caught and brought before Richbell. All were notorious bad characters, known to the Thames Police, and had been before the magistrate on lesser charges not long before, but had escaped a custodial sentence. This time, they were initially charged with wilful murder. However, of the four, only William Kennedy and William Brown were later indicted with murder and stood before Mr Justice Patteson at the Old Bailey. At the trial, a verdict of murder was returned and death sentences given, but these were later commuted to transportation.

More broadly, with regard to the 1850s and 1860s, a trawl through the court records makes it clear that the detective forces were becoming very effective, and they were working together. The London Detective Force had been in existence since 1842 and gradually, in the next twenty years, regional detective forces were formed, particularly at the ports and larger provincial towns. When the Thames Police needed detectives, they had the City of London men to call on, and also detectives from the Metropolitan divisions bordering the river. In 1856, for instance, a big-time forger called Joseph Wilson, from Leith, was pursued across Britain and his case highlights the advanced communications which could be used even at that time. Wilson had been in Australia, and boarded a ship called the *Adele*; a telegraph was sent telling the London police that Wilson's ship would arrive at Deal. The villain had anticipated this and he had landed somewhere in the Channel, but that did not deter the detectives: they got their man in Folkestone.

The liaison between the Thames Police and the City detectives may be seen clearly in the case of Christian Sattler. The story is impressive in its success regarding co-ordination of various law officers involved across London and the Eastern counties. The Thames officers found themselves merely a part of a long and impressively co-ordinated chain of policing strategies and sheer dogged detective work.

In 1857 Baron Martin, a judge who had begun his career at the bar rather later than usual at the age of twenty-nine, found himself sitting at the Surrey Assizes with a very nasty and brutal killing of a police detective presented before him. Baron Martin was much respected as a lawyer who understood mercantile affairs and he was in demand at the Guildhall as well as in Liverpool and on the Northern Circuit. He was respected as the judge who never had a *remanet* – a term used for a second sitting at the Queen's Bench. In other words, he got on with things and had a practical, no-nonsense turn of mind.

The case before him was that of the murder of Detective Charles Thain, who had been shot on board the *Caledonia*, while sailing back to England from Hamburg. The man who shot and killed him was Christian Sattler, a desperate character who had been born in France but followed a military career in Germany before landing in England and starting a career of crime.

In the trial, Benjamin Eason, Chief Warder at Wisbech Gaol, remembered Sattler well. He said that the man had been on remand for a week and then convicted of a petty theft. But the warder's recalled conversation with Sattler was a significant one. He said that he advised Sattler, on release, to 'endeavour to obtain an honest livelihood' and he opined that the good Christian people of England would not allow him to starve if he could not find any work. Sattler replied, 'It's not a Christian country, I will not ask for relief; if I cannot get employment I will thieve, I will steal, and if anyone attempts to prevent me, I will shoot him like a dog.' The man was fond of that last phrase. He was to repeat it on board the *Caledonia* after he had shot Thain. When asked to report on the accused's general attitudes and submission to the gaol discipline, Eason could bring to mind merely one small misdemeanour that cost him extra hard labour for an hour. But otherwise, he was not exactly recalled as a crazed sociopath.

At the first hearing at the Mansion House the charge was put explicitly and clearly: Chief Clerk Samuel Goodman repeated it later before Martin: 'For shooting on the high seas at 4.15 p.m. on the 22nd instant, detective sergeant Charles Thain in the right breast, with intent to murder the said officer.' There were plenty of witnesses, and it soon became clear what had happened. The story began with Sattler stealing a carpet-bag with clothes and cash in it; he pawned the clothes in Cambridge and then made for London, and the man who had been robbed was a stockbroker in the city. At the trial all kinds of people came forward and soon the narrative of Sattler's escape from Cambridgeshire to London was closely documented.

A pawnbroker in Cambridge, Robert Cole, stated in court that Sattler had gone to his house to pawn a mackintosh and had pledged it for five shillings in the name of Pickard. After Sattler had returned with banknotes to buy a watch, Cole was suspicious and checked the notes; then he heard about the robbery and told the police. Information was given to the City police and two detectives, Jarvis and Thain, were assigned to the case. It became a fast-paced pursuit, as Sattler had gone from his lodgings in Gracechurch Street and the sleuths discovered that he was heading for Hamburg. They set off in pursuit.

Thain got his man in Germany, and the next record we have of this case is from the first mariner witness, Stephen Robertson, at the trial. He said:

> On 20th November last I embarked on the *Caledonia* at Hamburg for London – I had been shipwrecked and was a Consul passenger … I did not see the prisoner personally until he was down below … I was standing on the gangway a little after ten o'clock … the deceased officer, Thain, came on board by himself – three other gentlemen behind him – the prisoner came on board after Thain accompanied by two gentlemen.

He saw Sattler later, in his cabin, handcuffed. Thain had been given a small separate cabin and he was by all accounts looking after Sattler, as many seamen commented, 'with kindness'.

The stories given by various witnesses built up a picture of

Sattler as a moaning complainer, irritating those around him and yet being well cared for by the detective. Robertson heard Thain speak and respond to Sattler's request that his handcuffs be taken off, as they were giving him considerable pain. He heard Thain say, 'I have been warned of you, but I will take them off when we get to England, if you behave yourself.' Robertson heard the gunshots at around four in the morning of the Sunday (Thain and Sattler had boarded on the Friday night). This was the scene before him as he ran into the cabin: 'The prisoner was sitting on a chest, Thain was standing up, holding on to him with one hand, and with the other at his own breast. He said, "The prisoner has shot me" – I seized hold of the prisoner and dragged him out of the cabin.'

There was then a very nasty scene, after Sattler had explained how and why he had shot Thain. He had loaded his concealed pistol by the side of his bed and then fired at Thain as he came in. He said that Thain had not 'kept his word as a gentleman' and had said earlier that he would 'shoot like a dog' any man who broke his word. A gang of seamen on board, led by some American sailors, grabbed Sattler and some were for lynching him there and then. Some shouted that they wanted to 'stretch' him, meaning to pull hard on all his joints as a torture, and then hang him. A Mr Lilley described the situation: 'He was dragged on deck rather roughly ... he was not in a very excited state at this time, he only cried out with the pain of his arms being pinioned behind him. He had the handcuffs on and a handkerchief was placed around the muscles on his arm.' The gunman was then tied hard to a large bolt on the fore hatch.

As for Thain, he had not yet expired when the *Caledonia* docked that Sunday. He was taken to Guy's Hospital and there he made a statement for the magistrate. He wrote that, 'At about twenty minutes before four o'clock I got up and left the cabin and went to the water closet, having locked up the cabin and left him there. I returned in about a quarter of an hour and found him sitting on a folding carpet stool.' Thain asked if Sattler wanted any tea, and as the man answered in the negative, Thain turned with a folded coat he was offering Sattler, and then he was shot.

Other police officers gave testimony and it emerged that not only had Sattler hidden a gun on his person, but he also had a knife, and told one man that he thought about knifing Thain earlier but changed his mind.

Thain died on 4 December and the house surgeon, Alexander McDougal, said he found three pistol balls in the officer. He showed the balls to the court and said that he was holding up a piece of the man's diaphragm with the ball in it. When asked about the likely position of the deceased when shot, he thought that Thain would have been stooping when shot. Detective Jarvis, who came to the dock and found his colleague lying there severely wounded, said that he asked Sattler to show him how he managed to fire the gun while wearing the handcuffs, and that Sattler demonstrated how he had done that. The killer told Jarvis that he had estimated the powder required: 'There might have been enough in the pistol for two, three or four charges.'

The defence counsel had obviously reasoned that Sattler's only chance of escaping the noose was to argue that the custody was illegal. The court report gives the man's account in this way:

> Mr Lilley then proceeded to contend that the prisoner was not in legal custody; that his apprehension was forced and unlawful; that being a foreigner he was not amenable to the English law; that no proof had been offered as to whether or no any treaty or convention with Hamburg was in existence and therefore...The arrest was clearly wrongful.

Baron Martin would have none of this and saw it for the desperate plea that it was. He said that he 'entertained a doubt' about the issue of the lawful custody, but nevertheless he conceded to the actions of the jury and moved on to the question of murder. He confirmed that the action of the shooting was one of 'express malice' with a clear intention.

The decision was guilty of wilful murder and Christian Sattler was destined to become a client of the hangman, William Calcraft, a man with a reputation for not being too accomplished in matters of execution. There were still public executions at that time (these being abolished in 1868) and Sattler walked out to meet his fate at 8 a.m. on the morning of 9 February 1858. The watching crowd must have morbidly enjoyed the man's last dramatic antics, as he bowed in all directions before stepping forward to have the cap put on and to be pinioned ready for the drop. Calcraft liked to use a short drop – and that meant that usually his victims were slowly strangled – so he tended to put his weight on them as they struggled, and thus hastened their end. Luckily for Sattler, the drop gave him a quick 'clean' death. According to one contemporary report, 'The body was cut down at nine o'clock ... and there was a tremendous yell.'

From the mid-Victorian period, offences we now call 'white collar' increased, as banking and all branches of commerce expanded; it follows logically from this that detectives were more than ever in demand, along with their support networks. A typical case was that of Robert Shandley, who forged a delivery note with intent to defraud in 1858; he had taken a number of valuable items from a Captain Lloyd at the West India Docks, mostly chests of clothing. One of the City force's best men, Detective Brett, called on him at Princes Square, St George in the East, and asked for a confession. Shandley opened a cupboard where he had stored most of the clothing. He was charged and later convicted, being given a term of penal servitude. This would be exactly the kind of crime committed every day in the docks. Formerly, before detectives existed as a properly organized force, that search for the culprit would have involved the excise officers, staff at the docks, Thames Police and any other constables nearby, from the Ratcliffe Highway area.

Of all the crimes in the chronicles of the Thames Police, that of piracy is arguably the most pernicious, nasty and violent. The river pirates and those convicted in London for piracy offences across the seas form part of a story extending back many centuries. In the eighteenth century, this kind of report was common in the papers:

Execution of the Pirates

Brett, the Dover pirate, when he got into the cart at Newgate, shook hands with many of his friends, seemed quite composed, and had a smile on his countenance; when he sat down in the cart he took off his hat and threw it to his friends; he was a well-looking young man about six feet high and twenty two years of age. Clark ... paid particular attention to his devotions. Hobbins, convicted with them, five minutes before he was turned off, declared his innocence of the crime.

Smuggling may have been the more common offence – 2,115 people were convicted for it in 1848 alone – but pirates were, as Colquhoun had written in 1798, 'the most desperate and depraved characters'. He wrote in strong terms as he defined their nature: 'Their attention is principally directed to ships, vessels and craft in the night, which appeared to be unprotected; and well authenticated instances of their audacity are recounted.'

Colquhoun explained how they often worked with an example from East Tier Lane in the 1790s. A ship was boarded in the night, and the pirates actually brought up and stole the ship's anchor, taking it across to their own vessel. As the captain came up on deck, the rogues, rowing away, told him they had his anchor and cable and hoped that he would have a good day!

Mayhew, in the 1850s, explained in more detail how these crooks worked:

In the river, the chief object the thieves have in view is to enter the vessel at midnight, as they know that when vessels arrive the seamen are often fatigued and worn out. ... They steal from all classes of vessels but chiefly from brigs and barges. They take any boat from the shore, and go on board as if they were seamen, dressed as watermen ... Their chief object is to secure wearing apparel and money.

Mayhew's account includes several dastardly deeds of these thieves, including the incident in which a clever ruse played a part in the pirates' success. This happened at Bermondsey and, during the robbery, one of the thieves was caught by the crew and detained. The sailors called for a police galley and one drew up alongside, and took the captive on board. The next day, the ship's captain went to the Thames Police office to ask about the pirate; imagine his amazement when he found there was no such man in custody! The boat that was supposedly occupied by police was actually one with more pirates on board. The usual outcome followed: the ship was about to set sail so nothing further was done to chase and apprehend the thieves.

Another adventure against the river pirates was, in fact, a plain clothes operation. Mayhew tells the tale:

> Three constables went on duty at midnight in consequence of a number of robberies having been committed over the river, especially at Deptford. They went out in a private boat in plain clothes. On getting to Deptford they proceeded up a creek. After remaining there in the dusk for about an hour they heard a loud knocking, and suspected that someone was taking the copper from the bottom of a vessel lying there.

The officers were right: they found two men in a boat with a pile of copper next to them and tools in their hands. They were arrested, then the galley took them away, and fortune favoured the law on this occasion, because two other pirates were at the time climbing down the chains of a vessel, trying to escape from the crew, who had been disturbed by the police raid. They were arrested too.

Traditionally, pirates were tried in maritime cases, meaning that the Admiralty took charge, and also that trials of pirates were held at the Old Bailey. However, the law changed in the eighteenth century, so pirates could then be tried in courts other than Admiralty courts. Pirate prisoners were generally held in the Marshalsea Prison, and their fate was usually to hang on gallows at Execution Dock. There were several places of execution along the Thames, and as far as pirates were concerned the guideline was that their bodies should be, in the words of the

Tudor historian, Holinshed, 'hanged on the shore at low water mark, where they are left till three tides have overwashed them'. In the past, some offenders had in fact been executed by having weights tied to them and being thrown into the river, but at Wapping, Execution Dock was used, and after hanging, bodies were taken downstream to a gibbet at Bugsby's Hole, at Blackwall. Today, the garden of the Town of Ramsgate tavern (just a hundred yards from the Wapping police office), over-looks the spot where the gallows stood. There was also another hanging place – at the mouth of one of London's hidden rivers, the Neckinger. This was at a wharf on the western side, and as a 'neckinger' was a name for a neck-cloth, the term 'Devil's Neckinger' became a common name for that execution site.

During this period, piracy provided one of the most sensa-tional trials and hangings of the whole nineteenth century, although it did not directly concern the Thames Police. This was the *Flowery Land* case, a trial for mutiny and murder on the high seas. Some of the crew of the *Flowery Land* had committed the offences, with six crew members being killed, and so they were also guilty of piracy. The offenders were Spanish, so translation was a problem at the trial at the Old Bailey, but eventually five of the pirates were sentenced to hang, and the notorious hangman William Calcraft stretched their necks outside Newgate on 22 February 1864. The importance of this case with regard to piracy was in the public reaction, which was generally one of repugnance. But one letter to *The Times* expressed the opposite attitude very powerfully, and in fact explained exactly why public hanging was to end just four years later, in 1868:

> Sir, I am not ashamed to avow that I went this morning to the hanging of the five pirates at the Old Bailey and I am concerned to state my impressions at this public spectacle, because they were so utterly different from all which I had heard or read....As I watched from a commanding position an enormous crowd of spectators, which I should not hesitate to compute at as many as 20,000 or 25,000 chiefly men, and surveyed the sea of faces at the fatal instant when the drop

fell and their expression was generalized by a sudden and common emotion, I should say that the pervading feeling was a cordial acceptance of the act then transacted before them, and a complete recognition that it was just and inevitable.

A more influential reaction to public hanging was expressed by Charles Dickens: 'I pray to Almighty God to cause this disgraceful sin to pass from among us and to cleanse our land of blood.'

The old sensational tales of pirates still persisted in the penny dreadful publications and in boys' adventure stories, but as far as the Thames was concerned, there was nothing of the high seas yarn about what the Thames Police had to cope with.

5 Mutinies and Other Disturbances

IN THE YEARS *c.*1850–1870 the incidence of crime in London was alarming. One work, by J. Ewing Ritchie in 1858, informed the public that in 1856, 73,240 persons were taken into custody; of these, around 16,000 were for theft or larceny, and there were 6,763 common assaults. Add to this the 18,000 arrests for drunkenness and we have a picture of a city whose forces for law and order were trying to turn back the waves, like King Cnut, such was the alarming scale of urban crime. The police force in London was, at the time, constantly accused of indulging in corrupt practices, and the problem of drink within the ranks of the constabulary was still there, as it had been since the first Peelers of 1829. In 1863 alone, 215 officers of the Metropolitan Police were dismissed for drunkenness.

In terms of the Thames Police, by *c.*1860 their methods of work were well established; they had begun to increase their efforts towards preventive policing, and some of the reports of criminals at this time give us an insight into this work. This may be seen from the case of Joseph Williams, who was indicted for the murder of a Hastings gaoler in 1856. The criminal's track record went back many years, and after his most extreme crime, the press report noted that he had been 'well known at the Thames Police Court for many years and to the constables of K Division under the cognomen of "Bluey" which he obtained by having for some time worn a pair of old blue naval trousers'. Eight years before the Hastings murder he was linked to a Spitalfields gang and was before the magistrate at the Thames office. His future after that offers a glance into how the Thames Police and magistrate tried to do more than simply dish out sentences: 'The magistrate who heard the case questioned Williams, then a boy of 14, and the lad expressed a desire to shun bad company and lead an honest life, and said the gang of thieves he had been with had threatened to murder him for impeaching Jem the Lagger.' What happened next is important with regard to policing generally at the time. He was provided with clothes from the poor-box fund and sent to sea, but the optimism was not well placed, as he lasted for just one voyage but was then back on the streets. In an age before probation (which was not in existence until 1907) this case gives an insight into basic reformative measures taken on by the police divisions when and where they could.

As all divisions of Peel's new police had gradually learned, the basis for the best policing was to understand the *modus operandi* of the crooks in each category of offence. With that knowledge, the chain of communication among the criminals could be broken. Colquhoun, in his account of the 'light horsemen' or 'night plunderers' explains exactly the kind of thinking necessary in this way:

> These corrupt watchmen did not always permit the lighters under their own charge to be pillaged. Their general practice was to point out [to] the leader of the gang those lighters that were without any guard, and lay near their own, and which might be easily plundered. An hour was fixed on for effecting the object in view. The Receiver was applied to, to be in readiness a certain hour before daylight to warehouse the goods. A lug boat was seized on for the purpose. The articles were removed into it ... and conveyed to a landing-place. The watchmen in the streets were bribed to connive at the villainy.

This was exactly the kind of chain of events which led to the closer integration of 'uniform' and 'plain clothes', and so to a certain level of unease in the general public on the subject. The fact was that 'plain clothes' as a concept was not really far removed from what the previous generation of Londoners (and others of a radical disposition in the provinces) had known as *agents provocateurs* or, in plain language, spies amongst the working men campaigning for their rights.

In the first decade of the City Police, the great Chartist movement emerged into prominence. The Great Reform Act of 1832 had disappointed large numbers of working men and artisans in a wide range of industries and occupations. The changes brought about in the electoral system by that statute had not significantly improved the breadth of suffrage and the majority of people still felt excluded from the practical politics of the land. The disaffected were, of course, a great cause for concern for the authorities. Across Britain, so profound was the fear of the large-scale public disorder the Chartists presented, that the authorities had used *agents provocateurs* to infiltrate their ranks. After all, one of their leaders, O'Connor, had been drilling men on Woodhouse Moor in Leeds.

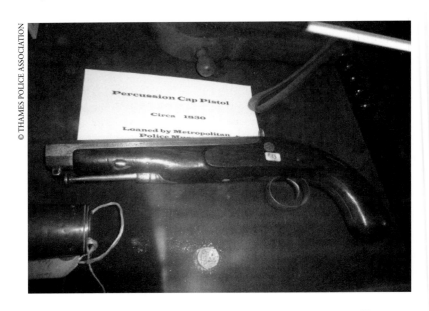

The new social unrest made armaments more important. The percussion cap pistol replaced the flintlock. This example (*c.*1830) was made by William Parker of Hatton Garden.

The main obstacle to the kind of police work needed in this context was the whole concept of plain clothes. The notion of 'police spies' was something that the British public associated with the Revolutionary regime in France and was considered to be ruthless, immoral and just not 'playing the game' of fairness and above-board dealings.

Donald Rumbelow points out that there had been a detective force in the City for some time before the recognized beginning of detective work in 1857. He states that: 'The exact date of the origin of the detective department is uncertain. For many years it was part of the Reserve.' By 1850 references to detectives in the City were common, as in one court report of that date in which Michael Haydon, 'One of the City of London police detectives', deposed that he had apprehended a prisoner.

The Metropolitan Police established a detective force in 1842, but there had been officers on plain clothes duties since the first police force as, naturally, knowledge of the criminal fraternities was essential and such 'insider' knowledge could only be gained by means such as infiltration. Nevertheless, there had been scandals. The MP and editor of the *Leeds Mercury*, Edward Baines, had written about and exposed a spy working in Yorkshire, and that had caused a stir. Therefore, when all the police forces in London employed men in plain clothes, there was debate and dissent, and the Thames Police were in the thick of this, because their work demanded a high level of specific and localized knowledge – of the river, the docks and the riverside communities.

It is possible to absorb some idea of what the topography of the Thames Police work was from the documentary evidence in the middle years of the nineteenth century. When Henry Mayhew and John Binny compiled their monumental work, *The Criminal Prisons of London*, they explained and described the kinds of locales and working conditions that East Enders working on the river would have known. They describe the docks, for example, in terms that convey precisely the kinds of terrain and environment the constables would have known:

Along the quay you see, among the crowd, men with their faces blue with indigo, and gaugers with their long brass tipped rules dripping with spirit fresh from the casks they have been probing. Then will come a group of flaxen-haired sailors, chattering German, and next a black seaman, with a red-cotton handkerchief, twisted turban-like round his head. Presently a blue-smocked butcher pushes through the throng, with fresh meat [...] in the tray on his shoulder.

From the 1830s to the 1860s, the context for police work was subject to the tremors of extreme social change and countless professional pressures, as the organization developed, and as other statutes were gradually implemented by rural constabularies. Not until c.1860 did any real semblance of a national police network emerge. But the Thames Police had gained some support in terms of help in their own locality: in 1841 the Dockyard Divisions of the Metropolitan Police were established, and by 1845 the expressed aim of the government was to have one police officer for every 450 heads of population. (However, by 1849, when the population of London was 2,473,758, there were just over 5,000 men available for duty.)

The Thames Police were in an anomalous position, with several confusing and paradoxical aspects: they were part of a network, at least on paper, consisting of Customs and Excise, Docks police, other Metropolitan divisions and some regional officers, but regarding their day to day work, they were really alone. In fact, before the establishment of the Metropolitan Police, when the Thames Police magistrates dealt with absolutely anything 'on their patch' so to speak, they could even be involved in affairs which, in other contexts, would have involved the process of civil law at a high level, as in 1828, when the St Katharine's Dock Company set about ejecting householders who stood in the way of development.

Magistrates for the Thames Police, Ballantine and Broderip, heard the pleas of several householders who argued that warrants issued by the Company should not be enforced. Mr Toms, acting for the Dock Company, had a year earlier purchased property from a head landlord and now, in 1828, he was requesting a warrant of ejectment for those people who refused to quit their homes. Both parties argued the legal applications of the phrase 'shall be purchased' and eventually Ballantine saw that the Company had wanted warrants before actually seeing demolition done. In other words, they could only work on demolished property, not eject people from their homes. Ballantine summed up that taking demolished property was 'the only mode by which they could become entitled to any of the houses'. Through modern eyes this is alarming in terms of the sheer disorganization of the commercial interest; the Dock Company clearly thought that they could do anything they liked to the residents, and instead of a lawyer standing in their way, there was a police court magistrate.

Multi-tasking was part of the job description of the Thames Police from the start. The magistrates and superintendents held the key positions, and with those roles came a never-ending stream of minor administrative tasks and the onerous burden of regulation. The Thames was such an incredibly busy river (then as always) and, naturally, the regulation of river traffic, along with the responsibilities of protecting the various categories of vessel, from pleasure to business boats and from large craft to rowing-boat, was a constant demand.

In 1832, a typical example of this occurred with an infringement of the Waterman's Company by-laws. The London watermen had been working on the river since medieval times. In 1514 came the first Act to regulate their conduct; they were firmly established by the seventeenth century and they had apprenticeships and professional codes of conduct. In the late seventeenth century there was one estimate that there were 40,000 watermen on the river, but that probably included the fishermen also. True watermen specialized in taking passengers in their wherries, and there was also a tilt-boat which ran from London to Gravesend. The painter and caricaturist Thomas Rowlandson loved to take a boat from the Strand to Greenwich, which was another popular destination. With all this happening, regulation and control were essential. Magistrates Richbell and Ballantine were faced with two captains, Hallsey and Rule, who had incurred penalties of five shillings each for exceeding 5 mph while taking their craft between London Bridge and Limehouse Reach.

Hallsey's boat, the *Rose*, was seen by an old man called Oliver as he was coming back to the City from Greenwich in a wherry with his son and a waterman; from Limehouse Reach they saw the craft going exceedingly quickly and causing small craft to be, as the witness put it, 'Tossed about, and the Thames appeared like a rough sea.' He also saw the *Essex* behind, doing the same. The two boats were steamers, and the witness said that he reckoned they were doing a speed of 12–15 mph. What made it worse, in the old man's opinion, was that the *Essex* was trying get past the *Rose* and the press report said that, had it not been for the waterman pulling close to shore, 'nothing could have saved them.'

The question was all about the speed: were the craft really in excess of 5 mph? Other witnesses stated that such was the case. Hallsey claimed that he always slowed down when going near boats with passengers, and went down to 11 mph. If they had been racing, then that would have made things much worse, and Hallsey claimed that they were simply coming up together at the same time, by chance. Then Richbell, a sea captain himself, had the knowledge to respond to Hallsey's argument that, in the broad water of Limehouse Reach, no boat could be in danger, regardless of the speed of other craft. Richbell said that what Hallsey had done was enough to stave all small boats, and that boats going past the Wapping office at 7 or 8 mph had had the effect of making police galleys 'often injured and upset'.

Both captains had to pay the five shillings, and Richbell ended with some strictures, entering the men into sureties to keep the peace, on penalty of £100 for the coming year. The writer for *The Times* commented that the decision 'Gave great satisfaction, as it will prevent any captain of a steam packet from navigating at a greater speed than that allowed by law.'

In that same year, the watermen had published *The Laws and Constitutions for Watermen and Lightermen on the River Thames*, and far from there being 40,000, their numbers were, in fact dwindling: thirty years after this case it has been estimated that there were only 1,500 licensed watermen. But regardless of rules and regulations or the insistence of the guild to maintain behaviour and proper use of river craft, the fines were something that had to be seen to be done, as a warning to others, of course. The Thames Police had everything to gain from such public assertions of their authority.

In contrast, this same period presented the magistrates with cases of serious mutiny. In 1830, Richbell and Ballantine found themselves having to conduct the first hearing of two cases which would eventually be tried at the Admiralty Court, and these tales reveal the brutality and tough suppression of any dissent by sailors out on a voyage. The definition of mutiny is that 'a combination of two or more persons subject to service law overthrow superiors or resist lawful authority in the sovereign's forces'. Such a wording means that mutiny has to be distinguished from other offences such as assault or bodily harm, or even conspiracy. Once again, here were two Thames Police magistrates shouldering the responsibility, and their responses would play a part in the decisions of higher courts.

In the case of the *Lowther Castle*, a seaman called John Hawkins was charged with mutiny on the homeward journey of the ship: he had refused to be put in irons and had drawn a knife with which he attacked an officer. At Wapping, this was one of the most sensational hearings the magistrates had to conduct. *The Times* reported the scene: 'The office and every avenue thereto was crowded to excess, and in the street nearly 500 sailors, composing the crews of the China fleet, were assembled, anxiously awaiting the result.'

The captain and crew of the *Lowther Castle* had been conducting a reign of terror, with floggings being extreme and all punishments very harsh. While the vessel was lying off St Helena in June 1830, Hawkins hailed a man-of-war, the *Ariadne*, as he had the intention of being transferred to that ship to escape the regime. He was ordered to go aft but refused, and a fight between Hawkins and the fourth officer took place, with the seaman being punched and then calling out 'Murder!' Hawkins was ordered to be put in irons and the Master at Arms came to do that; Hawkins was overpowered by several officers, but that proved to a dangerous task, as Hawkins drew a knife and almost killed the fourth officer. The vengeance then taken by the officers was such that the badly wounded seaman had to be sent home on another ship, where he was tended to by surgeons.

Ballantine listened patiently to all this, and in his response he said that Hawkins had previously served well on a man of war and had had no problems. Further inquiry revealed the brutal nature of the regime he was faced with. Ballantine concluded that Hawkins had been within his rights to hail the other ship, but of course, he had assaulted the officer. Ballantine and Richbell left the further inquiry into this case to the Admiralty Court, where there was an acquittal.

The case regarding the *Inglis*, heard around the same time, revealed another atrociously cruel regime by the captain. Following the alleged mutiny, the main culprits, as the court was told, had been in irons for seventy-two days before being taken to Wapping in a Thames Police galley and released from their shackles. At the first hearing in Wapping only one witness, Mr Dudman, was available, and both Evans and officer Moody of the Thames Police had received a very poor opinion of the ship's officers, who had not attended the hearing, but sent a message that said, 'Do what you like with 'em!'

The prisoners were defended by a lawyer called Flower, who said that the men had been in close confinement and shackled for two months, and that they were ready to meet any charge against them. What emerged was a case of horrendous cruelty: the bosun's mate had received five dozen lashes on the journey, and had since supervised the defence of the accused. There had been punishments on board, carried out without a previous court of inquiry (a court held on board by officers and men), though the captain claimed that was not so. Officers had used foul and degrading language to the seamen, and after a young boy was lost and drowned, the callous report in the log simply noted that there had been severe weather.

A group of men had gathered to resist punishment – that could have constituted a mutiny of course – but Ballantine gave a common-sense response, saying that if the officers exceeded their authority, 'The laws of this country were open to the men.'

The press report notes that the magistrate said that the case was a misdemeanour, not a mutiny and, as with the *Ariadne* case, there was to be a trial at the Admiralty Court.

One of the most high-profile cases of mutiny the Thames Police had to deal with was also a murder case. This concerned *The Queen of the Teign* on her way to California in 1853. In October of that year Mr Yardley of the Thames Police found Captain Stooke and two seamen called Northcote and Goldsworthy standing before him on a murder charge. Mr Bokin, for the Crown, and advised by Lord Palmerston, defended the accused, and was against lawyers Humphreys and Clarkson. An alleged mutiny had followed a confrontation in which five lascars (oriental sailors) died, and witnesses against the captain and the two men had since been confined and sent home in a steamer, *The British Queen*, from whence the Thames officers had taken them to Wapping.

A witness called Fairfold said he could not recall full details, but it seems that the incident began after the captain took exception to a man who said he would take the ship to California, as the present commander was incompetent. Two of the lascars told him who had spoken those words, and it turned out to be Fairfold, who was implicated in an action that followed an attempt to put him in irons. He was hauled before a court of inquiry at Gibraltar and sent home in irons.

The chief mate, William Treatt, gave evidence, saying that he had been surprised on deck by four of the men together with the lascars and that there had been a fight. The mutineers had daggers and one had an iron bar. Treatt's account of the incident, as spoken in court, was as follows:

Ion Cre was on deck, and he raised the iron bar and aimed a blow at me ... and another man stabbed me in the arm. Tindal made a blow with his weapon at Northcote who was at the wheel, and Tindal stabbed me in the belly with his dagger. The attack was sudden and unexpected.

Another of the lascars was armed with a grains – a kind of harpoon with several prongs – and that also hit Treatt. The lascars had come on board with all these weapons at Singapore and had not been searched at the time.

Treatt had been wearing a thick coat, and *The Times* described what happened in court regarding this:

> Mr Evans, Superintendent of the Thames Police, opened the coat, a very thick and heavy one, which was probably the means of saving the mate's life. It was cut through in several places, and Mr Evans said that there were scars on the mate's body corresponding with the cuts in the coat. The magistrates and counsel closely examined the coat.

Treatt said that four or five lascars were 'on him at once' and that: 'One stab went through my coat pocket and trousers pocket, shirt and flannel and 13 layers of cloth.... I attribute the saving of my life to the captain who acted promptly and bravely.'

Yardley accepted that there was no charge against the captain and seamen, but felt that the two remaining lascars, Ali and Ahalt, should be remanded. At the next sitting, an interpreter was present, and there was still some difficulty in understanding the accused. One of them had no idea what the word 'danger' meant and so the interplay of the defence and prosecution in court was a scene of confusion at times. Eventually another man was found who could do the interpreting better, and made sure he said the right thing for the record. The two men were again put in prison cells.

A week later, the British seamen still stood to answer a murder charge, along with the lascars. Eventually a story was ascertained from the lascars – that Goldsworthy and Northcote had swords, and then that one of them fired a gun. A witness said that he saw three men killed – lascars named Awang, Drumma and Sidur. Another man came into court, being sworn in on a copy of the *Koran*, and he said that he saw three men, including Awang, attack the mate. At last a retired Thames officer, who knew Hindustani, was called to help when another lascar called Cassim was in the dock and finally there was a lucid account of what had happened. Cassim stated that he had seen the attack by Fairfold and the lascars, and that after the attack on the mate, the lascars had been shot and others made fast on deck.

There was insufficient evidence to charge the British seamen with murder, as it appeared that their actions had been to quell a mutiny and that the deaths involved were in the course of a response to the murderous attack on Treatt. But they were committed for manslaughter and they were awarded bail. Ali and Ahalt were charged with mutiny and remanded. The two lascars were later tried at the Old Bailey, found guilty and sentenced to fifteen years transportation. Stooke, Goldsworthy and Northcote were acquitted.

These kinds of cases show that the Thames Police Court had a key role to play in matters that were really the concern of the Admiralty. In fact, when it is recalled that the Thames officers had to deal with the normal flow of river traffic, such as the massive amount of coastal trade in manure, bedding and hay on barges between London, Kent and East Anglia, dealing with the daily transportation of the 2,500 tons of material for the horses which kept the city's transport going, then this additional burden is notably extreme. The magistrates had to switch from basic matters of regulation and supervision to very serious cases which affected a whole of a fleet of the navy, and such switches could happen at any time.

The Marine Police Force, as it was called at the time of its formation, had metamorphosed into a body of men with an annual cost of £5,000 – this being shared by the Exchequer and by the West India merchants. If we recall the first mission statement: 'To combat theft, looting and corruption in the port of London', then it can be seen just how much its remit had been changed by c.1850. The original force, as it was before amalgamation with Peel's new men in 1829, had comprised a small group, with the main focus on the work of the surveyors, inspecting unloading processes, and some thirty quay guards, a mix of officers and surveyors. By 1850, although the rowing-boat galleys were still in use and other police forces had arrived to work alongside, the core of men and magistrates were clearly overburdened and were very much an organization that would be asked to do anything, according to pragmatic decisions.

This overburdening was increased later, notably after 1879, when the Summary Jurisdiction Act allowed minor cases of smuggling to be tried at magistrates' courts across London, at courts other than the Thames Police office.

Arguably, as time rolled on and the last decades of Victoria's reign brought huge social and industrial changes, the most challenging role for the Thames Police was a greater emphasis on preventive measures. By the 1890s the Customs and Excise service was to have launches on the Thames, with a continuous patrol, but steam launches for the Thames Police were a long time coming, the first tenders for supply being advertised in the 1880s after the awful tragedy which is described in Chapter 7.

Otherwise, before any great technological change, it was a case of the officers coping with changes in the nature and scale of offences, and with the repercussions of social change, many of these being elements of accidents and disasters on the one hand, or individual tragedies on the other. The Thames continued to provide a location for an end to lives of misery and despair as the metropolis grew at an alarming rate, along with the Empire, which Britain had to feed and sustain. In the very prosperous middle years of the century, the police also had to live and work among the expanding workforce on their river beat: Henry Mayhew, in 1862, wrote that there were 'not less than 20,000 souls living by Dock labour in the metropolis' and that 'the Docks are worked by between 1,000 and 3,000 hands according as the business is brisk or slack.'

6 Explosions, Fires and the War Rocket Factory

CRIME IS, OF course, not the only concern of the police: they have always had to deal with accidents and disasters as well. The records of Victorian coroners' courts are packed with the most horrendous accidents, common in an age when health and safety regulations did not exist and negligence claims were just beginning to become an issue as the new railways were subject to endless nasty accidents in which there was great loss of life. Fires were also a constant threat. In the years c.1840–1870 there were an increasing number of fires in the city and in 1865 the Metropolitan Fire Brigade Act was passed; previously, fires had been the responsibility of the local companies but then the responsibility was passed to the Metropolitan Board of Works. (Edinburgh and Manchester had fire services in the 1820s, but in London there was dependence on the insurance companies, some of which had been formed straight after the Great Fire of 1666.)

A system developed whereby those businesses that were insured by a particular company had specific fire-marks displayed on their buildings so that, in the event of a fire, the crews of engines run by that insurance company would know that they were in the right location to start work. As early as 1710 there were 13,000 members of one company alone: the Amicable Friendly Society. These companies existed by mutual contributions and the only thought was to save property, not the lives of the unfortunates caught up in the infernos. But one important landmark in this respect was the establishment, in 1836, of the Society for the Protection of Life from Fire. In that same year, the first mobile fire-escapes were made. In the eighteenth century, fire engines were really simply mobile water tanks; then, in 1774, the provision of ladders was made compulsory. When the London Fire Brigade finally came into being in 1833, it was the creation of the main insurance companies. James Braidwood became the first Chief Officer.

Yet police also played a part in fire rescue, and the Thames force had to deal with wharf fires fairly often. In 1861 there was a terrible fire at Tooley Street in Southwark, at the premises of Curling and Co., and in that blaze, Braidwood lost his life. There were two wharves, those of Davis and Mark Brown: the fire started among some 8,000 bales of jute, and at Brown's there were 10,000 barrels of tallow and grease in one wharf, and then in a neighbouring one – Hartley Wharf – there were oils and resins, so the result of that fire can be imagined.

A constable from M Division first saw smoke billowing out of Brown's wharf, and the first desperate response was for men to drag out as many bales of jute as possible, risking their lives in doing so. The constable ran to a Fire Brigade office at Tooley Street and then the Thames Police moved in: Superintendent Brandford, five inspectors and Superintendent Evans himself had several galleys and other boats placed alongside the wharf, with fifty constables on board, there to protect the place from pilferers who had turned up sharply to salvage what they could and make off with it.

Clearly, there was very little to be done, although two brigades arrived and, in a few hours, they at least managed to confine the fire to a stretch of about two hundred feet on the wharf. Fire insurance assessors were observing, and they saw the fire burn all day long, not receding until late that night. Reports add that some private engines also arrived, one from Long Acre.

It was a terrible disaster, which destroyed new buildings: the brick and timber premises had been built just two years earlier. However, it is possible to detect a great deal in this episode that might be termed a learning curve in dealing with a major fire, including the fact that there were Royal Society fire escape conductors used, and these men also gave first aid to firemen.

The Thames men had been out in considerable force and had fulfilled an important role; they had been very close to the fire, and they must have been in great danger from falling fragments of building and other materials.

Accidents could arise from any number of different sources; in 1856 it was solid lock gates at the South West India Dock, part of the City Canal, that were burst after the effects of a strong gale. This was at the Limehouse entrance: a new lock of huge dimensions had been constructed the previous year at the Blackwall end, and each entrance lock was given two gates to cope with the great pressure of water. In May 1856 the outer gate was being repaired when the gale struck, making a huge swell of water up the canal.

The lock gates burst into the area where barges and lighters were waiting for full tide. The gates having cracked and snapped, their massive tonnage of thick timber fragmented and drifted into the river, where small craft were battered and many destroyed, their parts floating away in the water. This great swell continued for ten minutes and some eighty vessels were snapped from moorings along the canal, these being all kinds of craft, including diving-bell barges, dredging machines and grain-lighters. One large craft, a visiting brig, was left high and dry on the south bank, and many barges capsized.

The Thames Police had the main task of recovering as much of the wreckage as they could, and Inspector White took charge as every available galley went to the scene of the accident as speedily as they could. There were human casualties, including a family on board a canal boat. The officers tried in vain to trace and save them, but such was the force of the gale and the miniature tsunami that had hit the canal and basin, that the people were never found.

Police were always in emergency mode, ready for any developments, when accidents occurred. In 1847 the boiler of a steamboat, the *Cricket*, exploded near the Hungerford pier, and many people were killed. The company involved ran the steamboat from the Strand to London Bridge and it had been specially made with tillers at each stern to avoid having to turn on leaving the piers. That was very sensible, but the steam pressure boilers were another matter. There were a hundred people on board when the boiler exploded: this happened while the boat was at the pier and people were still boarding. There would otherwise have been even more loss of life owing to the over-crowding that was likely had all available spots been filled. In this case, officers from F Division led by Inspector Marsh came quickly after the explosion to stop dangerous crowd pressure at one place.

One interesting aspect of this accident in relation to police history is that it was revealed at the coroner's inquest that no one had taken on the responsibility of supervising the damaged vessel. A juryman asked who was at the scene and on the boat, and it emerged that the owners had asked the police to take charge of it, but they had refused. The coroner then directed the Thames Police, specifically Mr Lewis, a surveyor, to make sure that his men ensured that no people went onto the boat who were not officially sanctioned to do so. There had been no on-board surveillance by the Metropolitan men closest to the scene, so the Thames men moved in.

Sometimes the tragedies on the river were mysteries and remained so: they may have been the result of accidents and other disasters, or they may have been caused by criminal activity.

In 1865 Inspector Ralph Thomas was present at an inquest at the Town of Ramsgate, a pub very close to the Wapping office, speaking at a coroner's court. He had been in a police galley off Wapping when he saw the body of a woman in the water. The body had been in the river for several days and was naked except for stockings and boots. The woman wore a brass wedding-ring, but police could not establish her identity. The body was placed on view in the pub, as was common practice, to allow locals a chance to identify the corpse, but to no avail.

The medical report was very important, and Dr Wood said that the woman had been the mother of several children, was about 35 years of age and had been in good health at the time of her death. This was certainly a murder, and although her skull had been crushed and there was no brain in the cerebral cavity, it was thought that this damage was done after death; however, her body had been mutilated before being put in water.

The coroner concluded that the case was: 'full of anxiety and speculation for the manner in which the woman had been found in the river, naked and with terrible wounds ... and though the certain cause of death could not be arrived at, the medical evidence was such as to lead to the belief that the death had not been caused by the injury in the skull.' An open verdict was returned.

One of the most sensational stories in the Thames Police annals occurred in 1853 with the suspicions cast over Hale's war rocket factory at Rotherhithe. To recount this tale, it is necessary to explain the life of a Hungarian named Lajos Kossuth, as a note in *The Illustrated London News* in this year, states: 'In *The Times* of the 15th April appeared the announcement that upon intelligence received by the Secretary of State for the Home Office and the Commissioners of Police, active measures had been taken to substantiate the charges which have long been vaguely preferred against M. Kossuth and his adherents.'

The interest lies in the implications of the word *vaguely*. The story is in fact, in some respects, farcical and the Thames Police played a major part in it, as the factory was on their patch.

Lajos (or Louis as he was known in most countries) Kossuth was a major figure in nineteenth-century Hungarian history. Hungary was then part of the Austro-Hungarian empire, the Habsburg monolith, which was to be an ally of the Germans in the Great War. Kossuth was born in 1802, and was of Slovakian origin; he later became a lawyer, journalist and politician. He had become a national figure by 1841, when he edited an influential newspaper called *Pesti Hirlap*. His prestige increased still further when he was imprisoned for his nationalist views, and he became the main leader of the extreme Liberal Party. He moved on to the centre stage in European politics in the year of revolutions, 1848, when across the continent, radical movements pressed for reform and new libertarian values, notably more rights for those enslaved in the great empires. In that year he became Regent-President of Hungary, but he had to take command of armies on the move, and that was not his real strength.

Kossuth tried to reach a compromise with the Habsburg powers, even using an American diplomat in negotiations, but eventually he failed in his efforts to retain power and to reach his objectives, and he became a fugitive, as so many Europeans did at the time. He first stayed in England in 1851 and, from his activities then, we can understand why, when the affair of the Rotherhithe bomb factory hit the headlines, there was a lot of popular support for him among the British working-class. He was fêted by many, including the Lord Mayor of London, and he was a very talented and powerful public speaker. He also took part in a procession through London to the Guildhall, and there were approximately 75,000 people watching this, so he became very well known.

Unfortunately for the government, Lord Palmerston showed extraordinary amiability towards Kossuth and intended to invite him to his country house. The Queen saw this as totally undesirable: here was a populist leader and demagogue, who did not believe in monarchy, being welcomed by her Foreign Secretary. Palmerston, blocked in this intention to speak to Kossuth, invited trade union members instead, and they read a statement which included a good deal of praise for Kossuth. This played a part in bringing down the government of the day, led by Lord John Russell.

This is the background to the Rotherhithe affair and the Hale family. Obviously, the police and the Home Office were watching Kossuth closely. After all, they had a revolutionary in their midst. A link was found between William Hale and his factory at Rotherhithe and Kossuth. But Hale was completely legitimate in terms of who he was and what his track record had been with regard to armaments: he was, in an important way, potentially part of the ordnance provision of the British army, but he had never quite secured a government contract. Rockets had first been used in the field in the Napoleonic Wars and the War Office knew all about Hale and had worked with him. If he did turn out to be some kind of traitor or arms dealer, then that would be a shock.

Suspicions were aroused, however, and a warrant procured from a magistrate, as it was thought that Hale was contravening the Gunpowder Act of 1772, which specified that:

No person is allowed to have more than 50 pounds of gunpowder, and no dealer more than 200 pounds, in his possession at one time, in any premises or within three miles of the cities of London or Westminster; or in or within one mile of any other town or city, or within two miles of the residence of the Sovereign, or within a half-mile of any church.

Superintendent James Evans told the court that he had entered the Hale premises on the Surrey Canal, with the warrant, and he had Detective Sergeant Saunders with him. The Hales were not there, but an employee called Boylin was working there at the time. Evans said, 'I looked through a window and saw Boylin ramming a rocket at some machine.' He went in and said he needed to search the premises. When Evans searched the workshops, his aim was to find gunpowder, and there were rocket shells around the room; but a workshop called the magazine was locked, and Evans said he had to look in there, and when he was told that Hale had the key, he threatened to break into the room, and Boylin went to fetch a key.

Evans found an amount of gunpowder in that room and took some of it for testing. He reported that, as he stayed there for some hours, he counted the materials, and found that there were 79 wooden cases with 1,549 rockets. The next day, the Thames officers took the gunpowder by galley to the Royal Arsenal at Woolwich. Then, at Scotland Yard, Evans met Hale, who was not very happy and asked what was going on. He explained to Evans and other officers that he had no gunpowder, but that what they had found was a composition used for making rockets. The Thames men tested the substance they had found by using some to fire pistols. In court, Evans said:

When we tried the experiments with the pistols, Saunders and others were present. It was in a stable in Scotland Yard. There was no hissing noise when the rocket composition was fired. The report was similar to that made by the granulated gunpowder. I have been 20 years in the police and never executed a search warrant for the same materials before.

What happened then was that a succession of scientific experts were called to Bow Street to explain whether or not the material was, in fact, gunpowder. Hale was insistent that he had not used gunpowder, and there was a certain amount of frustration in his words when he said that he had offered his rockets to the government and that he should be glad if they would take them off his hands. When Hale added that he had been exporting his rockets for years to other countries, and that this had been supervised and monitored by Sir Thomas Hastings at the Customs House, there must have been a sense in some persons present that this trial was going to be a waste of time.

The experts gave long explanations, including statements by men who knew the practical use of the material and others who merely knew the chemical composition. As for the Kossuth connection, Auguste Usener was the key witness. He told the court that he had been in the Prussian Army and had served on the general staff of the Hungarian Army for many years; then, for several months, he had been employed by Hale making rockets (an amazing transition, and somewhat puzzling) and there he was introduced by the Hale family to Kossuth. That meeting explained why Usener was there: 'I saw the elder Hale in the company of M. Kossuth at the home of the latter ... Kossuth said to Hale that he could recommend me to him.' He was employed at sixteen shillings a week and he was told to keep everything secret.

A workman who stood as a witness also said that there had been something suspicious going on, adding that he was told, 'When you leave work you must not talk at the public house or anywhere about this factory, nor mention the name of Kossuth, nor even the word Hungarian, because this would be an occasion to betray our work.' This all smacks of a government set-up, as if the prosecuting barrister, Bodkin, had primed and paid witnesses. However, it has to be said that one witness who had searched export records for rockets back to 1843 had not found the name Hale, and the Sir Thomas Hastings previously mentioned confirmed that Hale had tried and failed to sell his rockets to the army. Nothing was resolved, and the accused were sworn to appear at the Surrey

Sessions at the next assembly. *The Times* followed up with a long accusatory feature expressing suspicion and a sense of wrong at the number of rockets held at the Hale factory, when it was now known that he struggled to sell them and had apparently lied about selling them abroad. Their principal question was: 'But what was the destination of these deadly projectiles?' followed by slightly worrying words about the factory carrying on its work 'with secrecy to avoid penalties that every common informer would enforce'.

Eventually this all blew over, and the press, though still interested in Kossuth, contented themselves with selling newspapers by making out that Kossuth was becoming a target of underhand and ungentlemanly police investigation, such as in these still critical comments on a break-in at the Kossuth house at which a case was broken open: 'What a pestilent writing-case it must be which is big with the fate of so many poor Hungarians, who, as we would venture to remark, are in their own country, while Mr Kossuth is enjoying life comfortably in the Alpha Road!'

Kossuth toured the country, speaking to working men about life and liberty, and such was his fame as a dashing and heroic popular celebrity that he even featured in the theatres, for example in performance at Hull in *King Liberty, or Kossuth, the Hungarian Patriot*. As for the Thames Police, they had experienced a taste of what must have seemed like a shady case affecting national security, at a time when there had been revolution in the streets across Europe, and when the new detectives had been busy working with them to snoop on a supposed arms dealer and agent of foreign revolutionaries, as close to them as Rotherhithe.

There was danger on the Thames from all quarters and on every scale from individual mishap to huge disasters. This state of affairs was expressed more strongly (and darkly) by Edward Lear in his *Book of Nonsense* of 1846:

> *There was an old person of Ems*
> *Who casually fell in the Thames.*
> *And when he was found,*
> *They said he was drowned.*
> *That unlucky old person of Ems.*

Superintendent Alan King, more recently, explained the specific dangers of the river well:

> The River Thames is a dangerous tidal river; in fact it is technically the sea until Teddington Lock and is just about salt water until that point. The river has vicious currents running in different directions and at great speed at many points along its journey. It was a river constantly threatening people at both work and play back in the Victorian years, and was generally treated with respect. The police officers at Wapping had to know their river like the watermen, and indeed many of them were exactly that. Even in the first years, when assistants to the officers, part-timers, were used, those men had a profound knowledge of great Father Thames and his moods and rages.

7 'A Day of Funerals': The Wreck of the *Princess Alice*

THE KALEIDOSCOPIC NATURE of the Thames Police roles and duties was in evidence early on in their history. Their area of jurisdiction had expanded rapidly. The first area, from Limehouse to Greenwich, had grown to cover thirteen miles of river by 1830. Even as early as 1810, their men had been in action, on loan to eight other police offices, mainly because they had fifty constables in their ranks and this was very useful for crowd control when the 'land coppers' could not cope. By 1830 their numbers had grown also, so that there were sixty-four constables and twenty-two surveyors. In most of the large-scale events in the city, the Thames men had played a part, as in the preparations for the massive Chartist rally in 1848.

The responsibilities of the force had originally included powers over the existing 'watch and ward' facilities. The magistrates had the right to dismiss any watchmen in their area who were seen to be inefficient – and, indeed, the constables working the riverbank could inspect watch houses there. The son of magistrate Ballantine described in his memoirs the situation of the Thames magistrates, and explained that the generation of Ballantine, Richbell and Broderip had achieved a great deal in their time there, up to the 1840s:

> The districts over which my father's jurisdiction extended included streets and alleys inhabited by a class very difficult to manage. Irish and Jews of the humblest rank occupied the wretched dwellings of which they were composed, and the feuds between the two races often ended in squabbles that

attained formidable dimensions. My father, after a time, was looked up to by the rival parties, and succeeded in creating a much more peaceful state of things. In his efforts he was greatly aided by the rabbi and the Catholic priest of the neighbourhood, with both of whom he had established a firm alliance.

This is an important aside, with regard to what had been accomplished by the 1850s: clearly the staff at Wapping were very much a part of the community and had carried out neighbourhood police work of a very high order. Ballantine recalled that, when he was younger, he had walked the beat with Thames officers, and he wrote about their work in glowing terms:

> Their duties were confined to the river and to localities adjacent to its shores. These included districts inhabited by very lawless classes ... I had many opportunities of witnessing their conduct, and the power they possessed was considerable. I have seen the most serious disturbances quelled in a few minutes by the presence of two or three of them, and I do not remember a single occasion when they received serious injury.

Generally, the serious crime in the Thames Police's jurisdiction was not that of offences against the person (except in mutinies and violence on board ship) but, as with the Ratcliffe Highway murders of 1811, their participation was always valuable and often they were the first on the scene, working with detectives (once that body was in action in 1842). This was the case with the Plaistow Marsh murder of 1864. That year was one of the most horrendous in the history of British urban crime, because it was darkened forever by the raging epidemic of garrotting attacks across the land, which involved a particularly vicious gang attack and robbery in which the victim was choked from behind while an accomplice deprived the hapless citizen of pocket books and wallets. The papers were full of lurid accounts of such attacks, and magazines such as *Punch* and *The Illustrated London News* offered cartoons and sketches of the garrotters to the extent that a general moral panic ensued, with theatre-goers paying men to escort them to safety in the dark streets, and sword-sticks enjoying unprecedented sales. In the Plaistow Marshes, men who had gone shooting found the headless body of a young man in the reeds. The police were called and it was Inspector Goode, of the Thames Police, who arrived and found the severed head in a rat hole. He was later joined by some detectives and by Inspector Howie of K Division. That was to be the pattern in such murder cases. The Thames men were an integral part of the first response actions.

Naturally, there was corruption, as there had always been, in the police ranks. In 1894, Colonel Partridge, who had been for many years a secretary at Scotland Yard, wrote, with reference to the first decades of the new police, 'The corrupt character of the police system was known not only to those in contact with the police themselves, but it was a matter of public comment and complaint.' In fact, in 1827 *The Times* reported on one common practice that occurred when people thought their stolen goods were in the hands of receivers: as soon as a complainant asked for a search warrant, the officer present would pass the word on to the 'fence' concerned and when the victims arrived at the premises with a warrant, the stolen goods would have been moved on.

A typical case for the Thames Police was that of Inspector James Fogg, in 1844. He was alleged to have taken part in smuggling a large amount of tobacco – with a value of £600 – and was hauled in front of the judges at the Court of Exchequer. One report commented that he brought several witnesses, and 'The testimony of one of them was, to say the least of it, of a most singular character, but it seemed to have the desired effect with the jury and they acquitted the defendant.' But Fogg was still suspended, and when an independent police inquiry followed, initiated by the Secretary of State, he was dismissed from the constabulary. What happened then was common practice: his notice of dismissal was 'read in orders' across the stations and section houses of London – the ratification of the decision made by the higher authorities, and, of course, a source of humiliation and disgrace.

Another problem for the Thames Police was the advent of steam-driven craft on the river. Of course, improving speed and power was, as it always has been, a priority with engineers and inventors. In 1836, Francis Smith invented a screw propeller, taking out a patent in that year, and there were trials on the Thames, in which Smith, after hitting something underwater and seeing a blade broken, saw that the vessel went quicker with just one screw with a single turn. Steamboats themselves go back to the end of the eighteenth century when Robert Fulton started designing a paddle steamer. Using an engine bought from Boulton and Watt in Birmingham, he made a boat that sailed on the River Hudson. In England, William Symington put a prototype single cylinder engine into a boat, and then in 1802 his vessel, the *Charlotte Dundas*, was working on the Forth. At that time there were fears about the boat causing damage on canal banks, and investors were not found, but in 1824 the General Steam Navigation Company was formed and the age of pleasure boats on the Thames powered by steam began.

As these craft developed, their speed came to be of concern to the Thames Police. In 1876, a Mr Hall was in front of the bench at Henley for driving a steamer furiously on the Thames highway. His boat, *The Flying Dutchman*, had caused such distress that there were nine summonses against him from parishes along his disastrous route. The occasion was an opportunity for *The Times* to complain about the policing of the river: 'As we have frequently stated in these columns, the control of our river navigation is in a most unsatisfactory condition', they announced, and put the blame for the shortcomings of river supervision on there being three separate organizations who played a part in control: the River Police, the Waterman's Company, and the Thames Conservancy. The same feature described the first-named and its nature as they saw it at the time: 'The River Police are subject to Scotland Yard; their only duties are to protect property and assist when called upon in preserving order, though we believe the authorities at Whitehall question much the extent of their power in this direction, and the River Police are consequently subject to red-tape tremors.'

The chaos brought about by Hall also encouraged an anonymous writer to develop a detailed critique of the three separate authorities, writing that they were all helpless to stop this new rage of steam launches:

> The steam launch nuisance has got to such a pitch that some sensible efforts should be made to render detection more certain. At present a luxurious citizen hires a launch for the day or uses his own and gives a picnic to his friends. The faster the screw goes the more delighted are his visitors ... they fairly scream when the harmless fisherman is almost rocked out of his chair in his punt. ... Let us picture a man swamped by a steam launch, how can he detect the culprit? By the time he has recovered his self-possession, the launch is miles away and pursuit impossible.

Steam power was in one sense the new enemy, and also the new source of pleasure on the river. Recreational use was inevitable, and the police on the river were about to have a fresh swathe of offences to deal with. The writer of the article in *The Times* was aware that the Second Thames Conservancy had a remit to control a large stretch of the river – 177 miles in fact, from Cricklade to Yantlet Creek. This body had been formed in 1866 with the responsibility of taking care of all locks and canals; this meant maintenance and inspection, along with any tolls in existence in some places. The question of anyone using the river for recreation had not perhaps occurred to them in their early phase of work, but by 1885 the Thames Preservation Act stated: 'It is lawful for all persons for pleasure or profit to travel or to loiter upon any and every part of the river.' That statement must have placed a few worries in the minds of the police.

But before that statute was implemented there were some landmarks in the nature of policing on the Thames, and indeed in the nature of steamboats and how they worked. The Thames Police were well used to dealing with collisions and in January 1878 a steamer called the *Benbow* had collided with the *Ostrich,* a London steamer en route to Newcastle, both being owned by the General Steam Navigation Company. The weather was calm and clear, and the vessels were going in opposite directions; two people were drowned and two firemen seriously injured and taken to the Dreadnought Hospital at Greenwich. The Thames Police had the unenviable task of finding the bodies, and Inspector Varley, with some constables, found them in the fore cabin of the *Benbow* and brought them out. That was fairly routine, but later that year the whole city was to be rocked by a massive accident which led to the deaths of around 600 people. This would test the Thames Police to the limit, and in many ways illustrate the point made by the feature writer of *The Times*, who had complained about the state of integrated services between the river authorities.

The *Princess Alice,* a boat formerly known as the SS *Bute* when working in Scotland, was bought by the Waterman's Steam Packet Company and set to work as a pleasure cruiser, being named after the daughter of Queen Victoria. On 3 September she was cruising back up river to the City after taking people out to Gravesend; she was heading for Swan Pier, but by about a quarter to eight that evening she was at Gallions Reach near Woolwich when the captain, William Grinsted, saw a large ship called the *Bywell Castle* coming towards him. She was on her way to collect coal at Newcastle and was commanded by Captain Harrison, who saw the *Princess Alice.* To stay well clear, he ordered his ship to turn to the southern shore. Unfortunately, Grinsted appears to have misunderstood the actions of the larger ship and he also turned south. The merchant ship was huge – 890 tons – and in the ensuing collision the pleasure steamer was split, sinking in about four minutes. Many of the passengers were down in a cabin or seating area, and had no chance of escape. There were over seven hundred people on board the pleasure boat and because the *Bywell Castle* was almost empty, her decks were too high for swimmers to reach and climb aboard.

What made things much worse was the nearness of a sewage effluent point at Beckton, along with other industrial waste channels from Silvertown. The Thames Police and Conservancy barges were soon on hand to help. The sinking had been so swift and the drownings had been rapid, as there had only been shreds of wood to grasp, and the first police were only able to search for bodies. Heat made bodies rise to the surface, and Superintendent Alston, with two constables, brought up a man, woman and child; they also compiled a list of property that could be given to the London Steamboat Company. The Thames men also searched the lower cabin, using hooks. A reporter called Vincent was a witness at the time, and he wrote later that 'Soon policemen and watermen were seen by the feeble light bearing ghastly objects into the offices of the Steampacket Company, for a boat had just arrived with the first consignment of the dead.'

Matters were made much worse by the disgusting behaviour of the public; two men jumped on board a Conservancy barge and tried to take pieces of wood for ghoulish mementos. They were told to get off by police officers and one of them drew a knife. PC Vine was violently assaulted in the arrest, as the men were carried off to Woolwich to be locked up. There was further awful unruly behaviour by the souvenir hunters, hoping to grab pieces of the wreck.

In all, there were about 150 survivors, including a Mr King of the Thames Police, but Constable Lewis of the Thames force lost his small son and wife in the disaster. The description of his eleven-month-old son joined the long list of sad information filling the columns of the daily papers, which included details such as: 'A woman, 36, five feet six inches; hair light; dress, grey, waterproof, black jacket (velvet fringe, black buttons); grey skirt, grey stockings (white stripes); on person, gold watch and chain, 3 lockets, 4 coins, red coral trinket.'

The coroner's court met at Woolwich on 27 November for the twenty-ninth and last time. They had had to deal with a mounting toll of deaths, and at last the inquisition and verdict were concluded and decided. The final parchment document was a roll 24 feet long, with the names of 513 deceased people. The bland phrase 'death by misadventure' was a plain and unsensational closure for what was a massive tragedy on a grand scale; the coroner, Mr Carttar, thanked all parties involved, making a special mention of the Thames Police.

In its editorial for 5 September, *The Times* made a point of lamenting the frequency of such accidents, though most were on a much smaller scale: 'Collisions in the Thames are, as "Marine Insurance" writes us word, of incessant occurrence. From whatever cause they are brought about, from careless navigation or whatever else, they are to be counted literally by scores.' Naturally, reflections on what we would nowadays consider to be basic health and safety issues, such as the lack of any planning for emergencies, were made. People wanted to know, quite reasonably, how it was that the *Princess Alice* had no means of escape for its passengers in such a terrible eventuality. The statistics of the two vessels highlight what would happen in a collision: the *Princess Alice* was made of iron and had tonnage of 158 net and 251 gross. The *Bywell Castle* had a gross tonnage of 1168. There were dozens of heart-rending survivors' tales, such as that of a man whose wife fell overboard and drowned, while he was left holding their baby:

> When the steamer went down he kept the child as well as he could above water, and made towards the shore with the aid of the wreckage. In the end, however, he was obliged to let the child go in order to save himself as he was unable to go any further. He reached the shore just beyond the gasworks.

Captain Grinsted was drowned with his ship. Along with his passengers, he would not only have suffered this fate, but his corpse would have been bloated and coated with effluents from the polluted water. Peter Ackroyd has explained this: 'According to a chemist ... the effluent consisted of two continuous columns of decomposed fermenting sewage, hissing like soda water with baneful gases so black that the water stained for miles, discharging a corrupt charnel house odour.'

The question of sanitation and public health had been raised just five months earlier by a correspondent to *The Times* called Thomas Morgan, who asked who was responsible for the sanitation of the boats on the river. He went to see a supposed case of smallpox on board a barge and found his patient lying in a small space. His report shows the nature of the dilemma: 'On seeing the case on Tuesday afternoon, I at once ordered his removal, but the sanitary authorities on land declined to interfere. The Thames Police were then communicated with and in turn the Thames Conservancy and the latter sent an official on the Thursday morning.' As he pointed out, the barge was moored by lots of other vessels and the people all mixed. That was a recipe for disaster, and he asked who had the authority to act.

The larger question of the effluent in the water in relation to the dead after the *Princess Alice* disaster was shelved, but there were positive effects arising from the horrors. As far as the Thames Police were concerned, the recommendation after an inquiry was that they should be equipped with steam launches to make them more mobile and adaptable, so in the mid-1880s tenders were invited and the first launches were commissioned, although it was 1905 before the force discontinued the use of rowing-boats.

The later Board of Trade inquiry into the disaster blamed Captain Grinsted, although whatever had led him to misinterpret the manoeuvre of the other ship was always going to be a mystery. But there is an additional point to be made: after the collision, the *Bywell Castle* simply carried on her journey. Her movement away from the *Princess Alice* must have quickened the rate at which the latter sank so, basically, why did the larger ship not stop? The captain had already tried to reverse engines, when it had been too late to stop the collision.

As a coda to the tragedy, it appears that one of those who survived the wreck was Elizabeth Stride, a woman destined to be one of the victims of Jack the Ripper ten years later. In a local paper at that time, there was this report:

With reference to the identity of Elizabeth Stride, the Woolwich newspapers of the time of the disaster have been referred to, and it is stated that a woman of that name was a witness at the inquest and identified the body of a man as her husband, and two children, then lying in Woolwich dockyard. She said that she was on board and saw them drowned, her husband picking up one of the children and being drowned with it. She was saved by clinging to the tunnel where she was accidentally kicked in the mouth by a retired Arsenal police inspector, who was also clinging to the tunnel.

Coping with accidents and disasters was not the only challenge for the force. Throughout their history the Thames Police have learned to grow and adapt, to respond to the needs of the time. In the 1840s, the Thames Police office moved to a new court at Arbour Square, Stepney. That was not a welcome event in the minds of merchants, ship-owners and seamen because the new base was over a mile inland. But the office which was there at that time is still in existence today, being the small museum of the force, with a fine view across the river. In 1850 it was, in effect, the centre of a little island, with Wapping surrounded completely by water: there were water basins to the east and west, and the huge London Dock to the north. Just around the bend in the river were two contrasting places: Execution Dock, which eerily gave reminders of the barbarous days of the Georgian terror at the heart of law enforcement, and, a little further to the east, the Thames Tunnel, completed in 1841 when the enormous bore beneath the river was completed by the arrival of the shield at the shaft on the Wapping shore. The tunnel was officially opened in August 1842 and was, in the words of *The Gentleman's Magazine*, 'Rendered comfortable by the aid of gas lights, which are always burning ... the temperature of the atmosphere is nearly the same as it is on shore.'

The men who had to deal with major events such as the *Princess Alice* disaster were a very different group from those who had merely been on probation in 1800. Since then they had been given additional powers and overcome countless setbacks, not the least being the fire in 1800 which destroyed their office and station. Rebuilt after a vote in the House of Commons, it had become an established feature of the Thames that everyone knew by the middle of the century. In the 1840s one commentator, looking back on the history of the Thames men, said that their efficiency had never been questioned, and the same writer reflected on what had been the state of affairs before the force existed: 'Before the existence of the River Police and the erection of the docks on both sides of the river, it was computed that one tenth of the cargo of every vessel brought into the port of London was stolen, and men amassed enormous wealth through that plunder.'

Modernity and its industrial marvels had arrived by this period, but such advances brought with them new dangers, and the coroners' courts across the land were busy with horrendous deaths and injuries caused by industrial accidents and by something not entirely new, but on a new scale – terrorism and the threat from dissidents, anarchists and nationalists. Once again, the police adapted and reacted.

8 Explosion at London Bridge and Other Matters

ON 15 MARCH 1883 as Parliament debated issues around naval reserves, and the Home Secretary was in the Commons enjoying a meal, there was an explosion. Someone had put a bomb near the government offices in Charles Street. With an attack so close to the heart of the state and empire, it was time for urgent action. Five days later, because the American-based Fenians had almost certainly been responsible, an Irish Bureau was established in Scotland Yard.

Adolphus 'Dolly' Williamson took charge and his brief was to gather twelve top detectives and work with the intelligence department headed by Robert Anderson. The new office was in Great Scotland Yard, close to the Rising Sun public house. It did not take long for this new group to be called the Special Irish Branch. It was a development of the tendency to assemble teams of men with special expertise to tackle specific threats or new crimes, such as the garrotting panic of 1864 in which police had needed to rethink attitudes to street crime and to violent crime generally.

But this was different: it was not realized at the time but what was happening was the beginning of a split in the Yard that would become significant in the history of detection in England. From now on, detectives would be liaising with military intelligence personnel and the Home and Foreign Offices to work in pragmatic response to events on the world stage, rather than merely on domestic matters. This was to be the cause of rifts, jealousies and resentments in the ranks, but it also opened up the potential for powerful and ambitious individuals to make a name for themselves in new areas of detective work. Henceforth, some detective officers were to find themselves acting in quasi-espionage situations and, as time went on, in actual espionage.

It was the Fenians who had been the ultimate cause of these changes. After the history of absentee landlords and then the great famine in Ireland, a large number of Irishmen crossed the Atlantic to fight in the American Civil War of 1861–1865. There was a feeling that a war between Britain and the United States was possible and they hoped to fight on the American side. New York, with its thriving Irish-American community, provided the natural base for operations. Fenianism was a political and nationalist ethos, republican in aims and violent in its methods. One of the most important leaders, O'Donovan Rossa, was arrested in 1865 and by the next year the government began to see that bombing campaigns in London were going to be a constant threat.

A bill to suspend habeas corpus was passed in February 1866 and the Lord Lieutenant was given special powers of arrest. The habeas corpus principle is one of preventing both arrests on suspicion and the imprisonment of those arrested without trial. As well as making it illegal for a person to languish in gaol for indefinite periods, it also dictates that every person has a right to an appearance in court. In other words, the suspension was an act familiar to Britons today – it was a response to terrorism.

This move was controversial in the extreme: John Bright criticized it as 'a blot upon the reign of the Queen'. The most notable result of it was that Americans in Ireland who had been building alliances with republicans, went home. The focus of activities was going to be across the ocean and that would have important consequences for the new detectives. There was already a history of Fenian bombing and the Special Irish Branch was well briefed on that. Williamson had been active during the first real campaigns of 1867. That had been a period of desperation and extremism on the part of the Fenians. In 1866 a force of Fenians had tried to invade Canada after capturing Fort Erie. In 1867 they had attempted to attack

Chester Castle and in that same year they at last had a terrible impact on English life. Although a rising led by James Stephens failed in Ireland, the war was carried into England. On 8 September a police officer, Sergeant Brett, was murdered in Manchester while guarding two Fenian prisoners, Kelly and Deasy, and the killers were executed, thus providing the Fenian movement with some martyrs – they became known as 'The Manchester Martyrs'.

On 13 December that year came the Clerkenwell explosion. Twelve people died, over a hundred people were injured and sixty yards of prison wall were ruined. If nothing else, these events had the effect of making English people aware of the issues in Irish society. Between these first major terrorist activities and the new scares of the 1880s, Gladstone fought for reform on the Irish questions of Home Rule and changes in the established church. But even during the new bombing campaign of the 1880s, the Home Rule bill was defeated.

After the first bombings, the Metropolitan Police Act was passed in 1884 to establish two Assistant Commissioners, one for civil affairs, and one to head the Criminal Investigation Department; James Monro took over the CID responsibilities, and he was soon busy. The dynamiters left a bomb outside a government building in Whitehall, and there was an attempt to destroy Scotland Yard. A Constable Cole took action to stop an explosion at Westminster Hall.

There was more terror to follow from the 'Dynamiters'. In December 1884, they tried to blow up London Bridge; in the early evening of 13 December, a large amount of dynamite was fired against one of the buttresses of the bridge. It was a busy time of day, with crowds of pedestrians and heavy road traffic on the bridge; fortunately, damage was limited to some windows broken at the Hibernia Wharf and at the Customs House. Firemen and police were soon at the scene; the authorities had known that the bridge had been a target for some time.

The explosion had been timed for a busy period, with civilians as victims; as soon as possible, police inspected the buttress and the area around it to discover the narrative of the criminal activity. The first theory was that, because the walkway above was crowded and had places where people could hide from view, dynamite had been lowered on a string, and a time fuse used.

There was a general alarm and police from both City and Metropolitan districts sped to the scene. Crowds gathered, and in an atmosphere of excitement, the Thames Police arrived early the next morning. They always played a minor role in following up the prominent crimes committed by the dissidents and revolutionaries, but this was different: it was on their patch and they had special expertise. There was no damage to the bridge, but the effects of the blast were evident on either side of the river. Superintendent Stead of the Thames Division, along with other detectives, inspected the area around the blast again the next day, and still the main line of thought was that the explosive had been dropped from the bridge. Then an eyewitness told police that he had seen a boat with three men on board shortly before the explosion occurred. He had assumed that it was a police craft and thought no more of it but, after his statement, there were further checks and police found a piece of charred sacking about a foot square on one of the buttresses.

Just before Christmas it was announced that close inspection of the buttress by Stead and other officers had revealed that the dynamite had been covered with water and that explained the geyser which went over the bridge at the same time as the light from the explosion. The charge had been placed in a hole which had recently been made for drainage and it was soon understood that the spot chosen to position the dynamite was a place where the perpetrators would not be seen, as there was a stretch of the arch between them and the shoreline. They would have been out of view unless someone had seen them go under the bridge and had then crossed over to Fenning's Wharf, from where they could have been observed. Then, the police received a description of the men in the boat, and the craft was found. The owner of the boat they hired told police that the man he met was in the habit of hiring a boat: there had clearly been reconnaissance trips across the water.

It was later discovered that the bombers had been killed in

the explosion. The shattered bodies of the Fenians had floated down the river, and one of the dead men was William Lomasney, a bookseller from Detroit, known to the *Clan na Gael* terrorists as 'Little Captain'. He had volunteered to go to Europe to start a bombing campaign, travelling alone, as he feared spies. Another leader of the group called Lomasney 'a fanatic of the deepest dye'. Christy Campbell, in his book, *Fenian Fire*, has a footnote on this man and the London Bridge explosion:

> A Thames waterman named Carter gave a description matching Lomasney's as the man who had hired the boat for the doomed excursion. His brother and a man named John Fleming were also atomized in the explosion. In February 1885 a cache of Safety Nitro Company of San Francisco dynamite was found in a vacated house on the Harrow Road. The occupant's description matched Lomasney's.

The British spy, Thomas Beach, who operated with the name Major Henri le Caron, was involved in watching the American dynamiters, and in his memoir he wrote:

> The next group of dynamiters who visited England included Cunningham, Burton, Mackay, Lomasney, Luke Dillon and a man known as Ryan of Philadelphia. These men did not all come at the same time, but they worked together in harmony as far as possible. During their visits to London, explosions occurred in October 1883 on the underground railway; in February 1884 at Victoria Station; in May 1884 at Scotland Yard; in December 1884 at London Bridge ... the dynamite in all these cases was all brought from America, secreted about the persons of the conspirators, and of women who were sent over with it.

Cunningham and Burton were caught and brought to trial, and le Caron confirmed that Lomasney and Mackay both died in their attempt to blow up London Bridge. He also added, with inside knowledge, that 'so enormous was the quantity of nitroglycerine discovered that, according to experts, it was quite equal to the blowing up of every house and street in London from one end to the other'.

Inspector Stead had played a key role in the investigation, and it was becoming apparent by this time that the integrated police forces on land and on water, along with the Thames Conservancy, had found better ways of working together. In effect, the galleys were acting as floating police stations in terms of their preparedness for almost all eventualities. Naturally, coping with acts of terrorism was something altogether different from fights, collisions and the bodies of suicides. The galleys were increasingly engaged in inquiries focused on other divisions of course, and one outstanding example occurred just four years after the London Bridge bomb, when they played their part in a major police operation, as will be shown in the next chapter.

Meanwhile, the ghastly chores of dealing with death on the river went on, and the last decades of the nineteenth century saw a notable increase in suicides. In 1893 there were 3,412 deaths by drowning in Britain and of these only 581 were definitely confirmed as suicides, but of course a much larger proportion would have been suicide cases. Few such people leave notes or state their sad intentions to others. There have been a number of theories, some fanciful and speculative, about the allure of suicide by drowning. Some writers have seen in death by water a more comforting end than in self-murder by blades, poison or bullets. In the case of the Thames, there have always been particular places that suicides or those contemplating taking their own lives have found to be appealing in some way. One such spot was close to the Wapping station, a swing bridge on Old Gravel Lane, known as 'The Bridge of Sighs', but then a more famous place given that same name was Waterloo Bridge, after it was opened in 1817. Dickens crossed that bridge, and wrote of it: 'The wild moon and clouds were as restless as an evil conscience in a tumbled bed, and the very shadow of the immensity of London seemed to lie oppressively upon the water.'

Dealing with bodies found was as regular as pulling on an oar for the Thames Police, whether they were suicides, accidental deaths, deaths of the suspicious variety or cases of obvious homicide. When a body was found, there was often an investigation into background and circumstances, as was the case with Mary Williams in 1870. Her body was found and there was talk on the street that she had been murdered. This rumour began simply because she had gone out to the theatre with a lodger called Rudge, and she had left the theatre to go home and he had not seen her again. Mrs Williams' son found that several items were missing from her home and then, after giving one statement, Rudge had gone missing, implying some guilt.

The Thames officers thought that Rudge had also probably thrown himself into the river, and the coroner's court was told that it took around fourteen days for a body to be found floating on the surface. Then a witness came forward to say that he had seen Rudge jump from Westminster Bridge. Eventually, nothing could be done to determine the cause of Mary Williams's death apart from leaving the police to try to find other clues or evidence, and the final statement of the hearing was one which was heard a thousand times in this era: 'The deceased was found drowned ... but how she became drowned there was no evidence to show.'

There had been advances in forensic science since the early days of the police, and in 1844 William Guy published *Principles of Forensic Medicine*. Guy (1810–1885) was to have a distinguished career, taking his MB degree in 1837, and being appointed professor of forensic medicine at King's College, London, in the following year. He was also outstanding in the developing discipline of statistics, and was Honorary Secretary of the Statistical Society for many years. His work on forensics made his name, and it was re-issued and re-edited several times. Guy was in the background when police needed forensic information, available as a consultant but rarely in the public eye. However, he did have a special interest in the criminal justice system, being a member of royal commissions on penal servitude and criminal lunatics in his later years.

Guy's handbook gives us an insight into how the 'found drowned' clients of the Thames officers would be understood and handled; his book provided a guide to various ways in which a floating body may have died. For instance, he summed up the causes neatly:

> Death by drowning may be due to asphyxia, to shock, to syncope, and to apoplexy; or partly to asphyxia ... If in death by asphyxia the examination is made soon after the death and removal from the water the following appearances will be present – the face and general surface of the body are pale or slightly livid, with patches of deeper tint. The expression of the face is generally calm. The tongue is swollen and closely applied to the teeth.

In other words, a police officer with the plain explanations would be able to assist the surgeon, and report on basic features, as he would often have attended the deceased long before medical expertise was on hand. Guy also listed various guidelines in answer to the question of whether or not the death was due to drowning. But the doubts were still there when it came to suicide: 'This question is exceedingly difficult to answer, for if there are no marks of violence on the body, it is not possible to say whether the man fell in, jumped in or was pushed in.' Guy also offered guidance with regard to artificial respiration, and so his book was useful to many classes of readers.

The Thames Police were, of course, highly experienced in dealing with suicides, and there is plenty of material of the time explaining how they worked when searching for bodies. One of the most vivid examples is a piece written for the *Strand Magazine* in 1895 called 'A Night with the Thames Police', in which the writer describes the work done:

> And as the oars of our little craft touch the water, every man's eyes are fixed in order to catch sight of anything like the appearance of a missing person. A record of the missing, as well as the found, is kept at the station we have just left a mile or two down the river. Ten poor creatures remain yet to be discovered. What stories, thrilling and heartrending, we have to listen to! Yet even in such pitiful occurrences as these, much that is grimly humorous often surrounds them. Many

are the sad recognitions on the part of those 'found drowned'. Experience has taught the police to stand quietly behind those who must needs go through such a terrible ordeal, and who often swoon at the first sight. Where is there a more touching story than that of the little girl who tramped all the way from Camden Town to Wapping, for the purpose of identifying her father, who had been picked up near the Old Stairs?

The writer was curious as to methods of identification, as the Thames men must have tried all possible avenues of inquiry to ascertain the identity of a floating corpse. On his night out with the police launch, the inspector told a story of the detective work that such efforts necessarily entailed: 'When I came to search the clothing of the poor fellow, the timekeeper was found ... It was a gold one, and on the case was an engraved inscription, setting forth that it had been given to a sergeant of marines.' That led him to trace the person, but usually there were no clues.

The nocturnal excursion on the launch included an insight into the demands of the job:

It blows cold as we spin past Traitor's Gate at the Tower, but our men become weather-beaten on the Thames, and their hands never lose the grip of the oar. They need a hardy frame, a robust constitution, for no matter what the weather, blinding snow or driving rain, these water guardians come out – the foggiest night detains them not; they have to get through the fog and their allotted six hours.

The last decades of the nineteenth century were an age of intense curiosity about and documentation of working lives, and magazines such as *The Strand, Harmsworth Magazine* and *The London Magazine* opened up knowledge of all kinds of occupations and professions to the curious reading public. The tone and approach of the article just cited suggests that the readers knew very little about the men they would see on their river every day, but would not see in the dark and the mist while they trawled for bodies.

There were extraordinary tales of suicides and attempted suicides of course, as well as the almost daily sad stories of those found drowned. In June 1885 a police constable saw an old man jump off Chelsea Bridge, but instead of hitting the surface of water, he landed on the top of a buttress and lay unconscious. As there was a low ebb tide, he could be reached with a rope, and the officer went down to save the man. A Conservancy boat came alongside to help as well, but all was in vain as the man died shortly after being taken to St Thomas's Hospital.

The modern age is often defined as one of the dominance of celebrity and five minutes of fame, but the Victorians also enjoyed spectacle, dare-devil feats and circus-style risk in the form of entertainment. The Thames was naturally a draw to such exhibitions, and in 1888, just before the Ripper killings hit the headlines, an American specializing in leaps from great heights, Larry Donovan, hurled himself from Hungerford Bridge. A match had been arranged for him at Brighton – against another man for a wager – so he took a crowd of admirers to the London venue and dived in, to show that he was capable of doing well in the challenge. The *Daily Telegraph* reported on what happened next: 'He swam about thirty yards in the direction of Cleopatra's Needle steps, which were about a hundred yards from the bridge, and then sank. He did not cry out or throw up his arms, but sank like a stone.'

A week later Inspector Pullen of the Thames Police was in his galley off Horn Stairs in Rotherhithe, when he saw the body of a man floating in the water; his galley rowed as fast as possible to the spot, and the body was fastened to the boat. They then went to the stairs and took the corpse to the nearest mortuary. A description of the man was circulated, and he was found to be John Cooper, just twenty-four. He had been inspired by Donovan and had made a bet while in his cups in the Duke of Clarence pub in Tooley Street. He had then gone with friends to two other pubs before going onto the bridge, where he took off his boots and jumped in, going out of sight immediately. Ironically, he was reckoned a good swimmer, but what the Thames men had was a case of copycat drowning, death by misadventure.

Most cases of drowning were shown to be accidental deaths or suicides, and as mentioned earlier, the difference was not always known for sure; the last decades of the century brought a torrent of cases, as the demographics of the city had changed, with a massive increase in office workers and business people being at work and play on the riverside. There was also another class of course: the homeless. One inquest exemplifies this lamentable situation – one still with us today. Frederick Honeyball was a dairyman who had been living in Old Ford, but wandered down to the Embankment and talked about his troubles to a homeless man called Sutherland. Honeyball said that he was very hungry and had had no 'tommy' – nothing to eat – on the previous day. Sutherland told the coroner's court that he himself had eaten nothing for four days.

After Honeyball threw himself into the river, the subject of the homeless and of emergency arrangements to try to save those who were reclaimed from the river still alive was discussed. This story highlights the importance of the police at the time because, as the coroner said in his summing-up, the Waterloo Thames Police office was the only place where proper provision in the way of restoratives was made for the apparently drowned. He added that the French were much better organized in that respect, with a number of refuge houses along the Seine.

If we look for an explanation of the nature and function of the Thames River Police in the 1880s then we will see that their activities were largely on the peripheries of major criminal activity in the city, usually assuming a supporting role to leads taken by other divisions, mainly around the East End, but also further inland. This would be too reductive an assessment, though, because as the Fenian bombing and the various collisions and cases of violence show, they were increasingly integrated into an overall chain of command. By the 1880s the new steam launches were in action and the Thames Conservancy manpower and craft, along with the police of the docks, were part of the Thames Division as well – although it was not until the creation of the Port of London Authority in 1909 that the police forces of the London and India Docks Company, the

Surrey Commercial Dock Company and the Millwall Dock Company were amalgamated.

The view that the Thames Police played a secondary role in policing the river is untrue; they had their specialisms, as other forces did, and they were watermen through and through, recruited from the ranks of men who knew the moods, movements and material reality of the great river they moved on and respected. As such, they were called in when needed and were absolutely indispensable across a broad spectrum of crime, particularly as the century wore on and white-collar crime became more widespread and complex. The new technology of police work was on its way: fingerprints, for instance, would be in use by the turn of the century and detection methods were refined to cope with political crime. These advances did not sideline the Thames men. However, there were developments in the bigger picture of international politics, and these were bound to impinge on the Thames and on its docks and vessels.

Before such advances, the Thames men were prominent in some more major episodes in British criminal history, and their particular expertise would be called upon when, in 1887, the first of a series of torsos was found in the Thames. That meant that the river constables would play a minor role in the hunt for the Ripper, and would also have a major ongoing mystery to sort out that involved several police divisions of the city.

9 More Deaths on the River and the Torso Murders

IN NINETEENTH-CENTURY Paris the city morgue was an attraction for the curious, whether or not they had a reason for stopping by to view the corpses; inside, they would see a gallery of death. There were photographs of the deceased and their clothes were displayed. Naturally, this made a powerful scene for novelists to utilize, and Émile Zola did just that in his novel of murder, *Therese Raquin*, published in 1867. However, there were many practical reasons why a morgue of this kind was a useful addition to the amenities of a city. In 1882, a correspondent to *The Times* argued strongly for such a morgue in the face of so many anonymous dead and the ease with which murders could be committed on unsuspecting people out alone amongst desperate criminals. The letter was, in effect, a plea for much more organized police work in this respect.

The author was spurred to write by the fact that, in the five years prior to 1882, there had been 599 people 'found drowned' without coroners' juries being able to determine how they came to be in the water. In the course of the letter, rhetorical questions are asked: 'How many of the bodies were identified? Were photographs taken of them at all? What has been done with the clothes and other property found among them?' The writer then put forward exactly what the police authorities needed: a plan involving much more than a list of names or a bill stuck on a door:

> Our customs being different from those of the French, it might be deemed objectionable to set up a permanent exhibition of dead bodies in the heart of London, but a kind of

metropolitan dead-house might be established where the photographs, clothes and other belongings of persons mysteriously found dead should be kept on view ... At present when a body is pulled out of the Thames ... a description of it is posted outside the door of the district police station, but nowhere else, and unless the case presents features of an unusual interest, all that the public hear of it is through a short account in the newspapers.

The traditional habits surrounding coroners' inquests still held sway at the time: the focus was on the knowledge of the immediate locality, so it was assumed that a corpse laid out on a tavern table would almost always be identified as a local person and thus the mystery would be solved. That process made it all the easier for villains to murder hapless visitors by simply striking them hard in a nocturnal attack and pushing the body into the river. The author of the long letter was sure of his grasp of the policing situation, and may have been a police officer himself:

> Detectives and policemen may do their best to watch the river banks; the steam launches and gigs of the Thames Police may with noiseless vigilance patrol the waters: but it is doubtful whether the river can ever be made quite safe until scientific improvements shall enable all the London reaches of it to be lighted by electric buoys placed in midstream.

The population of London reached 3.3 million in 1881, and the great teeming metropolis was still a long way short of protecting its citizens; the vulnerability of all classes, ages and conditions was clear to all as problems of crime increased, often in consequence of rapid commercial and industrial expansion. Before the decade ended there would be riots, strikes and a seemingly endless flow of the heart-rending results of violent crime. The letter on morgues and deaths in the river proved to be not only perceptive and incisively argued: it was also dramatically informed by one of the most sensational and unsolved Thames mysteries in the entire history of the river: the so-called

'Torso' or 'Battersea Mystery' of 1873. This was to be followed by even more mysterious body-part mysteries in 1887–1889.

In early September 1873 a Thames PC was on patrol near Battersea waterworks when he saw something in the mud. He went closer and saw that it was the left quarter of a woman's trunk. He conveyed the information to his superiors and the news spread; meanwhile he had the body part taken to the Clapham and Wandsworth Union Workhouse. The doctor there, called Kempster, studied the remains, and while this was in process, a policemen employed by the South Western Railway proved particularly vigilant when he found the right side of the trunk at Brunswick Wharf; then Inspector Marley of the Thames Police found a part of some lungs; finally, off Limehouse, there was perhaps the most grisly find, the face and scalp – an image of which was captured by the artist for the *Illustrated Police News*. The killer had, as the report explained, 'taken revolting precautions to prevent identification, for the nose was cut from the face, but still hung attached to the upper lip'.

The police stated that they had searched and found some other body parts in the area where the Wandle joins the Thames, where barges congregated and regularly moved; this suggested that bargees were likely suspects and so investigations began on that basis. Dr Kempster did his best to provide forensic details on the woman, who was aged about forty and had dark hair, and a scar or burn on her left breast. He concluded with the statement that 'There is a large bruise on the right temple, which was caused by a blow from a blunt instrument or substance shortly before death. The scalp was divided at the upper margin of the bones, but I cannot determine whether before or after death.'

The Thames Torso Mysteries had begun. Medical minds were soon set to work on the mystery and, in *The Lancet*, the writer was desperate to point out that the body parts were not cast into the river after anatomy lessons by medical students wanting to create a sensation, insisting that such a hypothesis 'must appear preposterous if, in addition to the evidence that the death was a violent one, it is borne in mind [that the body] bears no trace of dissection'.

The general consensus was that the person responsible for the horrific fragments had the kind of knowledge a butcher, rather than a surgeon, would have of the human body and its anatomy. The details of the actions carried out by the killer hint at the kind of twisted mind that would relish the blood-thirsty elements of horror fiction, as in the note that the stunned body had been quickly deprived of a bloody section of its carotid artery.

The corpse was reconstructed, under direction from Dr Bond, the acting chief surgeon of the Metropolitan Police. One of the tasks accorded to the police was to keep the morbidly curious at a distance from this work; at the coroner's court, the verdict of 'Wilful murder against some person or persons unknown' was returned. By 9 September, there was also a foot and part of the right shoulder to work with. It was initially believed that the corpse was that of a Mrs Cailey, but then she was seen walking in Chelsea so once again the case was back in the category of total mystery. One of the strangest outcomes of this was that a group called The Association of Escaped Criminal Lunatics was not involved, and they announced that fact in *The Times*. This may well have been a sick joke by pranksters.

The Thames officers continued working with the detectives and other police professionals as further searches went on and, on 16 September, Inspector Edmund Walker, of the Thames force, was in a police galley with two other officers close to Easton's Wharf, when he saw an object floating in the water. He reported that he took hold of the object and 'found it to be part of the leg of a human being, from the knee to the ankle joint. I cannot say whether it was right or left ... I could not see any marks, it was so decomposed.' A carman called Patterson also found part of an arm.

In the occurrence book at Wapping – a record of those taken from the river by the galleys – there are brief accounts of the bodies found, such as: 'A gathering of people stated that they saw a man on the pier ... he was a wealthy person, perhaps a business-man, and soon he was in. Nobody could say what they saw except a splash'. However, Walker's report was a rare entry indeed: a few

An early fingerprint kit, kept at the Wapping museum. Lord Belper's committee recommended Edward Henry's fingerprint system in 1899. Henry was made Assistant Commissioner and fingerprinting then came into use at Scotland Yard.

© THAMES POLICE ASSOCIATION

words for each body part found. The luckless officer doing the recording would have found that a gruesome task, much different from routine. A mystery it was and so it remained. Surely if an argument was needed to support the anonymous writer to *The Times* in his appeal for a city morgue, then this would support the reasoning. This was not merely a suspicious death: it was a murder, and identification would have been the key to investigative approaches, because knowledge of the deceased often leads to witnesses and sightings, followed by descriptions of people who knew and who had been seen with the deceased. The reconstruction by surgeons was a bold attempt, and truly innovative in that time, but nothing came of it.

What was the nature of the Thames Police at this time? By the 1890s the manpower of the force exceeded two hundred, with eight galleys and three steam launches; the writer for the

Strand Magazine commented that by then, 'smuggling is in reality played out' and vigilance was effective, with the men constantly searching for suspicious characters. That writer also gives the reader a sketch of the interior of Wapping station:

> Inside the station-house you turn sharply to the right and there is the charge-room. Portraits of Sir Charles Warren [the Commissioner] and other police authorities are picturesquely arranged on the walls. In front of the desk, with its innumerable little wooden rails, where sits the inspector in charge, is the prisoners' dock, from the ground of which rises the military measurement in inches against which the culprit testifies as to his height.... In a corner near the steel rails of the clock, lie a couple of bargemen's peak caps.... Just in a crevice by the window are the telegraph instruments. A clicking noise is heard, and the inspector hurriedly takes down on a slate a strange but suggestive message.

That desk with its rails is still there today at Wapping, for visitors to see.

The telegraph message was about a boxing match, something that lit up the faces of the men with enthusiasm. Then we have a glimpse of the cells, cosy and clean, one of the two kept for women, painted yellow and with a wash basin, towel and soap, and even a cup. There are pipes for heating, and pillows and rugs are available too. Prisoners were allowed food to the value of fourpence before they appeared at the Thames Police Court. The reporter for the *Strand Magazine* also noticed that a door was badly dented 'from the boot-tips of young men endeavouring to perform the clever acrobatic feat of kicking out the iron grating through which the gas-jet gives them light'.

The men described by the reporter had their fair share of physical action and fisticuffs, so boxing was useful. Sometimes there were gangs to deal with, as was the case when four labourers ended up in court at Westminster for assaulting three constables. The trouble started when Constable Philpott landed a Thames galley to disperse a huge gang of what were then termed 'roughs' whom the constables pursued as they ran, but one turned to face the officers with a brick, threatening to smash Philpott's brains out with it. Another inspector then arrived and Philpott had help, but he was still thrown into a hole and attacked by a man with a knife. The crowd behind shouted for the knifeman to 'cut his ... fingers off!' There was a fight lasting half an hour and the police officers took a beating but a gang leader, Bagley, was arrested and other arrests followed.

Such was Wapping at the time of the Ripper and the Torso Mysteries – a combination that hints at more gory tales to come. Indeed, in 1887 and through to 1889 there were yet more torsos found. In the midst of that succession of revolting river finds, there was, of course, a serial killer at large down the road in Whitechapel. The Thames men were to play their part in that too and, naturally, torsos discovered were linked to the Ripper killings while theories were being worked out by the lead detectives.

The first body part was found at Rainham in May 1887 when some workers found a bundle in which was the torso of a woman; then other parts were found in May and June until finally virtually a whole body was found – as with the 1873 case – complete except for the head and part of the chest. There was no forensic certainty about cause of death, so this was another 'found dead'.

In September of the following year there was again a series of discoveries of body parts, one of which was found on the foreshore of the Thames near the Grosvenor Road railway bridge. It was taken by an officer to Gerald Street station and Dr Neville was called in. He announced that it was the right arm of a woman, and it had been in the river for a few days; there was string tied around it, and Dr Neville was sure that this was done so that it could be carried.

The Thames Police had the unenviable task of examining all the stretches of the river close by, and records of missing persons were examined. The only thing that seemed certain was that this was the result of a crime, not a medical students' joke. The horrible discovery was followed, less than a month later, by yet another: a workman found a parcel in a cellar in what was to become Scotland Yard. This was the trunk of a woman; a piece of black petticoat was the only clothing apparent. The medical opinion was that the limbs had been hacked off, with no evidence of any medical skill – more the act of a butcher. One of the strangest facts on this particular finding was explained by the reporter for *The Times*: 'The prevailing opinion is that to place the body where it was found the person conveying it must have scaled the eight-foot hoarding which encloses the works, and carefully avoiding the watchmen who do duty by night, placed the parcel where it was found.' One important part of police thinking was that the person who did this knew the 'intricacies of the underground part of these works', as the reporter put it.

Finally, in the middle of the hunt for the Ripper, in September 1889, the naked trunk of a woman was found in Pinchin Street. Was this a Ripper victim? The body was taken to St George's mortuary, and detectives were put on the case, one of them being Abberline, who was prominent in the hunt for the Ripper. There was a dispatch sent to all police, and the Thames Police were put on full alert. The message read:

> At twenty minutes to six a.m. the trunk of a woman was found under the arches in Pinchin Street. Age about forty. Height 5ft.3 ins. Hair dark brown. No clothing except chemise, very much torn and blood stained. Both elbows discoloured as if from leaning on them. Marks round waist, apparently caused by a rope.

There were detectives posted to the Thames Division just fourteen years before this – a detective sergeant and three detective constables. There had been men allotted 'nondescript' duties on the duty rota, and now, in the Ripper year, two of these men, DI Regan and CI Moore, took a team of constables onto the river and boarded all the vessels in the docks and at the river mouth. Stewart Evans and Keith Skinner, Ripper experts, explain:

> Attention was particularly directed to the cattle boats and those from Spain and America. Among those boarded in the London Docks were the *City of Cork*, the *Cadiz*, the *Malaga* and the *Gallicia,* and the *Lydian Monarch* in the Millwall

Docks. The operation of searching these vessels had not concluded until a late hour in the evening, and so far as the investigation had gone the captains of the various vessels were able to give satisfactory accounts as to their crews.

The Torso Mysteries were ultimately a source of great frustration and they remain a mystery to this day. The Thames Police had played a major part in the strenuous efforts to try to find some source or pattern in these gruesome events which might have led to a culprit. The nasty findings and investigations around the body parts do show something interesting though: a stepping-up of co-operation between police divisions, a specialized use of the Thames men, and the use of detectives. The river men were late in having their dedicated sleuths of course – over thirty years behind the rest of the city.

10 The Changing Profession: Constables Afloat

AFTER THE THAMES Court was moved to Arbour Square in 1842, the old Wapping station declined and was eventually demolished in 1869. A new one, with a wharf and a boatyard, was opened in 1872. During the middle and later years of the nineteenth century, as well as the riverside divisions and the Thames Division stations, there were floating police stations, and these included former hulks of the navy, such as the *Scorpion*, in service until 1864 and then replaced by the *Royalist*, kept at work until 1894. As Geoffrey Budworth has pointed out, the latter was known as 'the abode of Bliss' because a character called Inspector Bliss actually lived on board with his body of constables.

Routine for the Thames men in the last decades of the century involved a division of four watches, each for six hours; the interchange was arranged so that a new boat was on its way out on patrol every two hours. The result was that the river was always patrolled, night and day, and the staff rota gave the men a period of twelve hours off duty, replacing the former taxing routine of six hours on and off, alternated; but it was still a hard task to find a solid period of sleep and rest, because the system was such that an officer could be in a boat at any time, and with limited staff rolls, there were demands on energy and stamina.

A sense of greater permanence was achieved when the force purchased a boatyard from the Bridewell Hospital in 1891. The boats had been made by Martin of Greenwich, and they were the product of skilled craft and design; they were made of oak and coated in resin or tar. They had to be repaired, of course, and, as time went on, more mechanized support for such work was brought in, such as a Weston purchase (a chain hoist) to hold the galleys. Later in the century, steam launches, as noted in the *Princess Alice* story (see Chapter 7), came in, the first one in use being called the *Rover*. This was followed by a custom-built vessel, the *Alert,* and later this was superseded by a ship with a steel hull, the *Chowkidar*. By the end of the century, the force had eight steam launches and twenty-eight galleys. One of the notable characters in the Thames Division history, George Mitchell, enters the story here. He was an engineer who was supposed to be attached to the force on loan to instruct and guide staff on the new ships, but in fact he stayed and took control of repairs and remained there for the rest of his working life.

© THAMES POLICE ASSOCIATION

Oliver's Wharf: built in 1870, handling river cargo and also used for the tea trade, this was next to the police boatyard and repair shop.

Galleys were later converted into steam-powered craft after Mitchell devised a petrol engine to be adapted for use on them. A version of a powered galley was also created by Sir John Thorneycroft: called the Handy Billy, it was not initially reliable or easy to use, but was eventually improved and made much more useful. Early in the twentieth century, after all kinds of experiments, tenders were invited for the supply of powered boats for the Thames Division.

What about conditions of service? From the very beginning in 1829, the Peelers had been controlled in a framework of paternalism. This meant that, although they were in many ways a privileged group within the overall workforce, they were, nevertheless, managed by a combination of punishments and rewards, intended to keep the best men and to make constables think in a long-term, career-minded way. In the first decades of the Metropolitan Police, there was a very high proportion of men leaving the force, either through drunkenness or because of breaches of discipline in other areas, or sometimes through sheer hardship. On the other hand, there were some aspects of enlightened management, such as the fact that well before the legislation of 1880 and 1897 (the Employers' Liability Act and the Workmen's Compensation Act respectively) policemen had been given gratuity payments if disabled. But pensions were a different matter: the tendency was for men of the higher ranks to be given pensions, while lower-ranking men, of long service, often did not have a pension. (However, throughout almost the whole of the nineteenth century, few occupations had pensions, nor did they have security of tenure or support when sick.)

In introducing the original concept of pensions, the Commissioner and senior management wanted to have inducements for men to think of their police career as being for life. There was quite a reasonable prospect of promotion for constables, which may have assisted some to climb towards the pensionable ranks, but the statistics are not indicative of the early pension schemes being that successful. A Select Committee on the Metropolitan Police of 1877 reported that, between 1839 and 1860, of the 100,000 men in the force, only 13,855 were pensioned. The number dismissed was 29,923 and 3,730 had died in service. The pension fund had dried up by 1856 and there had been poor administration at the top.

There was a growing dissatisfaction with all this, and publications such as *The Police Service Advertiser* expressed dissent from the 1860s onward. However, a pension scheme for the police was made compulsory by an Act in 1890 and the Metropolitan men had a higher rate than that of provincial forces. In the statistics of total departures from the force, pension provision had risen from 30% in 1879 to 48.7% in 1891. There were various other good initiatives, such as reward schemes and awards, and accommodation for sick officers; there was even an orphanage for the children of policemen who died in police service. Medical assistance was also provided for officers, but sick pay had been at a reduced rate from the early days as a deterrent against malingerers.

In the bigger picture, crime statistics in the second half of the nineteenth century showed interesting declines, such as the comparison of the rate of indictable offences per 100,000 of population dropping from 448 in 1860 to 249 in 1989, while in the same two years non-indictable offences dropped from 323 per 100,000 to 229. Reading the accounts of the very busy police courts of London, however, suggests there was certainly a great deal for the police to do. As the nineteenth century wore on, the volume of petty crime increased so much that the old system of what were called summary courts was increasingly organized and administered by the police rather than by legal professionals of various kinds. It was becoming clear that preventing crime needed more emphasis and investment, and there was no probation service (that arrived in 1907). A massive influence on this accelerating volume of crime was drunkenness; so it is no accident that the police court missionaries, whom the Thames constables would have known well and worked with, had their roots in the temperance movement. The Inebriates Act of 1898 made it possible for the courts to send drunks to a reformatory, and there were a number of homes for inebriates. But back in 1876, when the idea of police court missionaries was born, there was nothing to help the women or juveniles on the streets, scraping a living through selling anything from trinkets and matches to sex.

The human traffic passing through the police courts reflected the dismal failures of the affluent society of Victorian Britain, with its proud boast of wealth and progress, displayed in the Great Exhibition of 1851. Beneath the glamour and the expansion of empire there was a growing class of people who found themselves before the bench for petty theft, hawking without a licence or prostitution. The police staff struggled to cope, and satires of the time, notably in *Punch*, revel in showing the swamping of the courts by the desperate and destitute. It is not difficult to imagine the chaos at the courts: a stream of people being brought in, and culprits in their dozens being loaded into the 'Black Marias' as they were shipped off to gaol; the missionaries squeezed in and worked when and where they could.

It was in 1876 that a printer from Hertford called Frederic Rainer, who was working as a volunteer with the Church of England Temperance Society (CETS), saw this problem at the courts and decided to act. He gave five shillings to the group of philanthropists who were working in a small way to help offenders. The result was a tentative placement of two missionaries in Southwark by the CETS. From there, a quiet revolution began.

After that, two former guardsmen, Batchelor and Nelson, became the first two police court missionaries. One snippet of oral history suggests that their friendship included one episode in which Batchelor saved Nelson's life. Nelson was in the Coldstream Guards in 1861, and was discharged with good conduct in 1871. In 1877 he listed his activities, and these included visits to 438 homes, 293 attendances at police courts and 149 temperance pledges taken. He made 117 visits to prisons and saw 20 women sent to homes.

By 1880 there were eight full-time missionaries in place and homes were opened. By 1896 there were six 'mission women' in the team and, in London, these staff would interview women charged at court. Some of these were sent to an inebriates' home at Gratton Road. The service offered by the missionaries was best summed up by Thomas Holmes, who said, 'Sir, I cannot carry Christ in parcels and distribute him. I can only do as I think He would have done ... I give them myself.'

There was someone else of note on the scene as well: William

Wheatley. In 1887 Howard Vincent, a former Metropolitan Police officer, saw through Parliament his Probation of First Offenders Bill; this did not establish probation officers, but brought about police supervision with Home Office backing. The most significant stipulation of this bill was that the offender being helped had to have a fixed 'place of abode'. In order that this could be fulfilled, Wheatley set up the St Giles Christian Mission and began to collect and work with young men who had committed a first offence. In 1890, a reporter from *The Daily Graphic* looked into Wheatley's work. His report included this information:

> It was not always so obvious as it is now that there are more ways of reducing crime than by merely imprisoning criminals. A great deal is left to missions such as St Giles Mission to Discharged Prisoners, with which the names of Mr George Hatton and Mr William Wheatley have been so long associated.... The headquarters of the Mission are in Little Wild Street, one of those narrow and not so sweet-smelling streets leading off Drury Lane.... But Mr Wheatley is usually found elsewhere, making his round of the prisons.

The missionaries went to extremes to help the fallen, the youngsters otherwise destined to be on the police 'Habitual Criminals Register'. Thomas Holmes even offered his own house at times; he wrote that he dealt with alcoholics by giving them 'the shelter and protection' of his own home. Perhaps his most lengthy and heart-rending account of one of the offenders he worked with was that of Jane Cakebread. This poor woman, after a life of crime, died in Claybury Asylum and Holmes went to her funeral.

But this does not imply softness and indulgence: on the contrary, the usual statement made about the aims of probation – to 'guide, admonish and befriend' – hints at the toughness required as well as the sacrifice of time, labour and personal comfort. What was very much an aid and support to the missionaries, though, was the First Offenders Act of 1887. This made it easier to give the missionaries the tasks of supervising young offenders who had been bound over, since voluntary supervision was undertaken for a designated period.

All this needed money, of course: the support could not be there without finance. A typical fund-raising effort was the concert given at Bycullah Athenaeum, which raised a great deal of money. The missionaries themselves were not particularly well paid – around £50 a year was average. But progress was made, and some of the main achievements of the Missions are very impressive, such as the boys' shelter at Bethnal Green, founded in 1893, in which around twenty boys would stay and be supervised for several weeks. The achievements are best appreciated with a look at some figures: in the area of what is now Greater London, missionaries visited over 5,000 homes, wrote over 3,000 letters and took over 2,000 pledges.

Police officers were bound up with all this; they knew that there was some kind of support network for the habitual criminals. We have some enlightening insights into this from the memoirs of Montagu Williams, a barrister who worked in the East End in the 1890s as a magistrate. In a letter written to *The Daily News* in 1891 he wrote: 'The London Police Court Mission have kindly given me the aid of the Thames and Worship Street police courts, who will be of the greatest use to me in my venture [to distribute clothing among the poor]' and it is clear that the Thames Division men were closely involved in this kind of work for the poor. Not only did they have a collection box at the station, but also a very special attitude of caring and exceptional concern for those in their 'patch' who were not necessarily criminal, but unfortunate and in distress. If an outstanding example of this need be found, it is in the career of Henry Lediard, who started with the Thames Division in 1877. Geoffrey Budworth tells the story of one of his acts of courage:

> While at Waterloo Pier he took the stand-by boat away single-handed to rescue a woman who had jumped off the bridge, hauling her water-sodden mass inboard over the roller fitted to the stern especially for that purpose. Having resuscitated and landed her, he secured his patient onto the hand-ambulance ... and pushed her to Westminster Hospital.

Despite their dedication and courage, the Thames men were subject to criticism, and this increased from the 1870s, when the volume of river traffic began to increase apace, and other bodies were more involved in policing. In 1884 a Select Committee of the House of Commons on Thames Preservation discussed the danger from criminals on the river. Sir Gilbert East of the Association of Riparian Owners, describing the villains, stated that:

> There were two classes of roughs who frequented the river – namely, the London ''Arry' and a superior individual, judging from his clothing and manners, yet one who did more damage than the first. The rough of the 'Arry class could be told by his peculiar dress and foul language. The other rough encamped on the property of the riparian owner, took hurdles for firewood, damaged trees, trampled among the hay, let loose dogs.

Policemen of the world would not be surprised to learn that the Select Committee, with these attitudes in mind, suggested that there should be a separate river police body under the command of the Thames Conservancy. In other words, the age of leisure along the Thames had undergone a revolution, and policing the new varieties of petty crime and public nuisance was something the established marine force could not prioritize when there were such things as murders, suicides, accidents and contraband to think about.

In fact, the Thames Conservancy Act of 1894 made clear the terms of employment of constables from across London:

> The Commissioner of Police of the Metropolis, the Commissioner of Police of the City, and Head Constables or other officers having chief commands of police of all counties, cities, boroughs or towns the Thames flows [through], if they think fit, at the present request of the Conservators, and upon such terms as to payment by the Conservators ... as may from time to time ... provide officers and constables of police to keep the peace, preserve order and prevent breaches of this Act.

In other words, there was to be no great reform or reorganization: merely a system of paying for special duties on the Thames when the need arose.

By c.1900, then, the Thames Division had been in existence for just over a century. The man aspiring to be a constable afloat had to be qualified in the management of boats, and would have to attend Wapping police station to be examined and to prove his fitness for duty. He had to be able to swim and had to produce a certificate to prove that proficiency. When an officer in another division wanted to apply to be transferred to the Thames Division, he had to apply to the Commissioner, and if considered suitable, his name would be put on a waiting list. He would then be appointed when the time came, as the queue moved on. But the handbook entitled *The Police Service of England and Wales* for 1900 pointed out that 'Owing to the few vacancies occurring in the Division it may be months before they are transferred.'

The jurisdiction of the police on the Thames was also defined at this time, and the legal expression was that their responsibility:

> should extend over the whole of the waters, bed, shores, banks and towpaths of the Thames and over any place within one hundred yards on either side of the Thames and over the whole of so much of any island as is in the Thames where that river flows through or by such area.

Also, what exactly was 'the Thames' in terms of policing? It was specified under the 1894 Act as:

> so much of the rivers Thames and Isis respectively as are between the town of Cricklade in the county of Wilts and an imaginary straight line drawn from the entrance to Yauntlet Creek in the county of Kent to the City Stone opposite to Canvey island in the county of Essex, and so much of the river Kennet as is between the common landing place at Reading in the county of Berks and the river Thames and so much of the river Lee and Bow Creek respectively as are below the south boundary stones.

Images of Thames officers on galleys or on launches suggest, at times, merely a steady patrol, with men's eyes searching the water for corpses or any other floating items of interest to them; actually, a more informative and explanatory account of what galleys had to do would be the story of what happened in 1841 when Inspector Charles Falconer and Constables George White and Joseph Doyle were helping to tow a sunken lugboat (a small square-sailed vessel) owned by a lighterman called Hinds, who was working for the brewers Hodgson and Abbott of Wapping. The lugboat was carrying a hundred hogsheads of ale on its way to India, when it hit ice, sank and lost its cargo; the boat needed to be towed to Wapping, and the job fell to Inspector Falconer and his men.

The boat was secured by a rope to a ring in the galley, but the boat was wrenched by the chain of the ballast engine; the strong tide turned the galley over and the officers were hurled into the water. They were good swimmers. White amazingly swam for half a mile to Alderman's Stairs and the other two were taken up by a ship. Even while the galley was going down, the intrepid White shouted, 'Don't be in a hurry master, I'll loosen the headfast!'

Falconer yelled back, 'Cut it man or the lug will drag us all to the bottom!' But White carried on cutting, saying, 'Don't be in a hurry master, never do things in a hurry.' Just as he cut the headfast, the galley turned over and was carried by the tide under a rank of other craft. Even when White had reached a schooner after his swim, he still called out, 'Don't be in a hurry master … but throw me a rope and I'll soon be on board.' It seems from reports that White and his coolness became a source of fun and storytelling in the ranks. It certainly entered the folklore and oral history of the River Police.

But going into the river was no joke. Not only were there hurricanes to contend with, as in 1838 when the police galleys tried and often failed to rescue men, but there was disease. In his book, *River Beat*, Geoffrey Budworth makes a strong point about the arduous and dangerous nature of the job:

The Roll of Honour at the rear of this book, listing the names of Thames officers killed on duty ... does not record the far larger number of officers ... who died, were injured, made ill or simply worn out by their arduous duty afloat. By the mid-nineteenth century a quarter of a million sewage outlets drained directly into the river Thames.

The weekly bills of mortality published in London included victims of the horrendous by-products of industry and of the sheer, unregulated mass of people whose waste products added to the foul effluent. Benjamin Disraeli said that the river had become 'a Stygian pool reeking with ineffable and unbearable horror.' In 1849 *The Quarterly Review* published a detailed article on the state of the water supply to London, and made it clear that most of the sewage facilities dated back to medieval times. It pointed out that, beneath some of the most wealthy and progressive areas, there was a pool of 'the foulest deposits' which often blocked the house drains.

One of the main enemies of the people in this context was cholera: there were major epidemics in the nineteenth century, the last being in 1865 and, in 1849, around 14,000 people died from that disease. Into that nasty, infectious river of foulness, the officers sometimes fell, and daily they had to deal with it as an integral part of their work. One notable example is that of PC Bond, who lived near the Wapping station; he dived into the Thames to catch an escaping prisoner, and died from the consequent pneumonia. Such deaths from the river in Victorian times were as great a common threat as that of gaol fever, which in the Regency and Georgian times had killed a massive proportion of the unfortunates who found themselves in prison. Even Conan Doyle used this matter of disease in his Sherlock Holmes story *The Adventure of the Dying Detective* (1887) in which Holmes has been working at Rotherhithe and becomes ill. Watson reports: 'He was indeed a deplorable spectacle.... His eyes had the brightness of fever, there was a hectic flush upon either cheek, and dark crusts clung to his lips, his voice was croaking and spasmodic.'

As mentioned earlier, sick pay had been one privilege of the

Metropolitan Police from the start: if an officer fell ill from such foul and unpleasant working conditions and risks, he had free medical care, although most of the funds for this were from officers' pay, as were superannuation, funeral and other benefits. All officers in London paid around 2.5 per cent of their pay as a superannuation contribution.

The Roll of Honour covering the years c.1860–1913 includes six police officers drowned or crushed on duty, and prior to that, from the early decades, it includes two officers killed and one drowned. One of those who perished, Inspector William Robson, was in charge of the station ship, the *Royalist*, in October 1884, and took a galley from there to visit a boat's crew on the shore; an hour later a boatman at North Woolwich said he saw a tug called the *Eclipse* towing two barges, and the man in charge said he had collided with a small boat. Robson's boat was then found, stoved in, and police comrades began to take out the drags to search for his body.

Of course, there were other officers' deaths not recorded on the Roll of Honour since they died off duty, such as 56-year-old James Goodhew in 1890. He was stationed at Wapping and lived in Star Street, Shadwell; his son said he saw Mr Goodhew leave the Princess Royal, and that he had had a few drinks. Later, a barge search saw the officer coming to the Glamis Road Bridge, and then there was a splash; he had tried to cross the bridge while the gates were open. He was soon taken out of the water but could not be revived.

Today, it would be obvious that the working lives of the Thames men in the nineteenth century were very hard indeed, and it is clear that there was heavy drinking across all the working classes, with a proliferation of beer shops as well as pubs. The constables afloat were no different than the other men in all the divisions, but the dangers confronting them were perhaps more insidious and always present, than were the threats to the land bobbies. From pollution to accidents and from violence to career stress, the enemies were legion.

11 *Fin de Siècle* Problems

THE YEARS *c.*1890–1910 were a period of accelerated change for the Thames Division. These changes were in work conditions and in the arrival of motorboats, but also in the context of broader issues for policing, as London experienced trouble from politically motivated groups as well as from the usual criminal fraternity.

Generally, the decade often defined as 'the naughty nineties' had far more to it than fun and entertainment. It was the time when social concerns grew in relation to what was thought of as 'degeneration' – the idea of the decline of the species in evolutionary terms – and this brought with it strange notions of genetics, and consequently a fear of what was termed the 'underclass'. The huge turnover of defendants at the police courts confirmed many thinkers' ideas that there was a sub-class of people, habitual criminals, heaving beneath the 'civilized' surface of life. In 1897 H.G. Wells wrote *The Time Machine*, a novel in which a futuristic world is envisaged consisting of the eloi, an éffete higher group living above ground with a sybaritic lifestyle, and the morlocks, a simian subterranean group who come to the surface to catch and eat the eloi.

It was also a militaristic decade, which featured the Anglo-Boer Wars (1899–1902). Journals such as *The Graphic* and *Harmsworth Magazine* were crammed with features on army manoeuvres, naval power and new military technology. There were volunteer groups and reservists of all descriptions, and an open fear of the growth of German sea-power was expressed generally.

The police were to play a major role in the primary domestic problems relating to anarchism and socialist militancy. To meet the new changes, developments took place in London: the Metropolitan Police had moved their headquarters to New Scotland Yard in 1888, and in 1894 the first borstal scheme was conceived, followed by the 1908 Prevention of Crime Act which established a network of borstals. The Thames Police Court records reflect this growing problem of juvenile crime, although the development of the probation services was one initiative aimed at counteracting this.

More pressing in importance for all London policemen was the Police Act of 1890 which, as explained in the previous chapter, included a reform of pension provision. There was, however, discontent at some of the consequences, and a test case was the hearing at the Queen's Bench of *Upperton* v *The Home Secretary* in 1900. Retired PC Upperton had questioned the decision of the Home Secretary regarding his pension provision. Upperton had carried out additional special duties at Westminster, and wanted his earnings for these to figure in his pension calculation. He argued that when he retired in 1899 he was due his thirty-nine shillings a week plus seven shillings for the special duties. This claim was rejected by the Quarter Sessions and again at the higher Divisional Court.

Grievances and dissatisfactions such as this would persist and would later play a part in industrial action. There was an immediate effect from the 1890 Act though: there was a decline in voluntary resignations and an increase after that date in the number of average length-of-service records. The higher echelons of police wanted officers to serve for longer periods and to have the 'carrot' of a good pension on retirement, but the paternalism remained and the thinking was still to use a system of rewards and punishments, with an increase in bureaucratic red tape in all areas of police administration. One of the main leaders of dissent and protest was John Kempster, who became editor of *Police Review*; he lobbied Parliament and in 1906 he sent a questionnaire to 1,500 parliamentary candidates.

Generally, across the land, constabularies saw that, despite legislation, their future was still in their hands; there was a growth in the number of burial and friendly societies within the constabularies almost everywhere, with contributions covering payments to relatives as well as to officers on retirement.

The turn of the century also brought a revolution in the policing and regulation of the Port of London. Through the nineteenth century, a series of docks had been constructed, from the West India Docks in 1802 to the Tilbury Docks in 1886. After various inquiries and reports through the 1890s regarding medical inspection, dredging plans and organizational ideas, the Port of London Authority (PLA) was created in 1908. The port had always been under the control of the City, but in 1908, when the PLA was instituted, it had repercussions for the Thames Division, because the PLA was to have its own police. Douglas Browne, writing in 1956, explained the situation: 'This body was given its own police which absorbed the various and very variously efficient ... police establishments of the dock companies ... the waterway itself is the responsibility of the Thames Division ... it was suggested at the time and has been advocated since, that this division should also be absorbed by the PLA.' But Browne explained that the independence of the Thames Division from other riverside forces was essential and had to be preserved. He added that a governing factor in the relations between the PLA police and the Metropolitan force was 'the division of powers' – the PLA officers could keep a suspect in custody 'only until he can be handed over to the regular civil arm for the normal processes of justice'.

For everyday routines and duties, the years around the turn of the century were marked by the use of the new motorboats. The police officer driving had to turn a crankshaft, priming the engine with petrol and then using paraffin when in action; there was an element of uncertainty about a journey taken in the boats, with the need to always have spark plugs handy, to restart, and also the need to have the oars standing by in case all else failed! The first of these petrol/paraffin launches was the *Sir Richard Mayne II*; all on board needed extra clothing to combat the cold, and it was the responsibility of the skilled driver to keep the gears and power in action.

A particularly fine vessel in this new breed of boats was the

Renavire, in service later in 1920, after being bought from Scotland. George Mitchell got to work on this vessel, which was re-born as the *Vigilant*, with an impressive line of brass portholes and cowls. Geoffrey Budworth has recounted the career of one of the *Vigilant's* crew: PC Bullion, who had fought at the battle of Omdurman against the Mahdi, served twelve years with the Thames Division, returned to the army for the Great War and then arrived to work on the *Renavire*, not retiring until 1927, and living to be 101.

The dangers of working with the new craft were made sadly apparent in 1913 when Sergeant Spooner was drowned and his body recovered off Rotherhithe. Sub-Divisional Inspector Hughes told the press that Spooner took two men in a motor-boat to patrol near Southwark Bridge; the officer admitted that he had heard of problems with the boats because the engines were not powerful enough in a strong current. A constable who was with Spooner said that the tide took the boat's prow down. The stern was in an eddy while the engine, of course, still went at full throttle. The result was that, near a buttress of the bridge, Spooner went overboard as the boat went under a barge. The two constables tried to find Spooner but he had gone. He had turned the boat in the way he had done many times before, but this time one slip in technique cost him his life.

There was a full statement from George Mitchell and then from Superintendent Mann; the latter said that the power of the engines was 'not altogether satisfactory' and he had told the Commissioner of this; an inquiry followed to look at acquiring more boats. The coroner at the inquest returning 'accidental death' added that the boats 'were at present under-engined, at least for emergencies'.

In support of the daily work there were the boatyard and the workshops. These had a first incarnation as floating police-stations back in Regency times; one long-serving vessel was the *Port Mahon*, which worked until 1836. From the start, civilian part-timers and assistants had worked alongside the constables, as was evident in the stories from the first decades covered in earlier chapters. There was no shortage of watermen and, as their profession declined in the middle decades of Victoria's reign, they would find some demand for their skills in the boat-yard. Obviously, shipbuilders, joiners and mechanics were always to be had in the greatest maritime city in the world, at the centre of a vast empire. (A similar facility was used in the Crimean War, where a floating workshop was employed at Balaclava, and the Army Works Corps employed smiths, navvies, carpenters and a host of other skilled men.)

By 1900 or shortly after, the Thames Division would have found that the days of its carrying on in splendid isolation were well and truly over: since the years of the great disasters and explosions, the rocket factory and the *Princess Alice* incidents, there had been the establishment of the Thames Conservancy, the inquiries of the Lower Thames Navigation Commission with its reports of 1895 into dealing with infection on ships, and then the Port of London Authority. All these were in addition to the arrival of a detective attachment and to liaison with the other Metropolitan divisions in the days of the Torso Mysteries and the Ripper. Another aspect of the *fin de siècle* that was new to the Thames men was the experience and repercussions of the strikes.

The docks were the focus. George Sala described the world of the docks *c.*1860, saying that these 'huge reservoirs of wealth, energy and industry' had bonded warehouses which were 'apoplectic with the produce of three worlds, congested with bales of tobacco and barrels of spices'. These were the heart of a fast-expanding city. Between 1831 and 1871 the population of Greater London more than doubled, rising to 3,811,000. By 1901, it was 6, 581,000. In the last decades of the nineteenth century there had been a huge influx of immigrants, many being Jewish, fleeing from pogroms in Russia. The huge volume of trade and the expansion of the docks meant that labour, in a world in which trade unions for the unskilled were only legal after the Trades Disputes Acts of 1871 and 1875, was always going to create problems.

In 1889 the dockers went on strike for their 'tanner' (a rate of sixpence an hour). The strike started at the south basin of the West India Dock in the ranks of the unskilled labourers, who struck during the unloading of a ship, the *Lady Armstrong*. As Ed Glinert puts it in his *East End Chronicles*, 'Wages were meagre, conditions barely human, work irregular. Men were hired not just by the day, but by the hour.' The General Labourers' Union listened to problems and demanded an increase in pay of one penny, taking pay to six pence per hour and eight pence for any overtime. The strike was to last a month, and the events brought to light the place of the Thames and Metropolitan forces generally with regard to companies' private dock police. The strike grew and 20,000 men marched seven deep, which called for massive police supervision, with 500 extra police being on duty.

What developed was a game of wits between James Munro, the Commissioner of the Metropolitan Police, the Home Secretary, Henry Matthews, and the dock owners. The union and strikers were caught in the middle, in a sense. There was widespread sympathy for the dockers, and this was from the rank and file police as well. Obviously, picketing and imported 'scab' labour made intimidation the central issue. Officers certainly protected lightermen from abuse and assault, but there were limits as to what they would do.

James Munro was the first Commissioner in place who did not have a background in the army; he believed in supporting pay and pension rights for his men and had enlightened views. He would not yield to pressure and cleared all thoroughfares to stop intimidation. He also applied an Act of 1875 in such a way as to ensure that violent confrontation between strikers and their opponents would be avoided. Eventually a Conciliation Committee agreed to the tanner, but delayed implementation for a while.

What became the main bone of contention for policing was the fact that dock employers having their own dock police meant that their assistance from the Thames officers and others was restricted. There was a strike at the Gas Works, and there the regular police were used – otherwise there would have been widespread consequences across the city. But that action was compared in some quarters to the failure of the police to give regular cover during the dock strike. This highlighted a major problem of policing in emergencies and during large-scale events. The MP for Limehouse, E.S. Norris, called for a mechanism to be set up by which the regular police moved in to support dock police when trouble was brewing. Monro's successor, Edward Bradford, was much more willing to go along with this, and so the foundation was laid for some of the police grievances that would emerge in 1918 when the police themselves went on strike.

The 'Dockers' Tanner' strike brought about what has been called 'The New Unionism', bringing in more unskilled labour. But, for the police on the river, it was important with regard to their relationship with the dock police. Not until the institution of the PLA did matters become fully rationalized in that respect. For twenty years around the end of Victoria's reign, letters to the press had complained about who was responsible for public nuisances and disorder along the river. Clearly, the Thames Conservancy legislation had tried to clarify the responsibilities of the various bodies involved, including the Thames Division. But, with limited manpower for such a long stretch of river and the bordering land, Thames Division had to prioritize. The events of 1889 showed that new thinking was needed regarding that issue.

A more mundane matter in the last years of the nineteenth century was the flood and gale of 29 November 1897. The road was flooded over the Victoria Embankment and water came through the wall; Temple Pier was affected, with water a foot over the top landing, and the press reported that Thames officers and Conservancy men were expressing 'serious alarm'; the Thames Police reported that there was considerable loss of river craft as moorings were snapped, and wharves and warehouses at Deptford, Rotherhithe and Blackfriars were severely damaged. It was announced that the floods and high tide had been the worst for thirty years.

As the new Commissioner made his report for the blue book of 1896, the Thames Division was playing its part in an overall decline in criminal offences: reported offences were down to 20,024 from 20,970 the previous year. As to the Metropolitan Police as a whole, there had been considerable expansion, the manpower in 1896 being 32 superintendents, 592 inspectors, 1,870 sergeants and 12,777 constables. The pay bill was £1,266,311. The manpower of the Thames Police then was around 170 and would rise to 200 by the early 1930s.

12 The Great War, Spies and Strikes

WHAT DID THE Thames officers do during the Great War? It is on record that many files were destroyed during the Second World War, so much detail has been lost. The fact is, though, that they were involved in everything one would expect as spin-offs from the major events of the period: spying, Suffragette protests, opium dens and anti-German or anti-alien activities. It was a period of paranoia. There was the Official Secrets Act of 1911 and the various regulations relating to the defence of the realm which influenced a lot of police activity generally, and this was made worse by xenophobia, particularly after the sinking of the *Lusitania* in 1915. A person was deemed to be a spy if (a) he had visited the address of a spy or consorted with a spy or (b) the name or address or any other information regarding a spy was found in his or her possession.

There had been immigration into Britain by German people for a long time: throughout the nineteenth century families settled in many major cities, bringing businesses such as steel merchants, engineers, cutlery makers, engravers and dentists. After political persecution, notably in 1848 and 1866, the numbers increased. Bradford had always had its German population and its own 'little Germany'. The German contribution to the British economy had been considerable, but then in 1914 we were at war with Germany. When war broke out, there were around 53,000 Germans living in Britain; by the end of the war there were just 22,000. Tens of thousands had been placed in internment camps

In an Order of Council of August 1914, it was decreed that

'aliens' would have to be registered at their nearest police station and they would have to have a permit to move beyond a certain distance from home; there was spy mania across the land, and much popular suspicion of any German names in business.

The popular press did not help to dispel any prejudice or irrationality. Publications such as *John Bull* explained that Germans in Britain were the 'hidden hand' of Kaiser Bill's Reich, and that there was a cunning plan to colonize Britain, starting with these 'aliens'. There was even a suggestion that Germans in Britain should wear a badge or button to show that they were really one of the naturalized citizens, and not aliens.

In April 1915, the nurse, Edith Cavell, had been shot by the Germans and, on 22 April in the trenches, there had been the world's first gas attack in a war. This was followed by an official report on 'Alleged German Atrocities'. This report, priced at only one penny, was 360 pages of myths and provocative statements about Germans doing unspeakable things to women and children. With hindsight, we can see just what an impact this would have had on popular opinion.

Then, on 7 May 1915, the *Lusitania* was torpedoed by German U-boats off the coast of Ireland. It was a celebrated ship: being launched in 1906, it was the first four-propeller-driven liner, and it was also the largest ship on the seas, weighing in at 40,000 tons. Its loss was a profound shock, and the casualties were very high: 1,195 people drowned. There was a statement by the Germans to justify this, saying that the vessel could potentially have been converted into a battleship. Not surprisingly, this attempt at justification was not well received. One report stated that the sinking was 'The most hideous of the many barbarous acts for which the Germans are responsible.' It was a signal for anti-German mayhem and disorder across the land. There were savage anti-German riots in Liverpool and special constables were called out in force, operating in makeshift armoured cars. The East End of London was then affected – the very area where one of the most famous of all Germans had lived just a few decades before: Karl Marx. It was clear to the authorities that this violence would spread like a forest fire.

There was widespread unrest and the police courts were busy; at the Thames Police Court there were eighty people in the dock, with charges ranging from insulting behaviour to unlawful possession of goods, taken from looted shops.

As the war waged in the trenches over the Channel, there was an assortment of odd cases related to the feeling of nervous apprehension at home, such as the trial of a seaman at the Thames Police Court in 1918 on a charge of removing a screen from a light while his ship was at sea. He was given three months in prison. Or the bizarre case of three teenagers who were found stealing a stack of waste paper from the War Office, amongst which there were confidential reports, plans of forts and photos of firing-line trenches. The boys had taken the bales of paper and dragged them to the Thames shore, where they were found, with a lookout, who stoned any watchmen who came to reclaim the paper.

There had been a spy mania during the Edwardian years, and any understanding of this derives from the nature of the wars Britain fought throughout the nineteenth century. They were distant ones. That simple fact explains so much, as the very idea of an enemy on the doorstep was terrifying in contrast to the previous concept of war – one in which regiments were seen off from the quayside at Portsmouth on their way to the Crimea, India, or South Africa. It had been the case for a very long time that one war followed another and the movements of troops had taken place to meet particular emergencies. Most were small-scale combats involving the normal groupings of imperial infantry, artillery and various deployments of cavalry. Intelligence had always been integral to those movements, either included with the Royal Engineers, as they did signalling and reconnaissance, or left to the control of the Adjutant-General. Slowly, ever since 1873, intelligence work had become something to be understood separately, with its own specialisms and responsibilities. The Fenian bombings at the very heart of the empire had shown that something new was needed, something as ruthless and efficient as the potential enemies could be.

Therefore, when the new century began and there had

already been talk of spies infiltrating the land, a common view of such a threat was that it could be handled in traditional ways, but with intelligence personnel involved. Sir George Aston summed up the attitudes clearly:

> Their idea was that Germans, spies and others, needed leaders, and that they were helpless without them. That they liked working 'according to plan', according to the letter of a plan.... No matter how big a swarm of German spies there might be in England, Scotland, Wales or Ireland in pre-war days, they would look for guidance to certain leaders ... and if the leaders were taken away the followers would be helpless.

In his memoirs, Aston was keen to show that the amateur image of the British was, in fact, a virtue, and that luck was on the British side because they had an enormous capacity for hard work. His connection of the intelligence success story with what he calls the 'John Bull legends' ties in well with the successes of Vernon Kell and his team at the new MI5 department. They may have had their insight into a spy ring because of a fortuitously overheard conversation on a train, but the implication is that that sort of thing happened because the British undaunted spirit was there too.

It has to be said that the German spy network was indeed beaten because of hard work. In fact, it cannot be denied that the established methods of the comparatively new CID men were at the heart of the success. Police work against anarchists and Communists was notably successful, as in one typical account of Special Branch men from 1909 involving two robbers who were Latvian immigrants. The men, Hefeld and Lepidus, were armed when they robbed a rubber factory in Tottenham High Road; there was a police station opposite the scene of the crime. The robbers waited for a car to arrive, in which two men were carrying the wages of the company's workers. A pursuit followed, including gunfights, and the two fugitives were so desperate that one shot himself in the head rather than be taken and the other later did the same, while under siege. But the salient point was that the detectives were working against gangs of anarchists and the chase involved local as well as Metropolitan officers. In other words, normal detective practice from which Kell could learn was there. Liaison between forces and agencies in different parts of Britain was well established by that time – in fact, decades before, in a famous case in which several detectives were corrupted by a forgery gang, regional undercover work had tracked down the culprits – and interception of mail had also been carried out. Kell was learning from experts.

By 1909, when Kell needed such help, the detective branch had become skilled in such basic strategies as disguise, using informers, infiltration and, in fact, some basic forensic science such as fingerprinting. They had also learned how to work with other organizations and how to use local knowledge. All this would become vital in the work against the German spies in the ports.

These advances and practices filtered down to all police work in London, so that, for instance, in August 1918 a man called Pitta Jacobsen, a Norwegian seaman, stood in the Thames Police Court charged with landing without permission from the Aliens Officer. He had done so and his conduct had been suspicious: he had twice tried to put the helm of his ship the wrong way while at sea. His fate was a month in prison and then expulsion from Britain. There were arrests at all naval centres, and suspicion was everywhere. In 1917, Thames officers arrested a man thinking he was a German spy who had been involved in an attack on a minister. In the end, he was found to be innocent.

One case which certainly involved a suspicion of trading with the enemy was that of a Dutchman called Pronk, who had a chemical dye business; his firm had allegedly obtained a licence by fraud from the Board of Trade. They had ordered permanganate of potash from Germany – and that may have been the extent of their transgression, but the case was prosecuted by the great advocate, Travers Humphrey.

In August 1914, Scotland Yard made a dozen arrests in London in connection with espionage, including two men who were arrested after visiting Woolwich Arsenal. A total of twenty-one spies were arrested that month at naval centres across the land. Without the records, we cannot be sure what part the Thames Division played in this; Folkestone was the only port open to visitors from Europe, and that was very well policed and supervised, but there must have been enemy activity on the London docks.

Otherwise, the war impinged little on the Thames policing; the main concern was still in saving lives and retrieving those whom they had not been able to save, such as one case in which Inspector Bullivant actually saw the man, named Bennett, who drowned fall into the river, at Harrod's Wharf. Bullivant went to the rescue and a hitcher was brought out, but as Bennett was almost out of the water the hitcher slipped. Constable Bailey then jumped into the water to help a man called Monk who had gone in to try to save Bennett. Constable Bailey had to keep hold of Monk, and so Bennett was lost. Bailey received an award from the Royal Humane Society.

Dragging the river was also a regular business, and had been so since the force began. To do this, a flat-bottomed boat was used, towed to where it was needed; the dragging then entailed probing a stretch of water with hooks on poles, and it is on record that some men had a fisherman's instinct for knowing what was being contacted by the hook deep down.

It was unthinkable to every British person that the police could go on strike. But they did, in 1918 and 1919. In the midst of agitation and discussion, when a police union was illegally in existence, Sergeant George Miles, a representative of the discontented officers, declared:

> Nowadays a policeman must be brave as a lion, as patient as Job, as wise as Solomon, as cunning as a fox, have the manners of a Chesterfield, the optimism of Mark Tapley, must be learned in criminal law and local by-laws, must be of strong moral character, be able to resist all temptations, be prepared to act as a doctor, a terror to evil-doers, a friend and counsellor to all classes of the community, and a walking encyclopaedia.

This statement was made in 1919 when the Desborough Committee, which was destined to influence the most advanced legislation on police work since Peel's Act, considered matters in the aftermath of two widespread and acrimonious strikes.

The basis of the problem was that it was simply not deemed acceptable that the British police force should have a union. The ideology of both civic defence and social and individual security was against such a concept. But the fact is that, at the beginning of the Great War in 1914, the lot of the police constables was desperate; some were on the poverty line and many were having to do part-time work (against regulations) to feed their families. Although the matter of police pensions had been resolved, and despite the fact that police officers had a day off every week, the constable's income was inadequate to meet the rising cost of living; when the war with Germany developed, all this was exacerbated. Some policemen had to watch their children earning more than themselves in munitions factories, and one man said that he was in such a bad way that he had to do gardening in his locality to survive.

Deeply entrenched in the growing grievances was the rule of 'co-conferring': policemen were not supposed to engage in discussion with regard to conditions of service nor to air grievances. This sense of isolation in the ranks, a sense that nothing could be talked about and that all discipline should be accepted without dialogue, was to create the circumstance that nurtured the leader of the first union agitation: John Syme. He had been involved in a case in which he defended two constables in his division and was reprimanded for his care. He did not take that lying down, and the argument ended with him being first transferred and then sacked. Syme was a meticulous man, and early in his career he had been arguably a 'barrack room lawyer' because he knew the regulations and related legislation on police work very well. The man he confronted and who sacked him was Sir Edward Henry, a former Inspector-General of the Bengal Police who was Commissioner of the Metropolitan force at this time.

Syme met the editor of *Police Review*, John Kempster, and an alliance was formed that was to lead to the clandestine first phase of what would become two police strikes in 1918 and 1919. Strictly by the criminal law codification, these acts were mutinous and, of course, the police held demonstrations and strikes when Britain was at war, so the repercussions of both strikes were profoundly influential on the state of the realm while manpower was being sapped over in the trenches of the western front. Nott-Bower, the City Commissioner, lost a son in that war, and he was certainly in no mood to consider compromise when his men joined in the first strike.

The trigger for events that followed could be seen as Syme's personal grievances becoming a catalyst to bring out the other discontentment and grudges brooding in the force, long-standing and often rankling under the enforced discipline of daily work. The publication *Police Review* had been in existence for many years, and one of its functions was to give some kind of outlet to the complaints of police work; constables could write, anonymously, to the editor, and their letters would be printed, thus airing certain disgruntled viewpoints and offering at least one way of expressing them. The journal was popular for other reasons – it was a voice of the profession and it carried informative features. But when Syme met Kempster and other men were gathered around, notably J.R. Penfold and Mackenzie Bell (a Liberal politician), the notion of a union gained strength and support. There was some support in Parliament, despite the deeply held notions of the police being an exception in that respect: Ramsay MacDonald in 1907 and Philip Snowden in 1914 had both spoken in Westminster in support of the idea.

When it came to the dismissal of a policeman for being involved in the union (then known as the National Union of Police and Prison Officers), the inevitable happened and there was a call to strike. The number of officers in the union was over four thousand – a number grossly underestimated by the top brass in the police at the time, despite the fact that, even though Kempster himself did not agree with the concept of a union, there was an advert in *Police Review* listing the union officials. In fact there was a certain complacency and inaction on the part of the leaders; they thought of John Syme as a crank who occasionally irritated them and perhaps never really believed that he would achieve anything. When Syme was imprisoned in Wormwood Scrubs for libel, it must have seemed as though the strike would never happen but, in the months following the appointment of a new Home Secretary, Sir George Cave (and in spite of a plan to have war widows of dead officers receive a ten-shillings a week payment), the final trigger for the strike occurred. This was the case of PC Tommy Thiel, a man who was very popular in the force, who believed in the union and had been encouraging union growth in Manchester. He had been reprimanded for that, and, having been called to Scotland Yard to face the music, he was dismissed from the force.

On 1 March 1919 the Desborough Committee was appointed to review police pay and conditions; their work was done in two months. This was to lead to a situation in which the concept of a police union was more visibly a central issue – at least for some. This was because the Desborough Committee recommended a pay rise, raising the constable's weekly pay by £2. The Police Federation was also to be established, and the bill went through Parliament and was law by 17 August. This federation was ratified by the 1920 Police Act, and that dictated that no police personnel could belong to a trade union. The following year saw the Police Pensions Act which standardized all police pensions, but there was one shortcoming: to qualify, officers had to serve for thirty years.

The strikes lasted over a year and led to a huge increase in the recruitment of special constables. This new element to the Metropolitan Police affected all divisions, including the Thames Police, and in emergencies, when specials were most urgently needed, they proved to be very useful in river work, being selected by virtue of their past experience.

So far as the practical side of the Thames Police is concerned, there were several developments before 1930. The era of the rowing galleys came to an end – this was first recommended by the government in 1921, but some remained operational until 1925, their demise finally coming shortly after the long-serving engineer-officer, George Mitchell, retired. Gradually, more motor launches were acquired, bought from the armed forces or elsewhere. Some looked attractive and efficient, but some were apparently far from perfect, notably the *Katalina*, which, as Geoffrey Budworth explains, was 'Too fine in the bilge, it fell over on its side as the tide receded, unless tightly tied to the berth, and one once sank unnoticed like this.'

Diesel engines arrived also: in 1926 Boat Number 14 was fitted with one and later, by the 1930s, there were more added. As for the men who operated them, there was still, *c.*1930, the special quality of seamanship at the heart of the skills required. This had been the case in the formative years, when the force was the Marine Police and watermen and seamen were recruited, but pride in the special nature and abilities of the Thames men was still very much alive in later days. Anthony Richardson, in his biography of Inspector Nixon, describes how, when Chief Inspector Dalton was in charge (1931–1933), he gave a lecture to the new recruit:

You'll find this work very different from the work on land. The Thames Division is unique. The river has peculiarities of its own. Practically all the uniformed men who are recruited to us have been sailors of some sort. You can't expect to learn about it all at once. In a sense it's a life-time study. You've got to get the feel of it. ... All the men in the Division are picked men. There's no other police Division in the world precisely like this one. We work as a team. There's no room here for idlers or men who aren't keen on their job. The river makes no mistakes. If you put a foot wrong you go over the side, and it's easier to go in than to get out.'

These words were spoken to a policeman who was a detective with the Metropolitan force, and with army experience. But what was obvious was that he had been noticed and had been picked. A desk sergeant at Wapping said that Nixon 'was the man we want'. An officer called Jock Angus commented that Nixon 'put fresh heart into the nick'. Word had circulated about him, and he was assigned to work with DI Raby, who had recently, just before joining Thames Division, been the man who arrested Constance Wright in a very sad case of the

CRIMINAL RIVER

attempted murder of her three children. Raby had charged her at Lee Road station; later she was acquitted of the charge and given probation. Raby had played a major part in the sensitive treatment of that case.

Nixon, who was to become known as 'Nick of the River', joined the Thames force at the time when the thirties decade was just warming up into the 'Jazz Age' and fascism was on the march. Exciting times lay ahead for the new recruit and for the Thames Division. As Nixon was soon to learn, a principal part of the job was still, as ever, searching for, handling and discussing corpses. As a detective, he was soon to know the great Sir Bernard Spilsbury, the forensic scientist, as he spent more time with the tragic dead of the Thames.

In the year that Nixon joined the force, the fight was still going on regarding police pay, and as the officers across the metropolis dealt with fights, suspicious deaths, assaults, robberies and frauds, in the boardrooms the struggle continued for the Police Federation to have a proper status. Lord Trenchard, who was to reform the whole Metropolitan force, wanted the Federation to be barred from holding meetings. There were reports of general unease and dissatisfaction in the police ranks.

13 The Thirties and the Blitz

COMPARING THE SITUATION of the Thames Division in the 1930s with that of its counterpart a hundred years earlier is very informative. In 1830 the organization was still officially in its trial period as the Marine Police; before being absorbed into the 'new police' in 1839 it had been very much on probation in most senses. David Johnson's account of police history in London brings this to light:

> From the day they were formed, the Marine Police did a magnificent job, catching thieves, arresting murderers and deserters, seizing 'underweight' bread and giving it to the poor ... In spite of all this, the Home Secretary kept a rather critical eye on them, and on one occasion wanted to know what an item of £2.12s 6d. was doing on the accounts. The magistrates replied that it was for six pocket almanacs and calendars which they bought every year for use in the office, and if the Home Secretary thought the expense was not justified, they would be glad to pay the bill themselves.

In the 1830s, the only boats were galleys, the magistrates were overworked in the court, much of the time was taken up with dragging and dealing with corpses and flotsam, and the police were certainly not seen as an elite or specialist force. A century later, as we know from the writings of Superintendent Dalton, the force was dealing with the Thames from Teddington Lock to Dartford Creek and was indeed an impressive outfit, with five police stations: Barnes, Waterloo, Wapping, Blackwall and Erith, and resources to patrol at all times of the night and day.

In 1935, when Dalton wrote for *Police Review*, he noted that there was a force of 200 men dealing with a 36-mile stretch of water and its embankments.

The fleet, in 1935, consisted of three motor launches, twenty-eight motorboats and seven rowing boats. Dalton gave plenty of information on the boats, being particularly proud of the *Vigilant*: 'She is 35 feet long, 7.5 feet beam with fo'c'sle and wheel-house forward, cabin amidships and cockpit aft. She is mahogany and teak built and is fitted with a 40 h.p. Thornycroft petrol engine.' Other craft available included the *Alert* and the *Watch*. There were three sizes of motorboat, the largest ones being used in the lower reaches of the river where rough water is often experienced. When Dalton wrote his profile of the force, wireless sets were about to be used in the boats, directed through a central point at Scotland Yard. He was eager to point out that the skilled labour in the workshops was still there and doing very well.

Regarding the training of newcomers to the Thames force, Dalton wrote: 'After six months they are given a week's instruction in the Engineer's Shop, when they are tested as to their fitness for duty as relief drivers.' Nixon, as a plain-clothes officer, avoided this and as, in fact, was the case with Inspector Raby, it was possible for an officer to try to forget he was supposed to be a seaman. The biography of Nixon recalled: 'Inspector Raby wouldn't go afloat. He wouldn't or couldn't swim. Though an extremely efficient CID officer, he was serving on the river under protest.'

In 1930, the Thames Police uniform was still distinct, with reefer jackets and forage caps; they still wore white shirts and black ties, and Inspector Dalton adds, 'They are also provided with heavy woollen boat coats, oilskin capes, leg bags and boat aprons and fingerless gloves: the cold and inclement weather to which the men are exposed during the winter months make such garments necessary.'

Inspector David Nixon had a lot to learn when he joined the force in 1932. His biography explains very clearly what the main duties on the Thames were. He explains that an officer needed to know the construction of ships and the kinds of cargo they had so he and his peers could 'work' them methodically. Policemen needed to know about such things as bills of lading and ships' manifests – the former a receipt for goods and the latter a detail of cargo.

Nixon's initiation into river work on ships opens up the world of the River Police officer at the time:

> He learnt what manner of goods were loaded by slings or nets.... He came to know that a lighterman must serve seven years' apprenticeship and that he could only work his barges 'overside' or 'ex-quay' to craft ... And he learnt the various types of barges used for carrying coal and other heavy goods ... and how these types were hatched, sheeted and locked down.

In other words, he had done what police officers had always had to do: know their patch in terms of the patterns of life inside it. The work, he learned, mixed a knowledge of local industry, working routines and population movements. He became as well known to his clients as he was to them.

In comparison with earlier times, the world of the 1930s Thames Police officer was not much different in terms of watercraft: even the Inspectors had to know how to work in the boats (which is why Raby soon left for another division!). Nixon could do so, with the help of his sergeant, but he also had to learn how to 'beat the tide' and 'shoot the water'. Some aspects of police work specific to a beat would be unknown to the general public, such as the art of climbing a Jacob's ladder onto a vessel, as Anthony Richardson explains, 'watching the swell lest his legs became caught and crushed between the side of a ship and the launch, never trusting a foothold but only his hands'.

In 1935, when Inspector Dalton described the duties undertaken by the force, he summed them up by saying that it was all about the prevention and detection of thefts from cargoes of all kinds. He pointed out that, at the time, there were around 12,000 barges in the Port of London and that these carried the equivalent of 500,000 road vehicles. His account of the working of the Port of London makes it clear that the task of the police was immense, supervising 58 million registered tons of shipping and over 35 million tons of goods in a year. The police knew the pattern of movements well but, as Dalton notes, the challenge was to find out where any theft had taken place – whether before loading, in transit or at the landing place. He gave one instance of a huge theft of goods valued at £6,000 (worth twenty times that today) reported from a river barge, but inquiries ascertained that the theft had actually occurred in Vienna.

One problem in 1935 that was surely still exactly the same as in 1830 and 1890 was the 'mis-tallying' – the difficulty of identifying exactly which goods were part of a consignment. Dalton notes in his essay, 'Insurance companies make a condition of insurance that losses must be reported to police. For one reason or another the losses are often not so reported, but the companies rarely trouble themselves to enquire of the police whether in fact a report has been made.'

The innovation of wireless transmitters came into service in 1931 and approval was gained for new boats made in the middle of that decade to have transmitters and receivers; these were built and six boats were made ready for them, but then there was the issue of the weight of the equipment to consider. The answer was to use mountings in a material lighter than the usual brass, and duralumin was used. This is an aluminium alloy containing copper, manganese and magnesium as a rule; it was developed by Alfred Wilm in Germany, after experiments done in 1903. It was used in frames for airships and in planes made by *Junkers* in 1916, so it was a familiar material with a wide range of uses by *c.*1930.

The Thames craft from that time were included in the Scotland Yard map tables at the information room. When Dalton wrote his feature on his force, the use of voice transmissions had come in. Generators and voltage regulators were needed, with heavy-duty batteries; then in wartime, two-way radios came into use.

Drowning, attempted suicides and actual suicides were still part of the duties in the 1930s of course (and always will be). One of the most important features of suicide is that it was a criminal offence until 1961. An old term for suicide is 'self-murther' and that encapsulates the legal idea: one's own body is not one's spiritual property, as it were. Penal process used to follow a suicide, in that the body could not be buried in consecrated ground. Suicide was also a felony until the Forfeiture Act of 1870, which meant that an attempted suicide was liable not only to be imprisoned, but to have his goods and inheritance taken away.

There was also the advent of the suicide pact, which involved one person influencing another to take his or her life, and when suicide itself ceased to be a criminal offence, a suicide pact remained a crime. In 1957, not long before this reform, 514,870 people died and, of these deaths, 5,315 were suicides.

As Sir Harold Scott wrote, just before the 1961 reforms:

> Until recently there was much preoccupation with its rightness or wrongness, but little on its essential causes. During the last hundred years or so, science has directed its attention to suicide as an aspect of human behaviour amenable to analysis. Whilst a great deal of knowledge has emerged from the intensive study carried out ... it is admitted on all hands that suicide is still something of an enigma.

Throughout history, suicide has been an act of shame; the coroners' courts give clear support to this. In a case reported in the *Leeds Mercury* in 1865, a coroner's court heard that James Smith had thrown himself into the River Aire with pockets weighted with stones, and still the jury was not convinced that this was suicide, so extreme was the stigma that would attach to him and his family. The verdict recorded was, as happened thousands of times in the Thames, 'found drowned'.

The fullest account of an attempted suicide and its handling at Wapping comes from a *Strand* article of 1895. The author tells of a young man picked up on a pier after throwing himself from Blackfriars Bridge. He had been picked up by a skiff and his head held above water until the police took him in charge. As a consequence of his attempted suicide, he was deemed a criminal and placed in a cell. In the cell there was a bed and a medicine chest and 'a dozen or so of tins of all shapes and sizes. ... These are filled with hot water and placed in contact with the body of the person rescued from the river'.

The writer of 1895 makes the situation with regard to prisoners taken for attempted suicide very clear. He explains the usual sequence of events after the unfortunate person was brought in:

> It is often an hour before anything approaching animation makes itself visible, and even four hours have elapsed before any sign has been apparent. The rescued one is laid upon a wooden board, below which is a bath, and rubbed by ready hands according to Dr. Sylvester's method, whose instructions are prominently displayed upon the wall, and are understood by all the police.

The thinking behind suicide in terms of the law and Victorian thought is expressed well by Churton Collins, the scholar and true crime enthusiast, who wrote in his journal, 'Suicide is the worst form of murder, for it leaves no opportunity for repentance.' Although suicides were supposed to be buried away from consecrated ground, individual clergymen might ignore this, as in the case of one of Francis Kilvert's references in his diary, relating to a girl who drowned herself. He notes: 'It was surmised that she be buried as a suicide without any service on the "backside of the church" but she was buried by Mr Venables with the usual ceremony.'

A woman was also rescued during the writer's night on the river by the police galley and taken to Waterloo station; there the point arises about the fact that male officers had to undress her, and it was a criticism offered against the force: 'We do not forget that great promptness is required at such times in order to resuscitate the body. But, when we remember that every branch in the police system on the Thames is so perfect, it seems a pity that some means cannot be devised.' At Waterloo, the writer sees the one cell, laid out just like the Wapping one, and he comments that, 'eleven enterprising individuals have been accommodated there at one time'.

The first woman appointed to the Thames Division was

Anne Hunt in 1893, and she must have occasionally been involved in such rescues, but generally, change regarding women police came very slowly; women were appointed across the constabularies in 1919 but were not sworn in with powers of arrest until 1923.

By the end of the 1930s, not only were there women police officers, there were even women doing detective work, the first three having been appointed in 1933 to Vine Street and Marlborough Street stations. In 1937 there were fifty vacancies for women in the Metropolitan Police and *The Times* reported on their duties: 'The duties that women police are expected to perform include the investigation of offences against women and girls, attending where required to the welfare of victims, looking after women found ill, injured or suffering from lack of memory.' Throughout the inter-war years and during the Blitz, there was an urgent need for women police. The attitude of the press was that the whole idea was a charming novelty, as evidenced in remarks about the idea that women criminals would treat women detectives 'with scant respect', as one reporter put it. However, by 1954 there were over 2,000 women police officers in Britain, 548 being in the Metropolitan force. It was generally thought that women officers were of special value in dealing with the frequent suicides or attempted suicides of young women, so recruitment of women constables became a high priority.

Suicides in the 1930s and 1940s, as Dalton relates, were still most commonly attracted to Waterloo Bridge. He noted in his article of 1935 that more than 120 dead bodies were recovered from the river at that time. As in 1890, the boat at Waterloo police station was always in readiness for the reclamation of would-be suicides. However, the technical advances for first aid and resuscitation had brought into use an instrument which employed carbon dioxide and the Schafer method. Dalton explained its use:

The object is to give a fillip to the moribund respiratory centre in the brain. A distinct advantage of the carbon dioxide gun lies in its being portable. It is only 9.5 inches in length and weighs just over a pound. Each bulb contains sufficient carbon dioxide for a 12 minutes' supply when regulated to inspirations only ...A flicker of an eyelid or a twitching of a hand is usually the first indication of restored animation.

There were certainly acts of extreme courage by officers and citizens in the context of rescues. In 1931, for instance, PC Harry Barwick saved a ten-year-old boy from drowning in Teddington Lock. The officer was off work, sick, at the time, but still dived in when he saw a child's hand appear above the water thirty yards from him. He was awarded £5 from the Bow Street Reward Fund.

Yet the repercussions of a suicide were just as serious in the days of Nixon and Dalton as they were to the new police in the 1820s, it still being a serious offence to try to take one's own life. In 1941 a woman called Helen Denton tried to drown herself, and Nixon, in dealing with the case after she was rescued, tried to find out about her situation. That led to him talking to her colleagues; she had been working as a shelter nurse at Wandsworth Baths. Nixon's biographer recreates the conversation Nixon had with one of Denton's friends, by which time Denton was in prison at Holloway:

'People like you ought to be ashamed of yourselves. Nurse Denton is just another incident to you. That's all you care. But it's her life isn't it?'

'I don't know', said Nick, very truthfully.

'All you policemen want is to chalk up another case.'

In the end, Nixon had to simply say that Miss Denton had tried to kill herself and that was against the law.

In contrast to this sad everyday policing there were also the repercussions of the Blitz to deal with. What happened on 7 September 1940 was always to be called 'Black Saturday' for obvious reasons. The Luftwaffe had been attacking the airfields in the south, but now the East End was assailed by 337 tons of bombs. Thousands of people went into the Tube and into other domestic shelters; by the end of the year, there had been 14,000 civilians killed. The bombings spread to other cities: in Coventry, on 14 November, the attack was relentless and terrible.

The artist Edward Ardizzone wrote, 'Look at that strange, half-ruined street – something terribly moving about it. You know you feel almost like weeping. What was it to do with civilians – that's always hurt me about the war – to do with people who lived in the place?' He saw children dancing and homeless people walking away, smashed by horrendous tragedy. The contrast struck him profoundly, as it did so many.

It was a time of horror and nightmare; imaginations created even more unreal perspectives and horizons. Marilyn Cameron wrote to the *Daily Mail* in 2009, to recall that:

> During night bombing raids we all had to sit in the mud under the corrugated roof ... we saw what appeared to be a gun turret sticking out of the railway embankment.... The air raid warden was called and we waited terrified until the sun rose ... and the gun turret was revealed as an ancient bush that had been there for years.

In Norman Longmate's great survey of life in Britain during the war, he notes the sheer determination of Londoners not to let daily routine be disturbed. But on the Monday morning after the first large-scale bombing, one girl's story was typical of the chaos and the challenge:

> The Tube was closed at Balham. I hitch-hiked a lift from a lorry driver who took me to Elephant and Castle and from there I walked to the City. We walked over Southwark Bridge as we were not allowed to cross London Bridge, and when I got to the office I understood why. Rubble and glass were all over the place. Firemen, who had been up all night, were standing round.... They looked so tired.

The firemen were destined to be the heroes of the hour, facing gales of hot air as fire-storms developed in enclosed alleys and inside buildings. Along with people lined up in underground shelters, the firemen and their hoses and hats have become iconic representations of that time and place.

At the docks, over a million tons of softwood went up in

flames in 1940, and when a fire broke out at Woolwich Arsenal after a raid, the men had to cope with the thought that there were stacks of ammunition around them. The docks had first been bombed on the raid of 7 September 1940, the very first bomb hitting the Surrey Commercial Docks.

The Second World War was going to bring new and strange challenges to the Thames Police, as had been the case in the Great War.

Much of the force's work around the docks was concerned with supposed evidence of illegal imports or gun-running. Inspector Nixon and other staff were called to check out mysterious packages at the London Docks, for instance. That was a typical wartime event; the packages were supposed to contain household goods and had come from Europe, so there was suspicion attached to them. Nixon thought that there was certainly reason to suspect that these might be weapons of war awaiting Hitler's much-vaunted arrival in England. The police, not wanting to unpack and probably re-pack every carton, decided to use a metal rod, piercing every box and hoping to hear the sound of metal on metal. They did not, but the ploy saved time. So much police work is, and always has been, tedious and demanding, necessary in principle yet often ultimately proved unnecessary, and that job could have been that kind of labour.

The greatest wartime challenge was arguably the fire from the docks after bombing; when the Surrey Commercial Docks were hit and fire spread, it was hell. The Thames men did what they could: the most fruitful procedure was to move alongside every barge they could and to jump on board to deal with minor fires or with dangerous debris; the bombs carried on falling and more and more burning fragments fell or drifted onto the river craft. The men were exhausted, as the firemen were; bombing periods could last for hours. Wapping station itself was very nearly hit, while Nixon was there. He recalled being flung out of bed and seeing plaster fall from the ceiling. The duty sergeant had to light matches to look for emergency lanterns and candles in the darkness. Two launches had been flooded and glass had been blown from the door. In the morning, there was a large piece of shrapnel in the wall of the office, by Nixon's chair. His papers were everywhere and, outside, smoke still hung in a cloud over the Thames.

Thieving from the docks had, of course, been an ongoing problem in the inter-war years; in 1920 a committee of several important business interests was formed to report on what they termed losses on a gigantic scale; these organizations included the London Chamber of Commerce, the Chamber of Shipping of the United Kingdom and the Port of London Authority. They explained the problem and provided some startling facts and figures: one ship-owner was paying £250,000 a year in claims for pilferage and non-delivery; the Lloyd's Claims Bureau in 1919 and 1920 processed payments of around £10,000 a week. The committee put together an urgent statement asking for measures to be taken to reduce this scale of loss, and they also gave reasons for what they saw as police failures and shortcomings. The secretary of the committee wrote that one of the causes was a failure in co-ordination in policing bodies. He also said that before the Great War there had been some detectives attached to the Thames Division and that these had been withdrawn in 1916. He wrote: 'As a result within a few years thefts began to increase, assuming alarming proportions during the final years of the war, with a still further increase since its cessation.'

The committee made suggestions, and some applied directly to the Thames Division work. *The Times* printed these in 1920:

(a) The provision of a detective force, which may be either attached to the Thames Division or directly under Scotland Yard as may be deemed fit by the authorities to assist in the instant apprehension of offenders.

(b) The working arrangements for the river and land forces should so dovetail as to promote cordial co-operation between the various authorities.

(c) The Thames Division should control the whole of the waterway within the limits of the Port of London Authority, and with respect to theft from vessels, have their Executive power extended on land.

The report also pointed out that below Erith at least four different police authorities existed outside the metropolitan area.

The appointments of detectives Raby and Nixon were, in part, consequences of this set of recommendations. Dalton's summary of the problems involved in preventing and investigating thefts from the docks explains why no simple solution was found. He placed special emphasis on the fact that his own detectives worked closely with detectives from other divisions, so the report had been listened to.

Matters of the river extended to far more than theft, though, in the inter-war years. Such topics as the white slave traffic and opium dens fed the sensation pages of the tabloids. The records of the activities of the Thames men in this period show that they were very much in a supporting role – the white slave traffic is a case in point. In 1910, Ernest Bell published his book, *Fighting the Traffic in Young Girls,* and he made an impact with his cases, backed up by the famous story of W.T. Stead who, in 1885, had 'bought' a young girl to sell to men in need of a young prostitute. The book caused a moral panic. In the 1912 Criminal Law Amendment Act there was legislation against offences 'for the purpose of habitual prostitution' related to the procurement of young girls. A letter to *The Times* by one ''Ettie Sayer' had told nasty tales of young English girls being lured to work in New York.

In an article written for *The English Review* in 1913, Teresa Billington-Greig set about questioning the idea that such a trade existed on the scale stated, but she did research the topic, summing up statistics supplied by chief constables with the words, 'One may fairly deduce that there is no abnormal cause of disappearance acting in the case of girls and women alone.' Nevertheless, she was prompted to write by a host of disturbing stories of men trapping young girls and exploiting them.

These criminal trends persisted into the 1930s, however. Nixon records one experience that suggests such an offence: his boarding of a German vessel on the Thames at Blackwall. Local officers joined him and the girls in question were in custody. His biographer wrote that the girls' condition was not clear when found: one girl was taken ashore unconscious and dumped. Nixon went on board with Sergeant Perry and they found a girl 'naked except for her vest. Her eyes were fast closed, her face congested. Only the twitching of her limbs revealed that she still lived.' She was taken ashore into the hands of a matron at Woolwich. The offence cited was 'concealing women aboard' and Nixon rather too boldly visited another ship for the same reason, alone. He found out that there were half a dozen girls due on board just before midnight. He searched all the cabins and asked direct questions; the captain could not produce the Seaman's Discharge Book and was in a difficult situation, but then a woman came on board, someone known to him, who worked the shore pubs.

There was no certainty that this was a case of white slavery: both instances cited may simply have been ladies of the night aboard ship, servicing the crews. The important fact here is that such inquiries came within the remit of Nixon and his colleagues. They were 'in support' of bigger issues, from this kind of thing to murder and smuggling.

When the war came, the black market accelerated the spur to steal and for gangs to 'work' the river and the docks. The war with Hitler was so massive, reaching into the darkest corners of life on the home front as well as on the seas, in the air and on land, that it inevitably invited unscrupulous types to exploit the situation. This meant much more than simply looting or appropriating government property to set up retail sidelines. At times it meant large-scale enterprises and a degree of violence in gangland. Ports all had their problems in this respect: first, there were the ordinary rackets such as trade in market-restricted goods. In a world of rationing, this was wide-ranging. Some trading was significant, like the 1945 scheme to steal a large quantity of watches, pens and lighters, up to the value of almost a hundred thousand pounds. It might have come off, but for the fact that there were detectives planted among the crooks, in the form of American staff from the Army Investigation Division, and in no time the British CID were stepping in.

Another easy source of income for the unscrupulous was the exploitation of the 'reserved occupations' – the categories of work which would exempt an individual from military service. Obviously, anyone who had the power and the means to switch or create identities could see to it that a man could avoid a battlefield by being classified as a miner, for instance. One man who was, indeed, in a position to profit from this was David Rowan, a businessman who was also on the city council. He indulged in forgery, false pretences and the large-scale production of imitation documents for use in this way. Mr Rowan was given a seven-year custodial sentence.

But the largest-scale case during the war was that of Frederick Porter. He was director of a company of ship-scalers and has been called a 'mastermind in crime'. His activities were frauds of mammoth proportions, reaching into Cumbria, and involving a whole ring of powerful people in Merseyside. Porter had not only made large quantities of cash; he was a master of stashing the money in various places. It all began with thefts from Grayson Rollo and Clover Docks Ltd. The Porter ring had falsified some Admiralty sales books. In only a few years Porter had made around a million pounds, the equivalent to around twenty million pounds at current values. As Donald Thomas has written, 'He could have financed the building of a warship out of his own pocket.'

Porter's main method of meting out the cash profits was to store sums of money in strongboxes in a string of banks; it seems that large sums were also stored elsewhere and were never found. But all this ended with Porter's suicide: just after an accountant from the Admiralty had paid him a visit on 30 January 1942 and had seen some discrepancies, Porter shot himself. The shady business had run its course.

The unfortunate firm of Grayson Rollo had more problems a year later, when there was more fraud. Amounts of money recorded as wages for staff were, in fact, never paid, but misappropriated. There were various frauds committed in the ranks of workers, some of whom were recorded as working far longer hours than they actually did. A scam called 'minesweeper' was exposed by an honest man who blew the whistle on the plan: the operation involved small payments by drillers to their bosses, who would then record full days of working hours.

The black market in wartime had many faces – including even the somewhat farcical but clever business of making women's underwear from shrouds (clothing no longer needed by the dead, of course). During this period, the main targets of crooks would always be clothes and food (particularly meat on the docks). In the year 1941 alone, over two thousand beef and lamb carcasses were purloined.

Finally, there were much less subtle ways of gaining some profit from the situation, such as the notorious case of a troop-ship's galley which was smashed by some ships' cooks with axes one day in 1943; they stole a massive stock of bottled beer and whisky, and they also cooked a special meal for the soldiers. Many were found drunk and disorderly when an officer investigated the noise.

14 Search and Rescue: Post-war

THERE WERE POLICE reforms on a grand scale under Lord Trenchard in the mid-1930s; he was a man with an impressive military record who was pressed into service to sort out organization and training, being appointed Commissioner in 1931. One of the persistent problems he was expected to put right was the ongoing statistic of depressingly low figures of arrests owing mainly to the speed of stolen cars in the crooks' escapes. Trenchard did the usual things: introduced economies and took measures that today would be called 'rationalizing'. What was due to happen was that training and recruitment were to be revolutionized and streamlined; since a Committee on Police Powers and Procedure of 1929 made a positive report recommending that the selection process for senior officers be more rigorous, changes were coming. Trenchard seemed like the man for that job: he and others around him wanted to recruit men with a high level of traditional education

Trenchard was Commissioner for just five years. He had previously served in the Boer War and in Ireland; he had been Commander of the Royal Flying Corps in the Great War and then played a major role in the creation of the RAF itself. His regime in the police brought about many radical changes, including bringing in a statistical department and a daily crime telegram; he created a detective training school and a police scientific laboratory. The police training school at Hendon was his work too. In more difficult areas he was arguably reticent, as in the known activities which were undoubtedly corrupt. But he challenged the policy, going back to the beginnings with Peel, of promoting from within. Trenchard saw the virtues of a short-service scheme. What he did with the Police College was make it the place where the real 'career men' would be trained and encouraged to use their talents, and he offered finite career periods to others. A short-term contract would allow a recruit to sign on for just ten years before retiring with a gratuity payment. His own short-lived regime was assured some kind of continuance, however, as he appointed Sir Philip Game to succeed him – a man who could be relied on to act as if he were still an aide-de-camp.

What happened in terms of detective work was that the world's first training programme was begun in 1936 on the Hendon Police College estate. By the Metropolitan Police Act of 1933, Hendon was established as the centre for police training. It was opened in 1934 and it was clearly an institution that became indispensable, being renewed after the Second World War.

We have memoirs explaining how men became detectives and these help us to understand what their motivations were. The middle line in this was discontentment with the beat work of the 'ordinary copper'. Leonard 'Nipper' Read, for instance, 'the man who caught the Krays', explains it in that way, and writes that the course at Hendon Police College, which he attended in 1947, was: 'Drilling and lectures on public order, diseases of animals, child neglect, company fraud, incest, rape, bigamy, sodomy, helping children at school crossings, suicide, infanticide, drunks, ponces and traffic control.' Read started as a detective when a senior officer said he had a job for him and that he would be working in plain clothes.

Before the new training, though, a bright policeman – or a restless one – followed a set procedure of application to become a detective. This is explained in the biography of Nixon, 'Nick of the River', mentioned earlier, who later became a detective inspector. The method was outlined to him by a senior officer:

An applicant wrote his name in the book provided for the purpose in the Station. In due course, as vacancies occurred, if he were considered by the Station Detective Sergeant as a possibility his name was forwarded through the usual channels and he was interviewed by the Divisional Detective Inspector. If the interview was satisfactory the applicant was posted for C I D duties as an 'aide' when he was tried out on his own.

Read was a man who went through that process twenty years later, and he explains that as an aide the idea is that you have a mentor. He began at St John's Wood and there his mentor was Martin Walsh, of whom Read wrote: 'I was put under the wing of one of the best detectives I have ever met.... He was an older man, in his forties, who was used as a "tutor" aide. He taught me what investigating was all about.' In that way, Nixon and Read learned to be detectives by working on the streets with experienced men. But what about the new men going to the college?

A great deal can be learned about that curriculum from the 1938 *Report of the Departmental Committee on Detective Work and Procedure*. That report outlines the whole course of training, from a review of general detective work, through to specific skills such as crime record-keeping and photography. The document was produced by a team led by Sir Samuel Hoare, Secretary of State for the Home Office. In terms of commentary on existing detective work, the report puts considerable emphasis on communication between individual officers and, indeed, at the group operational level, as in comments about detectives from different forces gathering to exchange information at race meetings. Men who were asked in the course of the inquiry relating to the drafting of the report had repeatedly suggested that detective work would be notably improved if a 'spirit of co-operation was fostered'.

The 1930s was the time at which it was properly understood that liaison across the country was becoming crucially important in police work. The report recommended bringing senior officers from different forces together so that they could work together at the earliest opportunity in the process of investigating a specific crime. The normal practice at the time, if a man had to go to work in another area, was for the officer to notify the CID concerned, but the report's authors noted a very uneven application of this principle. They advised individual procedures, but stressed that an effective system of intelligence about criminals was at the top of the list of requirements. In the years immediately before the 1938 report, 'lending' of officers had been on a very small scale, and it is clear that these instances were for particular expertise; just twenty such loans took place in the years between 1931 and 1936. Naturally, in murder cases, this kind of lending activity is more important, and the authors reported that the recent results in this respect were encouraging: 'In the five years 1931–35 there were known to the police 460 cases of murder or suspected murder of persons aged one year or over [murders of children younger than this had been known as infanticide since 1922]. In 181 of these cases the murderer ... committed suicide, leaving 279 cases to be detected ... arrests were made in 254 cases.'

Training of officers received close attention. After all, numbers of officers were increasing quickly and the force was huge compared to that at work in the Ripper years five decades earlier. In 1938 there were 1,198 CID personnel; Liverpool and Birmingham had equivalent forces of over a hundred men. As recruitment was clearly increasing, it was a good time to take stock of needs and methods. All the obvious issues were discussed in the course of exploring the nature of the detective needed in that time of inter-war expansion and of organized crime, rackets and robberies. One of the central points considered was the idea of a probationary period, the line of thought parallel to the 'aide' system. The panel concluded that no probation was needed but conceded that a detective is 'always on probation' in that he or she must always be 'subject to continuing to discharge duties successfully'.

Naturally, these reforms and the new effort to streamline records and communications impinged on the river as much as on the street work. The reports of the Home Office on police work and on forces' liaison had been meticulous and through – if rather idealistic and perhaps too optimistic regarding the maintenance of much that they advocated as daily practice – but in recruitment in particular, both Trenchard and the new 1930s reports had an impact on the Thames Division.

When the war ended there was a certain amount of revisionist thinking in the higher echelons of the Division. There was recruitment to be done, and also fresh notions on training to be implemented. Special courses on maritime law, seamanship and watermanship were provided for new recruits. There were also new boats, including three forty-foot launches, which were converted from previous use in the navy. Wapping had also seen changes shortly after the war ended: new workshops were constructed by 1949, employing thirty-two men in various capacities, including fitters, carpenters and painters.

One of the chief ongoing concerns was the problem of the theft of lead on the river; its value per ton had increased markedly and, in bars called 'blueys', at a weight of around 60 lb, it could be moved. Other metals had become more pricey and desirable also, such as copper. What was happening was almost a return to the bad old days when Colquhoun had studied the massive number of losses from barges: crooks were shifting metal at night from water to the shore, and then driving it away. Improvements in transportation since the early Victorian days – with railways, road freight and canal transport all being much more widespread and efficient – meant that goods could be removed speedily.

What was needed was more of something that had always been one of the foundations of good police work: sources of on-the-spot information. Along with 'fences', gangs spawn 'grasses' and other forms of inside information. But in this case, post-war and after a huge and burgeoning black market trade, detectives like Nixon needed new faces, new sources. Nixon worked as detectives had always done; cultivating rogues who were attached to large outfits and who had something to gain by passing on information. The tip-offs began, and what were then needed were patience and observation, waiting for the right time to move. Nixon describes one occasion when he had a call to tell him that a barge at Lovell's Wharf was to be plundered; he waited until the tide turned, and had a sergeant set on watch, then a barge under observation was reported being towed and, at Wapping, Nixon sprang into action. The barge was supposed to be carrying timber, but was very low in the water, so suspicions were aroused.

Early in the morning the staff at the wharf were asked to check two barges, and one had a large amount of lead missing. The barge with the stolen lead was on the move, so it was a case of trailing it; at Barking Creek it moored and the line of thought was that its destination was further up into the River Roding. This was a case in which the Thames and the 'land' men worked together. A string of officers were put in place, waiting to pounce, and the barge went up Barking Creek. Men on board poled the vessel through a lock. The shadowing continued until at last the officers were on board, handling pigs of lead where there was supposed to be timber. The proof was there, but more dogged pursuit was needed, so that the unloading could be seen and the arrest made. Finally, a lorry arrived and the police let the work carry on until the right moment. We can imagine the sense of triumph when the police stepped in and told the crooks that they had been watching them unload the lead for half an hour, and the thieves were taken to the police station at Ilford.

Some of the events of the 1950s were on a very large scale indeed, perhaps none more so than the case of Antoni Klimowicz. On 28 July 1954, men were unloading a vessel at Mark Brown Wharf. The ship was the *Jaroslav Dabrowski*, named after a Polish war hero. The cargo was wood and had come from the Baltic; but working in the hold, the men saw a human arm, and they moved some goods out of the way. They had a stowaway, and he was Antoni Klimowicz; his English was not so good, and the Englishmen unloading were stunned by his appearance, especially as Antoni wanted the police. When he recalled the strange meeting, a docker remembered that they had put the Pole onto a plank and lifted him up and on deck. He was then summarily seized by the crew and held captive.

The dockers knew that something was seriously wrong. They told the authorities and the local Polish community learned of the stowaway who was asking for diplomatic immunity. This was a bank holiday, so bringing in official help and making diplomatic and legal moves was going to be a problem. What was needed to bring the young man and his gaolers (for that is what they were) out to be questioned was a writ of habeas corpus, the ancient writ commanding anyone holding a prisoner to bring the body of their detainee to the Royal Courts of Justice for a hearing. A journalist called Boleslaw Wierzbianksi wanted to have the Lord Chancellor himself involved, and other Poles set about getting the High Court staff to come out for a special hearing; there were requests for a writ to be issued by the Lord Chief Justice.

The *Jaroslav Dabrowski* was on its way out of the estuary to travel back home to Gdynia, so the ship had to be stopped: that was a job for the Thames Police, and it has to be one of the largest, most sensational operations in its history. *The Times* gave the facts: 'A force of Thames river police, 120 strong, accompanied by the Commissioner of the Metropolitan Police, Sir John Nott-Bower, went to the Polish steamer *Jaroslav Dabrowski* off Erith … and took ashore the stowaway who had been found in the ship.' Behind the police there were two destroyers in readiness, and one of these, the Obdurate, came from the Pool of London to the scene; the other waited at Chatham. It was a moment of great diplomatic sensitivity: a series of communications took place between the Home Office and the court, then finally the Lord Chief Justice issued the writ on 1 August.

Before the habeas corpus was issued, there were ten police launches at Erith waiting for the order to move out, and it was late in the day before they went to the ship, taking an immigration officer with them. The period while the launches acted as guards and escorts was a tense one: *The Times* reported, 'The launches circled the Polish ship for some 75 minutes while the search was carried out. When they returned another posse of police lined the jetty at Erith as Klimowicz, wearing a blue jersey and his thin face half hidden in a muffler, was brought out.'

A large crowd had assembled to watch the confrontation, and witnesses recalled that the Polish crew had assumed a menacing attitude and it looked likely, as the launches moved around and the ship rolled at anchor, that the Poles might break through and head for the sea. Some noted that 'wild Cossack music blared across the water', but trouble was avoided and the police boarded the ship, going up a rope ladder. The

Commissioner read out the important wording of the writ and the search began. In fact, the stateroom was locked, and so officers smashed the door open, using fire-axes. It emerged later, as announced by Sir David Maxwell Fyfe, that the police had encountered much hostility and that a bucket of boiling water had been thrown over one of the launches.

As he had been lifted out of the hold by the dockers, Klimowicz had shouted 'I want freedom'. He subsequently found it, being helped by the Polish Ex-Combatants Association and the Federation of Free Poles; he lived with a Polish family after all the furore of the escape to freedom.

The years between 1950 and 1965 saw the emergence of striking personalities as well as chronicles of crime in a society of extreme deprivation and utilitarian recovery. In the history of the Thames Division of that period, it is clear that they played important roles in several major criminal investigations. One prominent example is the case of Alfred Whiteway.

On Coronation Day, 1 June 1953, the papers were busy with another story: a young girl named by many as 'The Force's Sweetheart' had been brutally murdered by the Thames at Teddington on 31 May, and her body thrown into the river. She was sixteen-year-old Barbara Songhurst, and her best friend, Christine Reid, also disappeared, her body being found eventually a week later, in the river at Richmond. The Thames police had the unenviable task of searching for the bodies, Scotland Yard having applied for the Thames to be partially drained from Richmond Weir to Teddington Lock. Seven days notice had to be given, and the idea was to lower the level of the river between 2 and 3 a.m. on the ebb tide – the Thames men were then to have the job of raking the area to find the corpse. Fortunately, this never had to happen. The hunt was intensified – 500 houses were searched on the Ham Estate and questionnaires were left with males, asking if they knew the girls.

The man called in to sort things out was DS Herbert Hannam of Scotland Yard. He is not one of the 'big names' from the Yard: his name does not figure prominently in the reference books, yet this charismatic figure always did police work with style and panache, and some of his most high-profile cases tell us a lot about the man and about the nature of extreme crime at the time.

Hannam was a career man for sure. His son, Kenneth, was also in the force, and Hannam was happily married, living in Willesden with a successful stint as a lecturer at Hendon Police College behind him. In the post-war years, he emerged as a currency specialist and was given some high-profile cases. He was a dapper man, always extremely well turned out; a photograph of him taken in 1957 shows a solidly built man, quite short, with a military bearing. He wears a trilby and a three-piece suit and his shoes shine with a regimental sparkle. It is an image of a man who means business.

Just before the Songhurst case, Hannam had been involved in a case at Eastbourne where there had been what looked like a double killing, and the popular section of the daily press mysteriously reported that Hannam was being helped by a certain Dr X and another enigmatic Dr Y. This was just the kind of sensation that followed Hannam wherever he went.

The Songhurst-Reed murders were particularly nasty. Both girls had been attacked on the Thames towpath, and on a cycle path – a detail that was a main factor in tracking down the killer. After Barbara's body was found on the bank between Teddington Lock and Eel Pie Island, the search operation was massive, as police were desperate to find Christine.

Barbara was a blonde and was considered to be brainy; her friend Christine was, in the words of her own mother, 'backward'. But the friends were outgoing types and loved to cycle around the area. On this fateful day they had left for a 'spin' just after 7 p.m. Events were pieced together after a group of young men who had been camping near the spot said they had been with the girls until 11 p.m. that night. An electrician, Albert Sparks, told officers that he and his mates were with the girls and that they had all arranged to meet after talking at Richmond on the previous Friday.

Another line of inquiry was with the American GIs at Bushey Park camp, as Barbara had a penchant for writing and talking to soldiers. Hannam said that Barbara had penfriends covering almost the entire world and was always prepared to correspond with lonely soldiers. She used to send her photo to most of them, and she had been seen dancing with a dark-skinned man, possibly an Indian, earlier that weekend. Hannam was sure that this man was an American at the camp.

The murderer had shown no mercy and the killings were remarkably savage. A coroner reported that the killer had wielded the knife with 'colossal strength'. Barbara had been stabbed three times in the back. Uncannily, she had been re-dressed after being attacked and stabbed, but the attacker was also careless; blood was found on the grass nearby and Christine's shoes were also left there. At this stage Hannam was sure that she had been killed also and told *The Express* that he expected to find her body soon.

She was found, and it was a terrible sight. Christine was 5 ft 6 in, with dark brown curly hair. Police knew exactly what she had been wearing that Sunday: a yellow cardigan, dark blue serge slacks and white ankle socks with black shoes. She had been battered relentlessly and knifed no less than ten times.

On 3 June, a lead was reported involving two men with scarred faces. But this went nowhere; the Thames was searched, and huge electro-magnets were used. Navy divers also took part. Some intensive and thorough work went on under the guidance of Hannam. Not only were launches dragging the river; a large patch of grass was carefully scythed in the search for clues, police dogs were used, and two pairs of shoes were found, but they appeared not to belong to Barbara.

Then came the link that proved to be the clincher, and led Hannam to Alfred Whiteway. The common factor between victims and killer was the cycling habit. Barbara's new maroon sports model (only recently purchased) was missing. Prior to the murders, two women had been assaulted in Surrey – one of them raped – and Whiteway had been held on suspicion for that. He was a keen cyclist. He was a married man, but separated from his wife; he was back living with his parents and they provided the alibi.

All seemed well for the man, until a vigilant police officer, cleaning out a patrol car, found an axe hidden under a seat. He realized that the car was the one that had recently had

Whiteway in it. Forensic tests soon established that the axe had been used on the two girls. It appeared that it had been used to fell them, in addition to the stabbing that had taken place, possibly during the sexual assault which followed. Whiteway confessed and was hanged on 22 December that year by Albert Pierrepoint at Wandsworth Prison. Hannam had got his man, after a long and very resourceful search and inquiry.

As a result of the Second World War, there had been changes and advances in the force itself and in its work, and for this Tom Fallon deserves a mention. He was Superintendent of the Thames Police from 1942 up to his retirement in 1948 and was the man who devised the 999 emergency call system. He had also been the officer in charge of communications at Scotland Yard and he developed the wireless and line communication system. More than that, he played a major role in establishing the air raid warning system in the war. During the war, an underwater drag using an electro-magnet had been devised by Fallon, working off an accumulator; this brought up metal of all kinds and shapes; it proved to be too troublesome to retain, though, and the idea was not pursued further.

Another advance was the establishment of the Underwater Support Unit (USU) in 1962. The first USU, devised by the Metropolitan Police, was only part-time and involved time allotted to train men to acquire the necessary skills. Geoffrey Budworth joined the unit in 1964, and it worked from Wapping, commanded by Inspector Bob Epps and Sergeant Alex Worth. Budworth, writing in 1997, stated that there were then twelve men (including the driver) in the USU team. He wrote that, in a typical year, the unit does 200 operational searches lasting 264 days. He added, 'They recover about twenty bodies, twelve firearms, ten edged weapons, fifteen cars and twelve motor-bikes, many of these items being clues in investigation or evidence for a subsequent court trial.'

The question must be asked: what happens to all the objects found in the river? Are they all retained, stored and tagged? Clearly, there would not be room for all this material, so most objects are monitored so that their location may be revisited if required. As may be imagined, a great deal of interest is aroused when such a unit arrives and starts work at a spot on the river. There is the same excitement and anticipation as when a modern metal-detector is in use – more so, in some respects, because in the Thames there is such a massive amount of discarded material, from centuries of busy history, that anything and everything may be found on a dive. The divers have a special part to play in gathering evidence from the river; one notable example was a gun retrieved after a bank raider threw it into the river following a robbery in which a man was killed; the gun was taken up with great care, and when the forensics experts worked on it, they had over a thousand fragments of glass still on the weapon. As the gun had been fired through a glass screen, the material was vitally important to the forensic study.

The underwater work naturally requires training. In the year 2000, the police service had two schools for police divers: one at Strathclyde and one used by London officers, the National Diving and Marine School at Sunderland. Nowadays, the work is regulated by the 1997 Diving at Work Regulations which impose three main responsibilities: holding an approved qualification for diving, being competent to work safely and holding a valid certificate of medical fitness to dive. Officers have to have a certificate from the Health and Safety Executive, and divers have to undergo a medical examination by an Approved Medical Examiner of Divers.

Budworth's account of the nature of the work of the River Police includes his personal experience of retrieving corpses, and he explains the training as it was *c*.1997, when the basic residential course lasted for two months. In that course, officers learned how to dive at sea and in docks, learned search methods and practised salvage work. He sums up the learning process thus: 'So although a new diver should become a useful team member after only a few months, it takes up to ten years to master the trade.'

Currently, within the USU, there is a sub-unit labelled the Underwater and Confined Space Search Team, part of the Wapping Marine Support Unit. The official police guide describes the work succinctly: 'The officers … search for and recover bodies, property, weapons and other evidence in support of police investigations. Often working in appalling conditions, such as freezing-cold, black, polluted water, the officers' skill, courage and experience are highly valued by the police and public.' As Budworth wrote: 'The U.S.U. has transformed underwater searches for clues and evidence. A suspect hoping to thwart investigators could, years ago, say "I threw it into the river"... Police divers can now state, "It isn't there."' Consequently, investigators can say with certainty that an object was not thrown into the river and detect a lie.

Overall, as will be discussed in the next chapter, the most marked change in search and rescue has been the establishment since 2002 of the RNLI running three permanently manned lifeboat stations.

Another innovation in the 1950s was the advent of the Thames Specials. Special constables, often jocularly called 'hobby bobbies', have been a part of the police structure since the reign of Charles II. In 1673 an Act was passed which made it possible for any man to be called upon to fulfil the role of 'temporary police officer'. In years following that, 'specials' were listed and ready to be called principally for use in exceptional circumstances, such as in radical protest, street violence and even the threat of open revolution. In the Georgian period, they appear frequently in the social history, most notably in deplorable episodes such as the Peterloo Massacre in Manchester in 1819, when soldiers confronted and attacked civilians at a public speech which became a riot.

The most formative legislation in this context came in 1831 with the Special Constables Act; these constables were then given full powers and equipment to put them equal with regular officers. Then, in 1834 (and largely in a climate of fear created by the Chartist movement) the specials were allowed to move outside their own parishes when necessary to be effective. For instance, a report of a Chartist disturbance in Bradford in *The Times* for May 1848 notes that: 'The police and specials then succeeded in capturing 18 of the most active of the Chartists.' The figure of the voluntary special constable emerged from this legislation also. Obviously, whenever there was trouble of a political nature, or crime waves too powerful to handle with the normal manpower, the specials were sworn in; during the 1830s 'Swing Riots' across the eastern counties, the Chief Constable of Essex employed temporary officers.

In the period of the world wars, specials were very important. From the end of the Great War, a medal for service as a special constable was established, and indeed they played an important role in defence actions, including taking part at one time in the capture of a Zeppelin.

By 1923, permanent special constabularies had been introduced. But, essentially, the use of specials has always been supplementary to the use of full time officers; there has never been any intention to replace permanent staff. When, in the 1950s, they were first used on the Thames, there were approximately a hundred special constables on the river. The part-time work attracted men who had experience of boats and working on the river, and they were given basic training, which included having to learn the regulations of the Port of London Authority and the laws relating specially to the use of the river. The specials worked in a launch, guided by the regulars, and had to use the two-way radio system based at Scotland Yard. The hierarchy they worked in was headed by a commandant and three inspectors, and employed sergeants, as well as the constables.

From the 1970s, the Thames Division moved with the times and acquired new varieties of boats. More modern replacement duty boats were found to work in place of the existing fibreglass ones, the order being filled by a firm on the Isle of Wight, Mustang Marine. What emerged was the TF9, with a Perkins engine and tanks of 150 gallon capacity.

The Division was shrinking, with stations at Blackwall and Barnes closing, so with this in mind, as Geoffrey Budworth put it, it was essential to 'go further and faster'. He points out in his book on the police that single-screw duty boats would take perhaps two hours to reach Erith from Wapping, even going 'flat out'. New, speedier boats were needed and so large, long-range craft were acquired, and a number of companies worked on different parts of the new boats, according to their specialities.

But these did not appear until 1992: before that, other major events had occurred.

There were cuts. In 1978 questions were asked in the House of Commons regarding the plan to cut the number of launches and police on the river. Mervyn Rees gave a reply familiar to thousands of employees in all trades, bland yet with foreboding: 'In the light of the changing pattern of policing needs on the River Thames and throughout the Metropolitan Police district the Commissioner has decided that a reduction in the number of police officers, patrol boats and police stations in Thames Division is justified.' Members of Parliament expressed disquiet, saying that there would be a slackening of security around the Palace of Westminster. But the argument from Scotland Yard was that more officers needed to be released for patrol duty on the London streets. In the previous year, there had been 884 resignations from the overall national police service, but there had been a net gain in strength of 150 after new recruitment. These facts were an attempt to reassure the crime-fearing public but, in the end, there were simply promises from Rees that 'the proposed changes in the Thames Division would not reduce the degree of protection I am able to afford to the Palace'.

To those who had served long, and from the war years, the contrast was stark between 1978 and 1949 when Chuter Ede, Home Secretary, reviewed the Thames Police to mark the 150th anniversary of the force. Then, there was a pageant from Greenwich to Westminster, and it must have seemed as though there was immense pride and satisfaction in such gargantuan growth and progress in policing the great river Thames. Ten years later, the floating police station at Waterloo had been towed down the river by tugs, on its way to be refurbished, and that was also a reminder to the public that the Division was moving with the times: the station was converted from coal to gas central heating and the overhaul was a major task, involving the fifty-two officers to be given temporary accommodation for three weeks while the work went on.

In fact, 1959 was one of those years in which there was more than usual attention paid to the Thames Division. The press provided substantial reports on the state of affairs and looked back to the origins of the patrols. In that year there were thirty-one patrol boats covering the thirty-six miles of responsibility. The long-oared boats had long given way to 30 ft patrol boats, and one reporter summed up the division's strength and duties: 'At present the effective strength is 182 uniformed officers and three C.I.D. staff, who are responsible for making enquiries ashore in connexion with missing property and in following up investigations linked to the river.' In a major feature in *The Times*, a constable told the press something that would have surprised the general reader: 'The chief difference between us and the land force is that if a police officer stops you for a motoring offence, then it's the professional lecturing the amateur; here we deal with people whose very life is the waterway on which they depend. The job often requires a lot of diplomacy.' The reporter was most eager to tell his readers that the division's work gave him and everyone on the river a feeling of security.

Just fifteen years later, then, there were cuts and the beginning of a gradual but inevitable curtailment in strength and resources.

15 From the *Marchioness* to the Marine Support Unit

IN THE EARLY hours of 20 August 1989, a river boat called the *Marchioness*, with a party on board celebrating the twenty-sixth birthday of Cambridge graduate Antonio de Vasconcellos, was rammed and destroyed by a huge Thames dredger called the *Bowbelle*. The boat party had been organized by Jonathan Phang, a photography agent and, after a dinner, guests had taken to the river in high spirits. The dead included Francesca Dallaglio, elder sister of Lawrence Dallaglio, the rugby star. The collision was fast and deadly: in poor light, the *Marchioness* went under Southwark Bridge and was close to Cannon Street Railway Bridge when the dredger hit it behind. The pleasure boat went down in just thirty seconds, with the *Bowbelle* being on top of the *Marchioness*, pressing her down rapidly. Witnesses commented that the pleasure craft was pushed under the water like a toy boat.

In many ways, the possibility of such a disaster had been of concern to the various river authorities for some time previously; in 1986 a meeting was held at Wapping at which Chief Inspector Patchett and other inspectors met representatives of the Department of Transport and the Thames Passenger Services Federation to consider a code of practice when dealing with disturbances of vessels. Inspector Patchett said that the police were happy with the draft of the code and he asked the Federation to circulate the text. The important outcome was that, as the minutes expressed it, 'Every boat will be requested to display the code in each wheelhouse.' Inspector Patchett told the meeting that there had recently been four calls to the police about disturbances on pleasure craft, that two were minor cases and in two cases there had been arrests.

One important subject discussed at that meeting was the drinking of alcohol on the cruises. The governing regulations on the relevant licenses stated that drink could only be served when the vessel was 'in passage' and this was clarified, so that, for instance, a brief stop to collect passengers would still be 'in passage', yet a number of other situations would not be.

This meeting's minutes have a subtext – a suggestion behind the words that there were police concerns about pleasure craft. The one aspect that everyone would have to understand was a key area of safety was visibility and, in the *Marchioness* disaster, that was the principal problem: the report of the inquiry of 2001, prepared by Lord Clarke, concluded that the incident was partly caused by the failure of the two skippers – Captain Henderson and Stephen Fald – to keep a proper lookout. The report made it clear that Captain Henderson should, himself, have kept a proper lookout. One important aspect of the whole affair was that Henderson had drunk several pints of lager the previous day, but it was concluded that enough time had passed for the alcohol to have had no effect on him by the time of the accident. Obviously, that remained a bone of contention for many years.

A full explanation of the police participation in the incident had come out in the report by the Maritime Accident Investigation Branch (MAIB) in 2000, and that followed questions in Parliament about the police actions during the disaster. The Home Secretary was asked, in 1999, how many police officers and boats were available to the Metropolitan Police Thames Division at the time of the disaster, and Charles Clarke replied that there were 146 officers attached to Thames Division and 23 boats deployed from the five bases. He noted in comparison that, in 1999, there were just 89 officers and 18 boats working out of Wapping, mainly dealing with monitoring river traffic and emergency response. He stressed that the fleet had been substantially modernized since 1989 and that two new boats were soon due to be delivered. He also reassured the

House that other technical developments were in progress, such as digital marine radio and vessel tracking.

The basic fact was that the *Marchioness* went under so quickly and with such violence, given the immense weight on her, that the number of craft and personnel available to help might not have made much difference to the death toll, though it would have speeded up the rate of rescue of those taken out of the water alive. The MAIB report was very thorough, and it detailed the police movements and reactions. Police launches were soon on the scene, and the tide was flowing at three knots, sweeping people upstream. More than half of the eighty people rescued were taken up by the four police launches. There had also been help from people on board the *Royal Princess* nearby, who threw lifebuoys out. Their spotlights also helped the police boats to locate swimmers.

The first call received at Wapping immediately put into action the Metropolitan Police Major Incident Procedure. The duty officer set up a control and rendezvous point on the Embankment near Waterloo and soon other support services were there, and co-operating. Following that, the Port of London Authority and the ambulance services played their part, and both the *Royal Princess* and another vessel, the *Hurlingham*, continued to help in the police search. At a point just over an hour after the accident, the police requested helicopter assistance and this was provided until just before noon.

From just after one o'clock in the afternoon, when various rescue and support services stood down, the Thames Division had the unenviable task of searching for corpses. The statistics were disheartening: of 131 people confirmed to have been on board, 51 had died. The most challenging phase of the work was surely when the wreck was pumped out and the police team had to recover 24 bodies. Searches of the river and foreshore continued for some time. The MAIB reported favourably on the police in its summary: 'The setting up of forward control points alongside Waterloo police station by the Police, Ambulance Service and Fire Brigade with their respective Incident Officers liaising closely, allowed a flexible response to a unique and changing situation.'

The MAIB has the job of investigating and reporting on all types of marine accidents on or to British vessels across the world; it is based in Southampton, and its powers are defined by the Merchant Shipping Act of 1995. This means that it is a specialist body for such reporting and conclusive recommendations, being linked to the Health and Safety Executive today. The report on the *Marchioness* had to look at every conceivable aspect of the accident, but the fact remains that poor visibility from the wheelhouse of both ships was the root cause, particularly as both ships were moving in the centre of the Thames. Captain Henderson of the *Bowbelle* was investigated; an inquiry into his competence took place in 2001 and he was allowed to keep his master's certificate. But, as one newspaper report summed up the investigation, in the end, 'The reports place the blame for the disaster fairly and squarely on the shoulders of the managers and owners of the *Bowbelle* and *Marchioness*, who, the reports say, fell below the standards which would have been adopted by any reasonable ship-owner.'

The whole business was made all the more distressing by the fact that the coroner, who eventually returned a verdict of accidental death, had ordered the hands of corpses to be cut off in order to systematize identification procedure; he was criticized for this in the Clarke report, and in fact the report went so far as to say that the relatives' human rights had been infringed. There were also extreme demands made on the police, not only in the handling of the bodies, but in dealing with the mortuary, set up in the basement of the boat repair workshop at Wapping: for the latter work, police staff were brought in from the Airport Division at Heathrow, keeping the Thames officers free to keep working at the retrieval of corpses.

In 1999, Superintendent Alan King took over command at Thames Division. In a lecture, he said that his brief was to 'restructure the Division and make it more relevant to policing 21st century London in preparation for the millennium.' In that same year, former Superintendent Rob Glen told the press that it was still not clear exactly who had overall responsibility for search and rescue. It was a time at which people were aware that there had been emergency service cutbacks. This statement was made at a public meeting at Methodist Central Hall in London. Glen pointed out that, at the *Marchioness* disaster, four police boats had been at the scene within six minutes, but, in 1999, there was just one boat operating in that area at night.

A separate search and rescue force, which Glen had advocated, came into being in 2002 when the Royal National Lifeboat Institution set up four stations at Gravesend, Tower Pier, Chiswick Pier and Teddington. Three lifeboats can be launched within a minute of an emergency call, and the official Thames Police site claims that these craft can be at any emergency scene between Canvey Island and Teddington in fifteen minutes. The Thames Divison became the Marine Support Unit in 2001 and was made a part of the Operational Command Unit, with a manpower of eighty-nine police officers.

The Maritime and Coastguard Agency now has the task of overseeing all search and recovery work on the river. Once again, the material history of the Thames Division still survives with a purpose, because the RNLI headquarters is at the Waterloo Pier police station. Today, there are rigid inflatable boats used by the Marine Support Unit, and recruits have a one-year probationary period, which includes a period of special training for search and rescue. The boats are manned by a sergeant and two constables, and nowadays the main police work is related to integrated work across the city against drug importation and terrorism.

One of the most recent developments, which took place in 2010, has been the amalgamation of the Kent and Essex Police and the Port of London Police. The Assistant Chief Constable of Kent has said that 'There will be no hiding place for criminals trying to use the Thames for illegal activity. Our combined resources take us to the forefront of river policing.' Those words could easily have been spoken by Patrick Colquhoun in 1795. Today, the rigid inflatable boats can move at high speed, co-ordinating with helicopters, to go to suspicious vessels, with the officers carrying semi-automatic weapons, ready to work as a raiding party. Yet, although the technology may have improved and the nature of crime might be very different in some respects from Colquhoun's time, the geography of the river is very much the same in respect of supervision and patrolling and policing still works essentially by persistent questioning, common sense and local knowledge. The twenty-first century has computer systems, whereas the nineteenth century had shouts, lights and Morse; in the modern world the officer might need knowledge of gadgets and formal procedure in triplicate, but instinct and a grounding in investigation techniques are still necessary. At the heart of the profession is the dogged will to succeed, to unravel a puzzle and to put information together so that a narrative of a crime is constructed.

Teamwork is more streamlined and more integrated now into every area of work; in the nineteenth century it certainly existed, but on a smaller scale. In the days of Harriott and Broderip, Evans and Ballantine, they had to cope with everything from minor incidents of theft to piracy, mutiny and murder on a regular basis. Accounts of police work in Victorian times often include face-to-face violence and the use of the truncheon; there was only a patchy sense of any duty of care to officers apart from supervising the beat system, and the constables must have wondered if anyone in the higher echelons really cared or ever thought about them as they faced a hostile mob, but somehow it worked, adapting and surviving as the patterns of crime changed with the times. Today, officers have to spend a lot of time reading various texts and have to know some criminology; in 1829 a writer to *The Sunday Times* poked fun at the educational shortcomings of the new police: 'University honours are not required to prove the fitness of the individuals applying for a situation which is to bring them in 3s per diem.'

The word 'international' is likely to be used regularly in London policing: that is possibly the most marked change compared with Victorian work on the river, you might think, but no – even in the early days, the officers were dealing with vessels from all over the globe. London has always attracted potential criminals from everywhere, and the more we take a historical perspective on the Thames Police, the more it becomes apparent that its officers have always had to be savvy in the microcosm of the London Docklands while, at the same time, knowing their larger mercantile world.

In 2011 the inheritors of the Thames Division are the men and women of the Marine Policing Unit. The Unit has specialist craft and provides a round-the-clock response service for all of London's waterways; work also entails checks and supervision of the river. Specific teams within the Unit include the Terrorism and Crime (TAC) team: these officers work with intelligence initiatives and liaise with other agencies and organizations in the contemporary world of terror threats and intelligence-reactive measures.

The latest incarnation of the underwater work discussed in the previous chapter is the Underwater and Confined Spaces team; such specialist divers are new in terms of some of the duties in their remit: that is, although they perform the kinds of searches related to accidents and recovery, they also work in areas concerning protection and safety for diplomatic purposes and when needed at any public event that may be a potential target for political or terrorist reasons.

Bringing bodies out of the river is essentially the same unpleasant but essential task that always confronted the Thames Division. But now there is a Unit Identification Officer with a specific job of identifying bodies brought out of the river, who works with the coroner. Obviously, any suspicious death will involve this officer working with the Senior Investigating Officer relating to the case in question. The job has more specialized medical knowledge included in the profile, with the officer having a good knowledge of the forensics of subaquatic death, a necessary requirement given the diversity of cases involving death by water. One of the most notable instances of this was the 'Adam' murder case of 2001.

The general public perhaps rarely stop to think of the immense range of knowledge that a police force needs to call upon. Most people are only aware of this when there is a sensational murder trial and an expert witness is called upon to pass an opinion based on no end of erudite research and professional expertise. The 'Adam' case is an outstanding example of this. The Marine Search Unit was faced with the task of handling the torso of an African boy, which was found in the river in September 2001. Everything about this find pointed to it being a case of ritual murder and so all the resources of forensic science were put into action. However, this turned out to be a case in which the circumstances were very unusual indeed. Ironically, it begs comparison to the Thames Torso Mysteries of the 1870s and 1880s although, in this case, the experts needed were anthropologists as well as surgeons and pathologists. In 1880 the press would have made much of the possibility that this was a joke by medical students who had thrown a corpse in the Thames after a dissection class, but in 2001 matters were very different indeed. One thing the basic pathology did establish was that 'Adam' had not been in Britain for long: this was based on the food in the stomach, which, together with pollen traces, indicated that he was a recent arrival. To add to the intrigue and shock, there was a potion in the stomach which suggested African magic. Science was equal to the task of asserting that the boy was from Nigeria, based on linking food and soil in the innards.

From that point on, the Metropolitan Police were dealing with the possible practice of ritual murders in London, and it seemed that mutilated corpses were going to be found again in the river, presenting the police divers with more exceptionally unpleasant jobs. Ten years later, the body was identified as being that of Ikpomwosa, who was just ten years old at the time of his death. His mother told police that she had given her son to a man called Bawa, and that he had taken the boy to London.

In 2005 a feature in the *Evening Standard* reported on an inquiry undertaken by Scotland Yard into the case; Richard Edwards told his readers that African boys were being sold for as little as £10 in Nigeria and then, in London, they were named witches and ritually killed. Edwards reported that police were trying to establish an open dialogue with the African community in Newham and Hackney, and they had been told of murders taking place because parents genuinely believed that their children were possessed by evil spirits. The claim of the article was that Scotland Yard had only traced 2 out of 300 such boys reported missing in London 'in a three month period'. Lecturers and academics passed opinions on the veracity of the research, and also on the ethical dimensions of the conclusions.

Inevitably, the whole phenomenon attracted close study by anthropologists and, in 2003, Professor Todd Sanders, now of the University of Toronto, published an examination of the police role in the torso murders in an academic journal. Sanders set out to discuss concerns about how Africans were depicted and spoken of in public discourse. He pointed out that shortly after the finding of 'Adam' there had been another similar discovery made in Holland, and that after the two cases were linked, the profile of the case was ratcheted up with a feature in *Crimewatch* about the supposed ritual killings.

The Serious Crime Group of the Metropolitan Police, headed by DI Will O'Reilly, was leading the inquiry, and a press conference was held to open up further discussion. There had been a meeting at Bramshill, at which a South African pathologist had confirmed the view that this was a case of a 'ritual homicide'. Then the media heightened the whole story by announcing that human flesh was for sale in London. Sanders concludes that the media and police actions led to a message that 'the Thames torso is the tip of a massive and malevolent iceberg, pointing to a thriving underground transnational trade in African children and body parts for occult purposes'.

The academic reactions, focusing, as Sanders does, on distorted imagery and denigration of African cultures, show one important aspect of the police work on the Thames in these strange new contexts of the twenty-first century: the ever-widening gap between 'hands on' police work and the increasingly elusive, complex and rarefied world of the detectives who have to deal with absolutely anything a multi-cultural city can throw at them. In other words, what was lost in all the discourse about the cultural and religious aspects of the Thames torso case was the task of dealing with the body and the forensic work involved.

This social phenomenon is largely responsible for the contemporary police identity as promoted to the public in the media across a wide spectrum: police reaching out for more liaison with people and communities, as in the Marine Policing Unit's Kraken project, which, as the website states, has a reporting line which 'provides a central point of contact for collation, assessment and analysis of all information relating to suspicious activity or behaviour that could be linked to all types of crime'. This confirms what many have thought about the revolution in police work over the last few decades: in a world of information overload, intelligence systems are the key to success. All information sources have to be brought together, and if those sources include matters as esoteric as ritual killings, then that knowledge is added to the database.

In 1840, the *Police Gazette* was circulated asking for information on crimes and suspects, deserters and con men; statistics were published to categorize offences; chief constables gathered information in filing cabinets and, later, typists tried to keep up with new information by the minute as London expanded and the pattern of crime changed with it. A century later there had been innovations in detective work: the murder squad and the flying squad existed, but there was still great reliance on word of mouth, on 'snouts' and local community sources. In 2011, information shoots along cyberspace in nano-seconds. Knowledge is both a boon and a burden, and the front-line officers have to carry on with the actual confrontation with crime. Arguably, the Marine Support Unit is the one section of the Metropolitan Police that is still closest to what it was in its beginnings: still searching, rescuing and responding to river emergencies. The technology has simply streamlined the work, but there will always be flotsam and jetsam, corpses and objects of sheer mystery floating in that great waterway that is the life-blood of London.

Events such as the Thames torso case in its time, and 'Adam' in 2001, will always be so extreme that there will inevitably be the official narratives and others 'off the record'. The *Marchioness* was a case in point: reading Lawrence Dallaglio's autobiography, we have a first-hand account of being at the coroner's court, and the perception from a grieving relative is that each person was a 'case' and was dismissed in turn by the word 'drowning' as the sequence of names was called out after the overall verdict of accidental death. Police work will always have that dual narrative, much the same as military professionalism seen through civilian standpoints.

16 The Policeman's Lot: Trials and Extremes on the Thames

GILBERT AND SULLIVAN were well aware of the demands and miseries of the new police when they penned the famous lines, 'A policeman's lot is not a happy one.' From the beginning, the recruitment of men was the most pressing matter, of course. For the Metropolitan Force in general, the desirable men were required to be under forty, literate and physically healthy. They needed to have basic arithmetical ability and have a suit of clothes. In terms of pay, it is estimated that, in 1840, an average family could just about survive on a guinea a week. Peel had started pay for his men at three shillings a day. But the real difficulty was that the pay had to cover housing costs, clothing and medical bills. Harvey sensibly set about increasing his own constables' pay by creating five groupings of pay levels conceived to reward the good officers. A dedicated and reliable man could earn the top of the scale – twenty-two shillings and six pence a week. By 1861 there was a desperate need for more men and so the guidelines then were that they should be under forty, over 5 ft 7 in tall and with the usual related qualities. The recruits struggled; many earned well below the twenty-two shillings of course, and those on the initial probationer wages earned much less.

The living conditions of the officers were generally poor. There were often sub-let rooms and most men could only afford to have two rooms. One of the most insurmountable problems was that illness led the officers into money troubles; an officer would be fined a shilling a day if his illness was not related to police work, and that was notably harsh. Their work was physically very demanding; they worked shifts of eight hours, but usually there was not much of a break between shifts. Often, the clothes supplied were inadequate and poorly made and that added to the general discomfort of the job. The most telling feature of the police work was the general tendency for most men to stay in post for around four years. Between 1840 and 1860 Harvey had over 3,000 men recruited, yet 2,562 of them left and 600 were sacked. Heavy drinking, insubordination and inefficiency were rife. Harvey's answer was to employ part-timers who would be hired on a casual contract. Finding the right kind of man was very hard indeed; from his recruitment campaign in 1861, Harvey had 570 applicants and only 38 of these were suitable.

In 1861, an anonymous correspondent to *The Times*, signing himself 'a police constable', wrote:

> There is now a considerable deficiency in numbers in the Metropolitan police and the Commissioner of the City of London police is advertising for men; but if recruits arrive they will not remain unless greater encouragement is offered than the police now receive. At present the great number of men enter the police service as a temporary refuge in distress and do not even stay long enough to learn their duties.

Clearly, the recruitment was rather desperate, and it is impossible to see how Harvey could have altered things, given the general poor health of Londoners at the time and the prolonged economic distress under which they had to survive.

Looked at in comparison with this profile of officers in the land divisions, it might be argued that the Thames men were well off in many ways: they were less conspicuous; their territory was not constantly thronged with potential dangers as there were no street corners and there was nothing above them; they were differentiated markedly from the start, but the river work was still packed with wrongdoers always likely to make their 'felonious little plans'. What does stand out is the sheer exposure to the elements involved in Thames patrols. The weather and the material discomforts and threats of the river itself were the cause of much misery as officers gritted their teeth and got on with the job.

In February 1895 the Lloyd's correspondent at Gravesend wrote that, at high water, the Gravesend reach was entirely covered with ice which was very thick along the south shore. In Bermondsey, the vestry water carts were busy taking water to parishioners. There had always been times when the Thames had been frozen over, as in 1788 and in 1814, when hundreds of people had crossed and re-crossed the river ice near Blackfriars Bridge. But in 1895 there was severe distress caused by the ice. It was the Great Frost – an event in the memories of generations of Londoners, rippling through oral history. The distress was so great that thousands were unemployed and 24,000 men were given work by the workhouses in their stoneyards, breaking stone or picking oakum.

In 1954 a Thames barge skipper called Thomas, aged eighty-two, was interviewed about his memories of the Great Frost of 1895. He recalled that he was skipper of the *Three Brothers*, a barge owned by William Gibb and Son of Duke Shore Wharf in Limehouse. One day he left Limehouse to sail to a dredger off Dagenham. He loaded deep and had around three inches of water on deck, and with a fair wind, off he went, noting that there was plenty of ice around.

He said, 'A great pack had drifted alongside the wharf and we could not moor, so we swung to anchor. Before we could get into a berth a great floe of ice came athwart us.' It fouled the moorings and Thomas managed to get a rope to the dredger and cast off. The skipper of the dredger was not co-operating, so the Thames Police were called. They arrived on foot, as it was too dangerous on the river to take their skiffs out. Skiffs and barges drifted by and Thomas could do nothing.

Such were the perils for the police and for everyone else when the Thames was frozen. That was just one of the many hazards the Thames Police have had to face in their history. They have worked in extreme cold, gales, floods and winter weather; they have searched and dived in polluted and stinking water; they have dragged out ice-cold corpses or would-be suicides and reclaimed the fragile lives of the latter. These pages have recounted the public history of the force up to now: the story of the Thames Police office, the significant events in the timeline, and the deeds of the most remarkable officers in the chronicle. But what about the experiences such as the one Skipper Thomas recalled – when officers could not even take the boats out and were operating along the shores? In 1823 the ice almost caked the river surface, and the Thames Police had to patrol the shores and confine their boats on the ebb, as it was too dangerous to venture out at night. The press reported that 'Many of the vessels that lie nearest the shore have dug pits for their anchors on land.'

In the Victorian years, the Thames men were very much everything to everybody. Public health was one issue in which they were usually on the front line too, as in 1881 when Mr Kennett had a master plan for dealing with the problem of establishing a smallpox hospital in London. He suggested a system of detached floating barracks, as were used in the Turko-Serbian War. Who was to have made sure that the patients were isolated? The Thames Police, Kennett suggested, as he argued for: 'An easily enforced system of quarantine and isolation of the entire hospital from the mainland, a small body of river police being sufficient to prevent any communication.'

There have also been floods. In 1841 the River Lea flooded and boys saw horses swimming in the flood. Prior to the flood the snow had obstructed the mail coaches into London. There was a rapid thaw and 'large bodies would rise well above their normal height and crash against each other', as *The Times* reported. On the river, in stepped the hero of the hour, Superintendent Russell of the Thames Police. While he was dealing with moorings, he saw a bold man jump from his ship as it broke up, and run onto the ice; Russell saved his life and he and two boys were placed in rooms at Wapping for safety.

How were the police equipped for all this challenging and dangerous work? Images of the officers from the articles by Dickens and the *Strand Magazine* writer almost suggest a leisurely dress and demeanour, owing to the straw hats and short jackets, but the truth is that the clothes were layered and very much a seaman's garb. In terms of weapons and defence, cutlasses were used at an early stage in the river policing, but these were not generally used across the city until 1832 when they were issued to all officers, with a warning that 'The police constable is given to understand distinctly that the sword is put into his hand merely as a defensive weapon in case his life should be in danger.'

The new police of 1829 had batons, rattles, lanterns, handcuffs and some cutlasses, and also pistols. But weapons and dress were just the surface; what really mattered was the stamina required to do the work. In 1856 a police surgeon working with the City of London Police wrote that men were being exhausted in their work, saying that they were prematurely aged and that they 'suffer from defective physical strength'.

For the Victorians, clothes were thick and tough for all labouring classes and indeed for all people doing military or public service work; photos of the middle to last decades of the nineteenth century show men wearing hardy and robust coats and trousers, often with thick cloth and added padding for labouring tasks. The Thames men were smart as well as sensibly dressed of course, along with their counterparts in the land forces. Constabulary handbooks contained details of clothing allowances, and even as late as c.1900 these tended to detail capes, waterproof overalls, leggings, lamps, handcuffs, staves and whistles 'issued as required'. Standard clothing was some kind of greatcoat and waterproof gear. All handbooks had words to the effect that 'constables will on all occasions observe a civil and obliging manner towards all ranks of the community, and will show special respect to every magistrate at all times.'

In the annual inspection of 1868 the authorities decided that an open neck for the Thames officers was not acceptable; reefer jackets and waistcoats were standard. For inspectors, there is photographic evidence of their garb, as in a picture of Inspector Bliss, who wore a double-breasted three-quarter length coat, almost certainly with a waistcoat and shirt beneath. One factor in this layering of clothing was the need to have lots of pockets, because fob-watches, smoking equipment, penknives and so on had to be kept on the person.

Such was the situation regarding protection against the elements and the appearance of these professional men in an age when appearance mattered for many reasons: clothes were a marker of one's place in the social hierarchy, but there was also a multiplicity of uniformed people in that age of empire and worldwide commerce, so clothes had to immediately define and distinguish status and responsibility.

In more modern times, naturally the Thames Police and later the Marine Support Unit still had to deal with the one aspect of Thames police work that never goes away. As long as there is a River Thames there will be suicides, suspicious deaths and accidental deaths. In the modern age, following the tentative Victorian beginnings of forensics, formative and influential minds in the field of forensic science have had their impact on the police investigations of mysteries in the river. A relatively early example of this was a talk given in 1909 to the Medico-Legal Society by F.G. Crookshank, police surgeon to the Thames Division, on cases of death by drowning. A Thames police surgeon also played a major role in the 'Brides in the Bath' forensic research by Sir Bernard Spilsbury.

As discussed previously, search and recovery of corpses has always been part and parcel of Thames policing, so Crookshank knew a great deal about the range of possible interpretations and conclusions about corpses in water. He said: 'When a living person enters the water and death occurs there is often, of course, a struggle and submersion alternating with appearance at the surface. In such cases death is due to asphyxiation from drowning.' However, he went on to say that death may sometimes be the result of something called 'inhibition' and this intrigued Spilsbury at a time when he was trying to understand how the brides of George Smith, serial killer, died in their baths.

Crookshank explained that inhibition may be demonstrated by a case of a woman who jumped off Waterloo Bridge. Her body was found at Barnes, and he described how he could tell that she died by inhibition rather than by other causes; this was death caused by the sudden impact of the person hitting the water, and Crookshank explained that such a death was 'mechanical rather than chemical'. Following this explanation an infamous experiment was carried out by Spilsbury and Inspector Neil using women in baths; one woman was pressed on the head and the other ducked into the water by a sharp lifting of her ankles. The latter method almost proved fatal, and it took strenuous efforts to bring the 'guinea pig' woman back to life. But the point is that Spilsbury had seen and understood how Smith had drowned his victims and left no traces of struggle or violence, and the line of thought came from Crookshank's lecture.

Interestingly, the pattern of suicides in London changed in the post-war period. A report published in 1954 by Dr T.M. Ling, a psychiatrist, stressed the loneliness behind so many self-inflicted deaths – a 'social evil' of the times. The distribution of suicides in the 1950s and 1960s makes an interesting comparison with those acts of desperation a century earlier: in the post-war years, Ling stated, they occurred to a greater extent in Holborn, Chelsea and Kensington than in Camberwell and Deptford. Ling's conclusions could have been applied in 1850, but to the East End: 'The suicide-prone areas of Kensington, Bloomsbury and Marylebone harboured many transients, while often the type of housing had been changed by economic circumstances from high Regency and Victorian family units to housing a series of isolates who led a lonely and dreary existence in a single room.'

Between 1961 and 1964, the years immediately following the Suicide Act, there was an average of around 600 suicides a year in London, the peak being 1964, with a figure of 646. Short items from police reports between the end of the war and modern times still pepper the daily newspapers: deaths by drowning, whether accidental or purposeful. Today the response from the police might be speedier and more efficient than in the past, but the phenomenon is still there and very much a major part of the police work. As Peter Ackroyd wrote in his book on the river, referring to a 2004 exhibition on missing people, 'No more appropriate spot could have been chosen for such an exhibition. The Thames is a river of the disappeared. In the records of the National Missing Persons Bureau, out of the first eighty unidentified bodies noted, some fourteen had been found in or beside the Thames.' Modern River Police would still agree with Victorian writer George Borrow, who wrote that there are points in the river which are like 'a grisly pool which, with its superabundance of horror, fascinated me.... The darkness and turbulence of the river exercise a fascination over the unwary'.

The chronicle of the Thames Police, as their identities shifted and coped with different labels, remained the same: men and women working on and knowing the Thames, making it as familiar over time as the streets that the other bobbies walked on their beats every day, month after month, year after year. Today there might be greater speed and more monitoring of every action taken, but the basis of the work has been dictated by the river and its traffic, and by the fringes of the water along the shore from estuary to Erith. In many ways, Patrick Colquhoun, a lover of statistics, reports and inquiries, might have found the modern world quite comfortable; he introduced a *system* – something the Georgians found problematical. They were talented at creating statutes which appeared to be doing remarkable things to improve the criminal justice process, but in fact it was a society working by backhanders and favours, monopolies and sinecures.

Colquhoun, like many of his contemporaries, was also a businessman and administrator, but he understood what was needed, and one of his statements made in his famous treatise could apply today as a problem of policing anywhere: 'The culprits seldom were restrained by a sense of the moral turpitude of the offence.'

Timeline

Key Dates in Police History

DATES OF SPECIAL relevance to the Thames Police are in bold: Roll of Honour and Thames officers killed on duty are in bold capitals.

1750s   Henry and John Fielding active as London magistrates. Bow Street Runners formed: 'originally consisting of the only six of the eighty Constables in Westminster not on the take' (Oliver Cyriax, *The Penguin Encyclopaedia of Crime*).

1792   Middlesex Magistrates Act.

1796   **Patrick Colquhoun's book, *A Treatise on the Police of the Metropolis*.**

1798   The West India planters committees and West India merchants fund the new Marine Police and the Marine police office opens at Wapping.

        GABRIEL FRANKS (MASTER LUMPER) shot in a brawl.

1813   **ABRAHAM BROWN (CONSTABLE) killed at Wapping.**

1820   **MARK ARNOLD (CONSTABLE) drowned.**

1829   Metropolitan Police Act: Robert Peel forms the first professional force, for London.

        Municipal Corporations Act: this brought about the formation of watch committees, created by boroughs.

        The Royal Irish Constabulary formed by Thomas Drummond.

John Kent, the first black police constable, joins the Carlisle force.

Formation of the City of London Police.

1839   **Thames Police absorbed by the Metropolitan Police. 'The power of searching all ships, vessels, barges, and boats hitherto performed by the surveyors, under the regulating orders of the Magistrates, will be continued to the superintendents and inspectors of the Metropolitan Police, with power to bring as many constables on board as they shall think necessary.'**

The County Police Act. This gave boroughs the option of forming a constabulary if the justices wanted to levy a rate for that purpose.

1842   The first detective force formed.

The Thames Police office moved to Arbour Street, Stepney.

1856   The County and Borough Police Act. This made it compulsory for all counties in England and Wales to establish police forces.

1866   Maximum pay of constables raised to twenty-three shillings and four pence per week.

FRANCIS HOLDER (CONSTABLE) drowned on duty.

1872   **GEORGE BROOKS (INSPECTOR) drowned.**

1874   The Criminal Investigation Department established.

1878   **The *Princess Alice* disaster.**

1884   **WILLIAM ROBSON (INSPECTOR) crushed on duty.**

1887   Police officers allowed to vote in parliamentary elections.

1888   Local Government Act abolished police forces run by boroughs with a population of less than 10,000.

1890   Police Pensions Act: receipt of a pension after twenty-five years service became a right.

1901	JAMES NEWBOLD (CONSTABLE) drowned on duty.
1903	JAMES WHEATLEY (CONSTABLE) drowned on duty.
1910	Steam giving way to motor power as the Thames Division expands.
1911	Captain Horwood becomes the Chief Officer of the Eastern Railway Police. (He later became Commissioner of the Metropolitan Police.)
1913	GEORGE SPOONER (SERGEANT) drowned on duty.
1915	The first woman police officer (Edith Smith, Grantham).
1917	The first policewomen sworn in for service in the Transport Police for the North Eastern Railway.
1918–19	Police strikes in London and Liverpool.
1920	The Police Pensions Act. This defines an age limit for each rank at retirement.
	The Palestine Police Force created.
1922	The Royal Ulster Constabulary formed.
1924	The Metropolitan Police start to relinquish dockyard duties.
	Ada Atherton starts work at Waterloo as a female detective for the Transport Police.
1930	A sign of changing times: large numbers of officers begin traffic patrol work.
1931	WILLIAM WARE (CONSTABLE) drowned on duty.
1932	The beat system abolished by Lord Trenchard.
	The Metropolitan Police College at Hendon opened.
1933	The Metropolitan Forensic Laboratory opened.
1937	FREDERICK PARNACUTT (SERGEANT) drowned on duty.
	ALBERT TAYLOR (CONSTABLE) drowned on duty.

1941   PC William Brereton awarded the British Empire Medal for gallant conduct. During an air raid on a goods depot in South London he saved the life of PC Rowing inside a burning building.

1948   The British Mandate for Palestine ends: the Palestine Police disbanded.

Essex Marine Police Unit formed.

1955   The Central Traffic Squad formed: there are a hundred men involved in this.

1963–75 Gradual rationalization of forces and disbandment of many smaller constabularies.

1965   The Special Patrol Group formed: 100 officers arrest 396 people in the first year of work.

Norwell Roberts joins the Metropolitan Police as the first black police officer in that force. (He receives the Queen's Police Medal in 1996.)

DENNIS COWELL (CONSTABLE) drowned on duty.

1989   The *Marchioness* disaster.

MARK PEERS (CONSTABLE) drowned on duty.

1991   An independent inquiry into the work of the Department of Transport and its responsibility for the safety of vessels on the Thames.

1993–94 **Service restructuring.**

1996   **The force becomes part of a new Operational Command Unit.**

2001   **The Marine Support Unit set up.**

2002   **The RNLI set up four lifeboat stations.**

2008   **The Marine Policing Unit formed.**

Appendix 1
The Curators at Wapping

W HEN THE FIRST vague feelings of writing this history occurred to me, all I had to start with was a discussion with novelist and East Ender, Jean Fullerton. She kindly took me on a walk around Wapping and the nearby docks, and then to visit the Thames Police Museum within the station at Wapping – the one built in 1908 to succeed the earlier one visited by Charles Dickens and by the *Strand* writer quoted in this book. Nothing excites a social historian more than the sight and feel of an artefact which is exactly the item as seen in books and magazines in previous research, and when Mr Joslin guided me around the mass of objects and documents kept at Wapping, there was the desk, as drawn in the *Strand* in 1895: exactly the same as when the duty sergeant stood at it and took down notes.

Even today, with modernity evident everywhere in the material world around Wapping, it is not too difficult to imagine the criminal and legal microcosm surrounding the High Street and the police office. Execution Dock was just down the river, the Ratcliffe Highway is a short walk north and the architecture of the docks is still evident. At the Town of Ramsgate public house (formerly The Red Cow) there are still reminders of the presence of Judge George Jeffreys, at the spot where he was supposed to watch the executions. The pub was used as the Admiralty Court, which covered crimes committed at sea, so pirates were of special interest to the 'hanging judge'.

John Joslin and Robert Jeffries are the honorary curators of the museum, and they have not only vast experience as officers working on the river, but also a profound interest in the history of the Thames force, in all its manifestations, from boats to cutlasses and from diving gear to ageing photos.

Robert Jeffries joined the Metropolitan Police in 1973 and served in the West End with the Diplomatic Protection Unit; he joined the Thames Division in April 1988 and retired in 2005 after thirty-two years' service. John Joslin, known as 'Joz', runs a newsletter of the Thames Police Association Marine Police Unit and his main project, as described in his newsletter of summer 2010, is to set up what he terms a 'proper reference library' in which records, reference works, articles etc. may be catalogued. He is on a crusade to reclaim and preserve all kinds of police records – many of which have been rather thoughtlessly classed as ephemera in the past, and not necessarily regarded as being of historical importance.

The Thames Police Museum is a very special place, and within the walls there are treasures from history of outstanding importance. It is to be hoped that the vestiges of police history across London are able to stake a claim in the wider area of what we now term 'heritage' – and at the moment the museum at Wapping is in very good hands. Historians of London would have to admit that the curators have one of the best-kept secrets of social and legal history within their walls and it is to be hoped that soon the massive work undertaken by Mr Joslin will see the light of day to provide a comprehensive chronicle of the Thames Police, in contrast to my selected highlights.

Appendix 2
The Thames Magistrates and Detective Work

A N INTEGRAL PART of the Thames Division, and its forebears the Marine Police, was the court or office: the magistrates and other staff did the rest of the work once the offender was in the dock. There has been some mention of these in the earlier chapters, but there is more to be said on the subject, particularly in relation to Patrick Colquhoun and his earlier experience before the founding of the force in 1798. There has been a fair amount of close academic study carried out on this, notably by Margaret Avery (see the bibliography). But this appendix deals with other aspects not much known with regard to the operation of the Thames Police Court over the years.

Some knowledge of Colquhoun's work, prior to writing his *Treatise on the Police of the Metropolis* in 1785, is important in understanding the establishment and work of the Middlesex magistrates, a body of men in place from the beginning of the new police. As a magistrate in London, Colquhoun was appointed under the Middlesex Justices Act (1792) and continued in that role until he retired in 1818, just two years before his death. In accordance with his theory, his stress was on preventive measures; one of his main proposals was a Board of Police, and that body was also to work in place of the Poor Law administration.

In 1988 Margaret Avery suggested that our view of Colquhoun should be revised, in the light of his work in Glasgow before starting out as a magistrate at Worship Street. She supports the view that he was one of a new urban elite who wished to normalize society. That implies a sociological imperative to eradicate radical thinking and open dissent. Although that may, in effect, be true, the fact was that Colquhoun was thinking and planning in the midst of a crime epidemic. He created the Glasgow Chamber of Commerce and established a coffee house as a focal point for meetings, communications and business decisions; this success made him known in London. When he became Lord Provost of the city of Glasgow in 1882, police regulations were foremost in his mind. The importance of all this is that in Glasgow we have a prototype of what he was to suggest for London: basically, that criminal justice and administration had to work closely with the movers and shakers in the business world.

Beginning as a London magistrate he was, as Avery puts it, 'to experience at first hand ... the distress and disorder of the labouring poor'. He was working in Shoreditch, a focus of the criminal activity of the underclass. What is often overlooked is that magistrates had to act as detectives in many cases. After all, they were at the very heart of every kind of crime, from petty offences to public nuisances, and all this meant that they had a special insight into how their community functioned – and what were the causes of social breakdown and malaise. Avery sums up Colquhoun's nature with these words: 'But always his charity was accompanied by a stiff dose of moralizing and his concern about indigence was always strongly motivated by his conviction that it was a major source of crime and a waste of essential resources within the state.'

As for John Harriott, he was very special in several ways; he worked for almost twenty years in the Thames office, administering all affairs with efficiency and order. Geoffrey Budworth defines his achievement succinctly: 'It was his strict leadership, brooking no incompetence or indiscipline, that moulded the men to their roles both afloat and ashore. They even did pike and cutlass drill.' From the end of the eighteenth century, Harriott and his successors had powers extending from Essex to Surrey; this was something quite new, a quiet revolution in some ways. In that we can perhaps see the germ of later detective work, with increased liaison with other judicial bodies and other constabularies along the Thames.

There are examples of magistrates in the eighteenth century, in Colquhoun's time, being detectives in the sense that they chased up leads and used connections across Britain. A look at one such instance highlights some of the ways in which the new magistrates worked. The popular history books and the media have given us a general picture of the eighteenth-century magistrate that tends to suggest an idle, overfed and peremptory fellow, too keen to have the next meal and put the felons inside to cool off. Perhaps this owes a lot to the novels of the time, although documents do indicate that a typical magistrate need not have stirred from a comfortable chair unless there was an extreme emergency such as a riot or imminent war.

But one particular exception to this occurred in the Bradford and Halifax area between 1751 and 1769. This magistrate concerned was Samuel Lister, a formidable man to have as an enemy, and unluckily for the men involved in the 'yellow trade' of coining and clipping at this time, and in the risky activity of forgery, he was more than capable of going out to make things happen, and to play detective when needed. Lister was based at Horton House, and he had been trained as an attorney, having thirteen years in that practice. However, he had to abandon the legal practice when he took up the magistrate's post.

There was a family tradition behind this; his father had served on the bench for the West Riding, and as the area covering Bradford and Calderdale was vast, mostly wild and empty, and in the first stages of the Industrial Revolution, a magistrate was sure to be kept busy. At that time there were around two hundred capital offences, and also plenty of lock-ups, stocks and houses of correction to keep the less serious offenders out of circulation for a while. In 1764, in the Halifax parish of Lister's area, there was most likely a population of some 40,000, and there was no magistrate in local residence when Lister stepped into the role. (Bradford had had three justices in the 1750s.) But we are dealing here with a remarkable man, one who was highly regarded by the Marquis of Rockingham, the outstanding legal figure for the West Riding, always busy at York Castle.

Lister had plenty to occupy him in dealing with the activities of thieves and robbers, and in this work he averaged about twenty-six sittings each year; but it was in the coining circuit that he really emerged from his usual role to become a detective, out to get his man. The man in question was one William Wilkins, who had been arrested and brought to the court for not paying bills at various hostelries throughout the West Riding. He had been searched and interrogated and on his person were found letters, one with a Gloucester postmark. More astonishingly, a promissory note was found for the huge sum of £1,100 – a massive fortune at that time.

Wilkins said that he was from a place called Painswick in Somerset, but the letters and notes he had were not actually signed by anyone of note. They were more than likely forgeries, and, if guilty, he would hang. But the problem was how to prove he was guilty. It was going to take extraordinary measures to achieve this, notably trying to communicate with the Painswick authorities, and this was something usually far too strenuous and time-consuming for an average magistrate of the time to bother with. Not Samuel Lister, though; he was a determined man with a sense of challenge.

The first step was to enlist some qualified assistance, so he turned to the Leeds man, 'the Recorder', Richard Wilson. The two men decided to keep Wilkins locked up while information was gathered; they put items in London newspapers and sent messages to Gloucester. They were pushed for time: Wilkins was to appear at the Lent Assizes in the South West and in a quite short time. He could have had friends there to stand bail, as well, so they moved fast. This is where the alacrity of Lister in using the 'grapevine' around Bradford paid off, as one of his contacts knew of a West Country man visiting the town, a Walter Merrett. He told Lister to write to a clothier at Uley near Painswick to ascertain information.

It was a triumph: 'Wilkins' was in fact one Edward Wilson from Painswick, wanted for forgery. The case was soon sorted out then: Wilson was sent to trial at Gloucester on 20 March 1756 and was sentenced to death.

Lister also got to work against the clippers. This 'yellow trade' involved filing or clipping coins down to an acceptable weight for local use, and so actually creating more coins with the clippings; it was very lucrative, and a capital offence – it was, indeed, high treason. The risks were high and the criminals involved acted with desperation and resolve, even to the extent of murder, as in the case of the exciseman, William Deighton, killed in Halifax in 1769. But the Bradford men still acted against the coiners, perhaps urged on by this murder. It was no easy task to work against the perpetrators though: the trade enjoyed considerable popular support. Lister was a part of this crusade to hit the coiners.

The best way to find out about the villains was to employ *agents provocateurs*, and Lister, together with John Hustler in Bradford, did this successfully, his work leading to the arrest of two men on an inspector's evidence, who were then packed off to York Castle. Lister must have known the risks: Deighton had sent some men to York Castle, and he paid for it with his life.

But Samuel Lister was indeed a remarkable man. He saw the magistracy as something opening up opportunities to act not only on behalf of the law itself, and civil order, but also as a means of reinforcing authority in an economic context. The action against the 'yellow trade' was taken in part because Lister had links with local industrialists, and he was, of course, representing their interests in protecting the value of coins in trade circulation. His principal biographer, John Styles, appropriately quotes Lister's own words as explanation of his motives: 'I think it my duty not only as a magistrate but as a private person to do all that I am able to bring villains to justice.'

Reverting to Colquhoun, he would have known the patterns of connections and communication channels across Britain, and being in London would have made him perhaps even more alert to criminal links than Lister.

The bill for the Middlesex magistrates was opposed by Charles James Fox in Parliament; he said that there were two objections to it: 'One, that it will do no good whatever, the other that it may do some mischief.' At that time, Bow Street was the only place where the victims of crime could find some kind of help in obtaining redress and satisfaction; the Middlesex bill established seven public offices with three justices working with each of them. All fees were collected by a receiver working with the Treasury, and that was a massive step forward, a way of reversing the trend of corrupt practices in the ranks of legal officials. Fox thought that the governmental control of the justices was the worst danger, as the men on the bench would be subject to central influence in all criminal justice matters. One MP insisted that the drawback to the idea could be seen in the fact that if magistrates voted wrongly they would lose their posts.

The practices of nepotism and favouritism, and the proliferation of sinecures in the hands of the government, were clearly possible influences in how the new justices were to work, but good men were appointed, and Colquhoun was one of them, along with a colourful character called Henry James Pym, who was also a poet. Pym was actually made Poet Laureate in 1790 and, later, he wrote a handbook for magistrates, which was notably successful. The implementation of the Justices Act was also successful and later, when the Act was renewed, it was in that context that the Marine Institution and the Thames Police office were created. The new police offices were, though, short of men and money, and so their initial impact was hardly going to be marked. The justices had a budget of just £2,000 per annum.

There was a clamour in the newspapers and among the MPs for magistrates to be men who had vast legal experience, and some even thought that magistrates should be barristers with many years of experience. But, in the end, as the Thames Police office ably demonstrated, the line of magistrates from Colquhoun and Harriott onwards proved to be impressively successful.

Insights into the culture and society around the Thames magistrates are hard to find, but in a feature written for *The Times* in 1963, there is a rare account of the courts and how they worked. The man in focus was not a magistrate, but a court usher. This was Thomas Livingston, 'one of the lowliest members of the staff' who was retiring in 1853 after a long period of administering the law in the East End. He was presented with £110 (a huge sum at the time) and 'an elegantly written testimonial, bound in green leather, gold embossed'. He had succeeded the very first usher, Benjamin Blaby, who was appointed in 1839, after amalgamation with Peel's new police.

Through the usher, we understand the workings of the court. His main purpose is to escort people and to command silence; he swears in witnesses, passes documents, cares for exhibits, liaises with advocates and controls the behaviour of the public who are present. The writer of the feature in 1963 noted that ushers have always been recruited from a variety of organizations but that 'until the First World War domestic service was a fruitful source.'

Livingston and Blaby were scarcely ever mentioned in the court reports, but as we know from Ballantine's memoirs, the Thames Police office was, for many years, a place in need of tight and vigilant security, overworked and rather vulnerable. The magistrates and the ushers had little help and support beyond whatever constables could be present, and in terms of statutory protection, the Protection of Justices and Constables Act of 1751 was the main influence. The wording of that Act was as follows:

> No action shall be brought against any justice of the peace for anything done in the execution of his office, or against any constable, Headborough [the head of a tithing, or person convening a court leet (a local community court)] or other officer, or person acting as aforesaid, unless commenced within six calendar months after the act committed.

Putting together the general state of the justices, as conceived in the late eighteenth century, and Patrick Colquhoun's particular nature and background, what we have is an example of a man of business who had read and reflected on the new philosophical thinking of Cesare Beccaria and others of the Enlightenment. They saw crime prevention as the key to changing the parlous state of affairs in most European cities in the eighteenth century, as commerce and industry expanded and population changes meant a shift from country to town and from stability to social disintegration. There is no doubt that the eighteenth century generated a glut of writing on penal issues. There were several attempts to place the theory of incarceration in line with such illusive notions as goodness, morality and religious precepts. Art and philosophy were turning the microscope on man as a phenomenon, in all his complexity and with all the contradictions that Shakespeare had expressed so powerfully in *Hamlet* for instance, in which the Prince reflects on the capacity for evil in a creature who has been made by a beneficent creator. In other words, the problems of evil and of different modes of transgression were examined at length. Even those who worked in the criminal justice system and in the ranks of writers and radicals of the time chose prisons as subjects for inquiry and reflection, as in Henry Fielding's *Tom Jones* (1749) and William Godwin's *Caleb Williams* (1794).

Colquhoun was aware of all this philosophical reflection, and his special achievement is that he not only understood the theory, but also ran a police court and succeeded. That is a very rare talent, and in that ability lies the very essence of the Marine Police as they were first conceived. Yet he and his successors were also, in many ways, doing duties we would think of as being defined as detective work, involving channels of communication on their 'patch' and beyond. Colquhoun was fortunate indeed to have John Harriott with him, as a practical, experienced man of the world was needed to consolidate matters: someone who knew the sea as well as the dark motivations of those who transgress.

Bibliography and References

Primary Sources

Books

Archer, Thomas, *The Terrible Sights of London and Labours of Love in the Midst of Them* (S. Rivers & Co., 1870)

Ballantine, Mr Serjeant, *Some Experiences of a Barrister's Life* (Richard Bentley, 1883)

Besant, Walter, *East London* (Chatto and Windus, 1901)

Booth, Charles, *Life and Labour of the People in London* (Macmillan, 1886-1903)

Collins, L.C., *Life and Memoirs of John Churton Collins* (John Lane and the Bodley Head, 1912)

Conan Doyle, Sir Arthur, 'The Adventure of the Dying Detective' in *His Last Bow; The New Annotated Sherlock Holmes* Vol. II pp.1341–1361 (W.W. Norton, 2005)

Cotterell, Gareth (ed.), *London Scene from the Strand: Aspects of Victorian London Culled from the Strand Magazine* (Book Club, 1975)

Dickens, Charles, *Reprinted Pieces* (Chapman and Hall, 1907)

Fletcher, Geoffrey, *London's River* (Hutchinson, 1966)

Gaster, Jack, *Time and Tide* (Amberley, 2010)

Guy, William A., *Principles of Forensic Medicine* (eds. Ferrier, David and Smith, William R.) 1st edn 1844, reprinted as *Victorian CSI* (History Press, 2010)

Harriott, John, *Struggles Through Life* (Hatchard, 1800)

Johnson, David (ed.) *London's Peelers and the British Police* (Jackdaw Publications, 1970)

Jones, Steve (ed.), *The Illustrated Police News* (Wicked Publications, 2002)

Kilvert, Francis, *Kilvert's Diary 1870–79* (Penguin, 1984)

Le Caron, Major Henri, *Twenty-Five Years in the Secret Service* (Heinemann, 1893)

McGrath, Melanie, *Silvertown: An East End Family Memoir* (Fourth Estate, 2003)

Mayhew, Henry, *London Labour and the London Poor* (John Howden, 1861–2)

Sala, George Augustus, *Twice Round the Clock* (1858) (reprinted by Leicester University Press, 1971)

Savill, Stanley, *The Police Service of England and Wales* (John Kempster, 1900)

Tristram, Flora, *The London Journal of Flora Tristram* (Virago, 1982)

Uffenbach, Zacharias von, *London in 1710: from the travels of Uffenbach* (ed. Margaret Mare) (Faber, 1934)

Periodicals

Anon., 'A Night with the Thames Police', *Strand Magazine*, 1892, pp.124–8

Dalton, Superintendent H., 'The Thames Police', *Police Journal* Vol. VIII no.1, 1935, pp.90–103

Maps

Maps: Medieval to Twentieth Century London (Oldhouse Publications, 2007)

Archives and Museum Publications

Costin, W.C. and Watson, J. Steven (eds.), *The Law and Working of the Constitution: Documents 1660–1914* (A & C Black, 1952)

Metropolitan Police Historical Timeline 1829–2000 at www.met.police.uk/history/timeline

'The River Thames – Policing and River Safety' at
www.the-river-thames.co.uk/police.htm
Surrey Cases Third Session, 1857–8, London Metropolitan
Archives, CLA/048/AO/10/003 (The trial of Christian
Sattler)

Other Sources

King, Superintendent Alan, 'Water: The Work of the Metropolitan
Police Marine Support Unit': lecture given at Gresham College.
See www.gresham.ac.uk/printtranscript.asp?EventId=790

Secondary Sources

Books

Abbott, Geoffrey, *William Calcraft: Executioner Extraordinaire*
(Eric Dobby, 2004)
Ackroyd, Peter, *London: The Biography* (Vintage, 2001)
— *Thames, Sacred River* (Vintage, 2007)
Amos, Sir Maurice, *British Justice* (The British Council, 1940)
Barnard, Sylvia, *Viewing the Breathless Corpse*
(Words@Woodmere, 2001)
Begg, Paul and Skinner, Keith, *The Scotland Yard Files*
(Headline, 1992)
Browne, Douglas C., *The Rise of Scotland Yard* (Harrap,
1956)
Browne, Douglas C. and Tullett, E.V., *Bernard Spilsbury: His
Life and Cases* (Companion Book Club, 1952)
Budworth, Geoffrey, *The River Beat: the story of London's
River Police since 1798* (Historical Publications, 1997)
Byrne, Richard, *Prisons and Punishments of London* (Harrap,
1989)
Campbell, Christy, *Fenian Fire* (Harper Collins, 2003)
Castleden, Rodney, *Inventions that Changed the World*
(Futura, 2007)
Clarke, A.A., *Police Uniform and Equipment* (Shire, 1991)

Clunn, Harold, *The Face of London* (Simpkin Marshall, 1932)

Cook, Chris, *Britain in the Nineteenth Century 1815–1914* (Routledge, 2005)

Davenport-Hines, Richard, *The Pursuit of Oblivion: A Social History of Drugs* (Phoenix, 2001)

De Quincey, Thomas, *On Murder* (Oxford University Press, 2006)

Dell, Simon, *The Victorian Policeman* (Shire, 2004)

Diamond, Michael, *Victorian Sensation* (Anthem Press, 2003)

Emsley, Clive, *The English Police: A Political and Social History* (Longman, 1996)

— *The Great British Bobby* (Quercus, 2009)

Evans, Stewart P. and Skinner, Keith, *The Ultimate Jack the Ripper Sourcebook* (Robinson, 2000)

Fallon, Tom, *The River Police: The Story of Scotland Yard's Little Ships* (Muller, 1956)

Fishman, William, *East End 1888* (Duckworth, 1988)

Glinert, Ed, *East End Chronicles* (Penguin, 2006)

Gooch, Graham and Williams, Michael, *The Oxford Dictionary of Law Enforcement* (Oxford University Press, 2007)

Gray, Adrian, *Crime and Criminals of Victorian England* (History Press, 2011)

Green, Jonathon, *Crooked Talk* (Random House, 2011)

Gregory, Jeremy and Stevenson, John, *Britain in the Eighteenth Century* (Routledge, 2007)

Hannavy, John, *The Victorians and Edwardians at Work* (Shire, 2009)

Howse, Christopher, *How We Saw It: 150 Years of The Daily Telegraph* (Ebury Press, 2005)

Hunt, Tristram, *Building Jerusalem: The Rise and Fall of the Victorian City* (Phoenix, 2004)

Jackson, Lee, *A Dictionary of Victorian London* (Anthem Press, 2006)

Jackson, Norman, *The Old Bailey* (Fletcher and Sons, 1978)

James, P.D. and Critchley, T.A., *The Maul and the Pear Tree* (Faber, 2000)

Jennings, Charles, *Greenwich: The Place Where Days Begin and End* (Little, Brown, 1999)

Linnane, Fergus, *The Encyclopedia of London Crime and Vice* (Sutton, 2003)

Low, Donald A., *The Regency Underworld* (Sutton, 2005)

Mitchell, R.J. and Leys, M.D.R., *A History of London Life* (Penguin, 1958)

O'Neill, Gilda, *The Good Old Days: Crime, Murder and Mayhem in Victorian London* (Penguin, 2007)

Osborne, Bertram, *Justices of the Peace 1361–1848* (Sedgehill Press, 1959)

Partridge, Col. S.G., *Prisoner's Progress* (Hutchinson, 1930)

Picard, Liza, *Dr Johnson's London* (Weidenfeld and Nicholson, 2000)

Porter, Roy, *Enlightenment* (Penguin, 2000)

Quennell, Peter, *Victorian Panorama* (Batsford, 1937)

Rawlings, Philip, *Crime and Power: A History of Criminal Justice, 1688–1998* (Longman, 1999)

Richardson, Anthony, *Nick of the River* (Harrap, 1955)

Robins, Jane, *The Magnificent Spilsbury and the Case of the Brides in the Bath* (John Murray, 2010)

Roud, Steve, *London Lore* (Arrow Books, 2010)

Schneer, Jonathan, *The Thames: England's River* (Little, Brown, 2005)

Shpayer-Makov, Haia, *The Making of a Policeman: a social history of a labour force in metropolitan London, 1829–1914* (Ashgate, 2002)

Slater, Michael, *Charles Dickens* (Yale University Press, 2010)

Smyth, Frank, *Cause of Death: A History of Forensic Science* (Van Nostrand Reinhold, 1983)

Stallion, Martin and Wall, David S., *The British Police: Police Forces and Chief Officers 1829–2000* (Police History Society, 1999)

Thomas, Donald, *An Underworld at War* (John Murray, 2004)

Wilkinson, Frederick, *Those Entrusted with Arms* (Greenhill Books, 2002)

Williams, Neville, *A History of Smuggling* (Shoe String Press, 1959)

Articles in Journals and Periodicals

Adams, Jad, '1911's Summer' in *Who Do You Think You Are?*, February 2009, pp.26–7

Anon., 'Long Line of Court Ushers', *The Times*, 12 November 1963, p.13

Anon., 'Parliament and London's Magistrates', *The Times*, 18 March 1964, p.14

Avery, Margaret E., 'Patrick Colquhoun: A Being Clothed with Divinity', *Journal of the Police History Society* No.3, 1988, pp.24–34

Ballhatchet, Joan, 'The Police and the London Dock Strike of 1889', *History Workshop Journal* Vol.32, issue 1, 1973, pp.54–68

Bazzone, A.T., 'Disturbance at the Docks', *Journal of the Police History Society* No.5, 1990, pp.42–48

Billington-Greig, Teresa, 'The Truth About White Slavery', *English Review*, June 1913, pp.428–446

Edwards, Richard, 'Child Sacrifices in London', *Evening Standard*, 16 June 2005

Sanders, Todd, 'Imagining the Dark Continent: the Met, the Media and the Thames Torso', *Cambridge Anthropology* Vol.23, No.3, pp.53–66

Styles, John, 'An Eighteenth Century Magistrate as Detective: Samuel Lister of Little Horton', *The Bradford Antiquary* Vol.10, 1982, pp.98–117

Newspapers and Periodicals: Texts and Archives

The Annual Register
Daily Telegraph
Freeman's Journal
The Graphic
Harmsworth Magazine

The London Magazine
London Metropolitan Archives: Surrey case reports: third session 1857-8 LMA/CLA/048
Morning Post
Notes & Queries
Penny Illustrated Paper
Police Journal
Police Review
Strand Magazine
Thames Police Association Newsletter
The Times Digital Archive

Websites

www.dur.ac.uk/alan.heesom/police.htm, Victorian Britain: police and crime
www.homepage.ntlworld.com/hitch/gendocs/police.html (Victorian London Research)
www.kenthistoryforum.co.uk
www.maib.gov.uk
www.met.police.uk/history/timeline1829
www.policehistorysociety.co.uk
www.policespecials.com/thames2.html
www.rjerrard.co.uk/law/city/city2.htm, 'City of London Police' by Donald Rumbelow
www.the-river-thames.co.uk/police.htm – features written by Dick Paterson.

Index